# DOING

# LESS

# AND

# HAVING

# MORE

# DOING
# LESS
# AND
# HAVING
# MORE

Five Easy Steps for Discovering What
You Really Want—and Getting It

**MARCIA WIEDER**

WILLIAM MORROW AND COMPANY, INC.

NEW YORK

Grateful acknowledgment is made for use of the following:

From *Breathing Space: Living and Working at a Comfortable Pace in a Sped-Up Society*
by Jeff Davidson (Mastermedia, 1991). Copyright © 1991 by Jeff Davidson. Reprinted with
permission.

From *Everyday Blessings: The Inner Work of Mindful Parenting* by Myla and Jon Kabat-Zinn
(Hyperion, 1998). Copyright © 1998 by Myla Kabat-Zinn and Jon Kabat-Zinn. Reprinted with
permission.

It is the policy of William Morrow and Company, and its imprints and affiliates,
recognizing the importance of preserving what has been written, to print the books we
publish on acid-free paper, and we exert our best efforts to that end.

Library of Congress Cataloging-in-Publication Data

Wieder, Marcia.
Doing less and having more: five easy steps for discovering what you really want—
and getting it / Marcia Wieder.
p.   cm.
Includes index.
ISBN 0-688-15824-2
1. Change (Psychology).   2. Simplicity.   I. Title.
BF637.C4W54   1998
158.1—dc21                                    98-15507
                                                   CIP

Printed in the United States of America

First Edition

1   2   3   4   5   6   7   8   9   10

BOOK DESIGN BY JO ANNE METSCH

www.williammorrow.com

*To Kevin,*
*Thank you for teaching me to live one day at a time.*

# A C K N O W L E D G M E N T S

A very heartfelt thank you to all these wonderful friends and supporters: Caterina Rando, Colleen and Myles Ericson, Beth Stelluto and Howard Dunaier, Lynn Flaming, Fran and Bob Beban, Teri Augustine, Luther Kitahata, Michelle and Steve Stern, Catherine Crowell, Fred Hampden, Lauren Eskenazi, and Richard Taylor. Extreme gratitude goes to my agent, Bonnie Solow, to Toni Sciarra, my editor at William Morrow, and to my husband, Kevin Zmarthie.

A special thank you goes to my family, for always believing in me and supporting my dreams.

I also want to acknowledge all the beautiful new babies that were born while I was birthing this book: Kiera Thompson, Sarah Mergen, Luke Novey, Samantha Gilbert, Casey Greer Seligman, Logan Ericson, and Riley Gaucher.

# CONTENTS

# PART I

# A NEW PATH

# 1

# The Ultimate Dream

I HAVE the privilege of traveling around the world speaking about dreams, hopes, and goals. In my audiences there are always many people who have dreams and some who don't. But they all seem to share a common concern: For many of us, life has become overwhelming. We have no time or energy to pursue our dreams, or perhaps even to know what our dreams are.

In this crazy world where life has become so overscheduled, overcomplicated, and often overcritical, it's no surprise that many of us often feel defeated, or at least dazed and confused. We wake up in the morning, rush around doing all the things we need to do, come home depleted, and pass out exhausted. Then we wake up the next morning and begin the process again.

How did this happen? What happened to our hopes and our desires? What happened to the kind of life you imagined you would live? What happened to your dreams?

And what about the ultimate dream? Can you imagine a life in which you actually do less and have more? Some people are talking about it, yet for many it's still a foreign concept. At first this may sound contradictory. Perhaps it sounds improbable or even impossible. But it is possible, and it's not all that difficult.

I will show you how to transform your life. You can get rid of many of the things (including people and situations) that don't support you. You can learn to say no and choose when to say yes. You can have free or leisure time and improve the quality of your life.

You can also begin to remember your dreams and actually have the time to pursue them. You can feel strong and healthy, as well as relaxed and calm. You can have more composure and competence. You can live life more fully.

## HAVING MORE

What does it mean to you to have more? Exactly what do you want more of? Do you even know? These questions require you to schedule a short date with yourself, for the purpose of exploring what really matters to you and what you are willing to do about it. The Irish political activist Bernadette Devlin reminds us, "To gain that which is worth having, it may be necessary to lose everything else." I know this takes unbounded courage and strength. Just remember, life is short. Live it your way.

If you could create your life the way you want it, actually live by your standards, exactly what would you want more of? How about starting with some of the essential basics? Would you like more time, more joy, more ease? How about some added extras: more money, romance, travel, friends, fun?

For some, having more is about material stuff. Not only is there nothing wrong with wanting a new car or home, or with taking a vacation, but you are empowered by deciding what you want.

Perhaps you have plenty of material wealth—maybe even more stuff than you need or want. Your "having more" list may actually turn into your "having less" list, as you purge and clear out the clutter.

Too much of anything can be burdensome. Excess weight, whether it be in the form of pounds, people, or worrisome thoughts, can be a drain. Are you aware of where you are being weighed down or overwhelmed? Can you feel where you are being pushed and pulled? Where has "more" become too much? Whether you want more or less material property, this book will ask you to look beyond that. We'll tap into your heart's desires and discover what has real meaning to you.

I once shared a cab home from the airport with an attorney. In his late fifties, he appeared to be successful, but he looked awfully tired. The cabdriver asked me what I did for a living. When I told him I teach how to make dreams come true, he felt compelled to share a little of his life with us.

"Twenty years ago I was fast-tracking up the corporate ladder, when I decided to quit my job and drive a cab. Why? Because life's too short to have stress and structure. The thought of continually doing more of the same made me nuts. In the last twenty years I've acted in a few feature films, written two screenplays, and traveled to every continent in the world. I work when I want to, for as long as I want to. I feel totally free, and I love my life."

I looked over at the attorney and asked what he was thinking. He said, "I've spent a lifetime working my tail off. I have a wonderful family who I hardly see, and great toys that I have no time to play with. I think I need to take a little break and revisit my priorities. But I'm nervous that if I don't keep this pace up, my family will suffer. It's just that if I keep going like this, I know I will have far greater regrets."

Beware of old programming that might immediately surface to squelch your creative process. Are you already starting to feel selfish or guilty? Does even the possibility of a life filled with more of what you want bring up doubts, fears, and concerns? We will deal with those sabotaging thoughts and behaviors in detail in this book. I will help you become acutely aware of them and remove them. They will no longer stop you.

Here's one thing I know for sure: If you create a dream or a goal that you are more committed to than your reality—which includes your worries and doubts—and if you do something to move your dream forward every day or even weekly, you will transform your life.

## HAVING MORE AT WHAT COST?

Andrea called me in distress, saying she needed someone to listen to her dream. Raised as one of five children in a poor family in Atlanta, she took out loans and did whatever was necessary to put herself through college. After graduation, she landed a social-work job. Although she found it rewarding, she was unsatisfied with the low pay.

Andrea believed that the more credentials she had, the more money she would make and, ultimately, the happier she would be. But it didn't quite work that way. She went back to college and got her master's degree. In her mid-thirties she had become a successful, high-paid consultant, but at what cost? She hated the work she was doing, where she was doing it, and whom she was doing it with. She wanted out, but was afraid that she would wind up poor. She felt trapped.

I pointed out how she had swung from one extreme to another and suggested there was a place in the center. We explored the idea that if her dream was to be paid well for doing what she enjoyed, she needed to get very clear about what she wanted to do. What was her truth? What did she really desire?

Andrea wanted to write a novel. As she described it to me, I could feel her passion and sense of devotion. She felt strongly that she had a message to share. Andrea also wanted to have a baby and start her family. As she told me her dreams, she began to cry. All her fears welled up. Should she quit her job? Would her husband become angry or afraid? How would they survive? Would he think her dream was crazy and that she had lost her mind? Would she ever take the risk and do what she wanted to do?

I looked at her and said, "What do you want to do? What really matters?" "I want to pursue my dream," she replied softly. We began the process that this book will walk you through. We separated her dreams from her fears, and used her passion to build a plan that would satisfy her needs. She now has a part-time job working about twenty hours a week, writing marketing brochures and articles, allowing her the flexibility to work on her novel (which is now in progress). Her body and mind are ready to conceive her child (also a work in progress). By the way, giving birth to a baby, a book, or any precious idea are similar processes in many ways. You need to be ready (which includes being rested), wanting, willing, and able. Creating the time and space in your life to give birth to your dreams is essential.

That's what Andrea did. She works less, doing something she enjoys, and she has more of herself and her life now available. The writer Marjorie Kinnan Rawlings said, "It is more important to live the life one wishes to live, and to go down with it if necessary, quite contentedly, than to live more profitably but less happily."

## DOING LESS

Doing less is not about doing nothing. It is about center and balance. It is about choice and freedom. And it is about ease. What is it you would like to do less of? Would you like to fret less? Would you like to have less stress and anxiety? Perhaps you would like to work less, or waste less energy.

Doing less is also about getting rid of garbage: old beliefs and emotional baggage that are weighing you down. Perhaps your idea of less is simply about lightening your load. Maybe it's moving to a smaller home, having a less complicated job, or having easier relationships. Maybe it includes losing weight, changing your mind, your attitude, or your image. It could even be all of the above.

I was working out at my health club when someone asked what my new book was about. I said, "Doing less and having more." A woman next to me perked up and said, "I do that. I've redesigned my life so I live that way." I took Jane to lunch to hear her story.

"When I turned forty-five, I realized I had segmented my life and began the process of integrating my work and home lives. Although I was very successful by most people's standards, I always felt as if I was in the wrong place. I had all the titles and prestige. I was the senior vice-president and chief financial officer of a Madison Avenue advertising agency, a high-level manager at a national bank, and I had CPA letters to put behind my name. But it all came from default rather than from choice.

"One day I realized I could no longer live in that world. I had lost myself and my soul, and I began the process of reclaiming it. I really simplified my lifestyle. I made a short list of the things that mattered to me most. They included important basics like owning my home and car, and some of my favorite extras like a personal trainer, two solo retreats a year and an expensive annual vacation, which my partner and I always take near Big Sur.

"I gave lots up, too, but what I gave up was great. I gave up worrying about money and life and my drive for more and more. I gave up my need to work harder and harder and my titles and labels. I felt like a new person, with a new lease on life. Instead of being driven by life, thinking I was in control, I moved into the driver's seat. I don't do anything just for the money, unless I really want to.

"It's not that I have huge amounts of money socked away. I changed my priorities. We watch our pennies and the dollars take care of themselves. I met a multimillionaire who told me that every dollar you save is worth two dollars that you earn because there are no taxes to pay. We do many things ourselves, like building an extension on our home. We do our own gardening, car-washing, and ironing. I've turned it all into a meditation, and I get some of my most creative ideas while doing these tasks. Then I can take all the money we're saving and invest in my ideas. I'm living the life of my dreams, and all it took was the courage to make the shift."

Jane made clear choices and decisions in her life. She got rid of much, making room for the new. Later in this book, we'll visit the Completion Corner. You will immediately feel lighter and a sense of relief just going through the completion process. As you create more space in your life, you can choose what you are interested in putting into your new life.

But before we delve into the process of purging and re-creating, let's take some time to find *you*. Under all those things you do, places you go, and people you see, let's get in touch with you. This book is designed to help you feel and find yourself. I will show you how you will actually create more by honoring what matters to you most, rather than by meeting everyone else's needs or expectations. Doing what you love will give you more energy, enthusiasm, vitality, and happiness. Wait until you see how much extra you have to give to the people and projects you care about!

If our lives are filled up with too much stuff—too many appointments and way too many commitments—it's difficult to live. It's hard to move freely, to breathe, or to really express your heart and soul if you are burdened and encumbered. This book will help you let go of old stuff and make room for new dreams.

## TO WILL OR NOT TO WILL

One of the most important tools to develop and utilize in your ability to have greater ease is the power of your will. When it comes to doing less, how well do you use will or willpower in your life?

If you don't have enough will, perhaps you are stuck in a rut or in a dead-end job or relationship. Not having enough will often keeps us from taking action or implementing a new idea. Some people think that will is about using effort and control. Or perhaps if you think of exerting your will over another person, it might be considered manipulative.

But will, in its most natural state, is simply about opening yourself, mostly your heart, to an energy that is already here and available. Life is already moving full force around you and actually through you, depending on how open and undefended you are. The simple key to using will successfully is intention. Intention is opening to what you want, and will is using your power drive to get there. By being clear about what you want or need and being open to what life may bring, you can blend will and intention into a magnificent moving force.

Will can be used for manifestation of your dreams and for greater ease. It is a focusing tool that moves energy through you. It is a free-flowing force available to be tapped. What you can clearly see and picture, you can create using your will.

But too much will can be awkward or even dangerous. If, like me, you have been driven by your goals, perhaps as an overachiever, consider this: Excessive work or effort will dissipate the ease, flow, and magic that this process provides. The improper use of will can be destructive.

Do you use your will to steamroller over your feelings? Do you force yourself to do things you don't want or need to do? Where in your life are you using will, control, and effort to manipulate yourself and others?

My life was built on this type of forceful energy, and you know what? It served me well. It helped me become successful, got me through tough times, and enabled me to go for my dreams. But there was a cost. There is always a cost and a payoff to any decision we make. I realized recently that at a certain level, I believe if I don't constantly have goals to pursue, I will die (after becoming a bag lady). But if I live my whole life primarily in the pursuit of my goals, driven by my will, at the end of my life, I will die unfulfilled. I will never know life. All I'll know is my own will.

So the choice here is die now or die later. Personally I've made the choice to die now. The death of a crystallized or habitual behavior is required to allow rebirth, new life, energy, and ideas in. I am practicing not always having my will lead my life. I still dance with it; it's just not always leading.

As I give up some control, I free myself to experience life. Surprises can happen, and I can relax. Although it may be difficult to imagine at this point, surrendering some control actually leads to greater self-trust, confidence, and ease.

Working with your will can be a bit tricky. Will can be elusive. If you try to kill it, you're using your will. To quiet your will is still using your will. What works is getting into partnership with it. Become aware of how much it runs you and your life. Identify trigger points or traits, so you know when your will has kicked in. Responding too quickly, demonstrating rigidity or certainty, even being aggressive, tells me that my will is intensely engaged. When I am unaware of my will, it often throws me off-balance. When I recognize it, I can use it effectively.

I now take a breath and put a pause or a little space between me and a "trigger" situation. I ask myself what am I feeling, knowing that doubt, fear, or worry often initiate my will. I practice taking some time, often telling other people I need to get back to them. In the interim, I might do some research, explore other options, sense my feelings, or just inhale and exhale a few relaxing breaths.

It is possible to use will without resistance, without judgment, and without effort. It can be used to manifest what you want through a laserlike focusing process. Get highly intentional, focus on what you want, and what you want will appear, or at least a clear path for getting it. This is a skill that can be learned. You *can* use your will without being driven by it.

Try these simple steps:

1. Get still and centered, by using your breath to become at ease, and open your heart. Do this by getting comfortable in your seat and taking three or four breaths, from your nose all the way down to your belly.
2. Feel what it is that you want and formulate it into a simple intention. (Example: Today I will spend time relaxing.)
3. Demonstrate your commitment to your intention by taking an action step. Even a small step is fine. (Example: Today I will sit in the park.)
4. Use the power of momentum to do the next thing, too. (Example: While in the park, I will meditate, watch the birds, or lie on the grass.)
5. Make your choices specific and easy. (Example: I'll do this on my lunch break, when I'm outside anyway.)
6. If you feel stuck and unable to move forward, take a breath and review your desire and intention, to deepen your connection to what you want. Open to more will and guidance. (Example: Ask, What else can I do today to relax?)

## ANOTHER WAY TO LIVE

When I first moved to San Francisco I had a dream of a much simpler life, but I also had a big concern. I was worried that force of habit would have me continue to live my life the same driven way I had been living it. I realized that I was moving three thousand miles away to create a new lifestyle, and if I wasn't careful, all I would get was a new backdrop for the same old life.

As a successful businesswoman, my three greatest strengths were my use of will, the power of my effort, and my degree of control. I was well versed in using these skills to make things happen and get the job done. Since the incentive for this big move was to deepen, stretch, and grow personally, I made a deal with myself. For the first three months in this new town, I would not use will, effort, or control. I would abandon my familiar behaviors and stretch outside my comfort zone.

Considering that I was launching a new image and business—in a city where I had few friends or resources—this was terrifying. But some part of me knew that if I continued to use only what I had, I'd be limited and would stay stuck. These kinds of thoughts began to run rampant: Was I crazy? How would I live? I had to market myself. I had to make things happen. These and a thousand other scenarios raced through my mind. Although I was afraid, I knew in my heart that if I didn't practice some new habits and behaviors, I was just going to get more of the same.

Picture this. I found a lovely apartment near the water. In my office, I situated my new desk near a corner window. If I looked to my right, there was the financial district: lots of structure, high-rise cement buildings, and unknown clients beckoning me to pick up the phone and use my will to make something happen.

If I looked to my left, there was the San Francisco Bay, with its flowing waters, sailboats effortlessly gliding by, and the wind gently blowing. I could literally see and physically feel the split I was going through. I sensed that the secret to ease was to find the center place of balance that would honor both. At any moment, I could choose seeing the beautiful flowing water or the dense, immobile towers. This became the metaphor of my life for the next few months.

Many mornings I would hear an inner voice bellowing, "Go knock on those doors. Go sell your services." I would then turn to see the Bay and decide to take a walk on the dock. I would have some moments of panic, but I realized that to use my will at this point would cut off something new, and (I sensed) easier, that was slowly being developed.

I found that if I could weather the storm, on the other side was often an amazing surprise, miracle, or opportunity. Calls for jobs would come out of the blue. I even met a CEO on the pier. He was out clearing his head and contemplating a problem. He wound up becoming one of my biggest clients.

Along the way, I began to develop new skills and a deeper sense of trust. I learned that if I didn't control every gesture and aspect of my life, I would still live. Trust is developed by trusting. It comes as we surrender, and as we surrender, we learn to trust that we will survive.

Surrender to what? How about to life? Life happens. It comes, it goes, and it takes us for a ride. I'm sure this is not news to you. What determines how much ease you will have in your life is how you meet it and deal with it. Surrender comes with practice. The great reward for deep surrender is often complete change. The world can literally be seen from a new perspective.

Had I continued to cling to my will, living life from a place of control, I would have never tapped in to ease. Amazing things happen in life as we create a balanced relationship with our will and learn to dance with it. Through this process, I began to develop belief in myself and my work. At the end of the three months, I began to use will again, as well as effort and control. But by allowing myself to try new skills, to actually put on hold the ways in which I had grown accustomed to dealing with life, my capacity grew. Now I can use will or no will, effort or no effort, control and release of control. Remember this: Everything serves a purpose.

It took letting go of what I knew to access a deeper place of wisdom and to expand my capacity. Having a broader repertoire of life skills to choose from provides less frustration, more choices, and ultimately greater ease.

## A DREAM LIFE

I remember the day I began to change my life. It was joyful and terrifying. Mostly it was confronting. It wasn't so much the asking of the question itself that threw me for a loop and eventually rewired my entire life. It was the answer.

The question was "How do you want your life to be, Marcia?" The answer, shocking at the time, was "Completely different from how it now is. I mean 180 degrees different."

Don't get me wrong. My life was not bad. Many people looking in on my life thought it was a fine one. I was president of a successful marketing and media agency based in Washington, D.C. I lived in a lovely condominium near Dupont Circle and had fun friends and clients. I was president of the D.C. chapter of the National Association of Women Business Owners and had met three United States presidents. Not bad, huh?

I had a little red sports car, with call waiting on the telephone. Uh-oh. Since I had offices in two major markets, I could often be found speeding down the Baltimore-Washington Parkway having some kind of a power talk, oblivious to the fact that the seasons were changing and all the trees were filled with stunning hues.

Then there was the food situation. I'd shop for groceries in D.C., get the crisis phone call from the Baltimore office, drop everything, and head north. By the time I returned home days later, all the food would be spoiled and I would toss it. After a few episodes of this folly, I knew what I had to do. Give up food-shopping and cooking. I didn't cook a meal for seven years.

Those of you who hate being in the kitchen may think this was quite clever. But buyer beware! This was indicative of my lifestyle. I was always going, doing, and accomplishing. There is one thing that's very difficult to do when you are in this overdrive mode. It's called being. I was never present. I was never there for a friend or for my family, much less for a date. And the biggest tragedy was, I was never there for myself.

This period of my life became the beginning of the end. Eventually it became the beginning of the new beginning, but not before the end.

## EMBRACING LIFE

If what you seek and dream of is more joy, juice, and jubilation, you have to open your arms and let it in. Do you meet life with open arms? How about open hands? An open mind and open heart? The ideal way to experience a life of ease is to meet it with all of the above: open-armed, open-minded, and, most important, open-hearted.

This is our goal. Together we will explore a simple process for doing less and having more. I will show you how to live with ease, so your precious life will be back in your hands. From this place you will have newfound dreams and passion. And from this place you will love your life.

This is not a book just about simplifying your life. Although that will be one of the results you can expect, I am not going to offer you 365 things you can do. I won't be talking about organizing your closets or clearing off your desk. These are useful techniques, but there is a deeper, more profound approach needed for having ease.

If you are tired or in need of doing less and having more, this book will help you. From the inside out, you can create so much more ease in your day-to-day existence that many of the overwhelming or incidental details will take care of themselves and go away.

Some of the ideas and premises of this book are ones you may have heard before. Hearing or reading something is useful, but putting it into a simple practice that you can use anytime and anyplace may well be what makes it life-changing.

Offered here are life skills that can be used in any circumstance. Please resist the temptation to make this process more complicated than necessary. Realizing that you already possess many of these skills should give you great comfort. But by the same token, don't write off these techniques as being overly simple or trite. It is how you use what you know and learn that allows you to develop yourself as a master. Transformation can happen in a day or even in a moment.

## THE PROGRAM

This is what's ahead. I will show you a whole new way to look at life, with a series of simple ways to access ease. I will teach you skills that can easily be integrated into your everyday life. I will provide you with a Roadmap to Ease and quick exercises that will literally help you transform your life. I will show you how to ignite or reconnect to your passion and purpose in life and how to use this passion as a force to inspire your dreams.

You will see how to get very clear and focused on any existing ideas or projects and many ways to create new dreams in all areas of life. We'll explore what you want in your personal life, professional life, relationships (both at work and at home), and your financial and physical well-being. I'll help you create your ideal life, and at the base of it will be greater ease.

We'll see how your attitudes and beliefs are moving you forward or holding you back. I will show you how to create a solid foundation for moving forward on your goals and dreams, even when there is no evidence that your dream is a good idea or that this is the right time.

By the end of this book, you will have a map for doing what you want, when you want. You will see how to live more from your passion and less from your calendar. You might even trash your Filofax. But don't panic. We'll replace it with freedom!

Finally, and most important, you'll learn a whole new process for partnering and teaming with other people. You will see how to build an awesome Ease Team who will not only stand by you, but who will actually cheer you across the finish line.

And just for good measure, the last part of this book is filled with additional tips and techniques for maintaining ease on an ongoing basis, every day of your life. Regardless of what you are doing, where you are doing it, and even whom you are doing it with, it is possible to be living in the stream of ease.

As I've mentioned, most of my time is spent traveling around the world, speaking to all kinds of people about their passion and dreams. I have spoken to teenagers (recently I addressed more than fifteen hundred kids for Take Our Daughters and Sons to Work Day), I've spoken at the Federal Penitentiary and at the Kansas City prison. I've spoken on cruise ships with Ann Miller and shared the platform with such greats as Zig Ziglar, John Gray, Marcia Clark, Jack Canfield, and the late Charles Kuralt. I've spoken all over Europe, in Asia, Australia, and Canada, and in cities so small they were hard to find. I've spoken at hundreds of corporations, churches, PTA meetings, and in front of audiences of thousands of people.

Let me tell you what all of these people have in common: They all want more of life. The number-one dream my readers and audiences are clamoring for is ease. If you are prepared to live the life you have always dreamed of, or if you are ready for a new dream, I extend an invitation to you.

I invite you to relax. Take a few deep breaths and say to yourself, "I am ready to begin this journey. I am ready for a new life. And I am absolutely ready for ease." Let's begin.

## FUNDAMENTALS OF EASE

1. In this crazy world where life has become so over-scheduled, overcomplicated, and often overcritical, it's no surprise that many of us often feel defeated, or at least dazed and confused.

2. Your "having more" list may actually turn into your "having less" list, as you purge and clear out the clutter.

3. If you create dreams or goals that you are more committed to than your reality—which includes your worries and doubts—and if you do something to move your dreams forward daily, you will transform your life.

4. Beware of old programming that might immediately surface to squelch your creative process.

5. Doing less is not about doing nothing. It is about center and balance. It is about choice and freedom. And it is about getting rid of garbage: old beliefs and emotional baggage that are weighing you down.

6. The death of a crystallized or habitual behavior is required to allow rebirth, new life, energy, and ideas in. Although it may be difficult to imagine at this point, surrendering some control actually leads to greater self-trust, confidence, and ease.

7. Trust is developed by trusting. It comes as we surrender, and as we surrender, we learn to trust that we will survive. Surrender comes with practice. The great reward for deep surrender is often complete change. The world can literally be seen from a new perspective.

8. You will actually create more by honoring what matters to you most. Doing what you love will give you more energy, enthusiasm, vitality, and happiness.

9. One of the most important tools to develop and utilize is the power of your will. By being clear about what you want or need and being open to what life may bring you, will and intention blend together into a magnificent moving force.

10. It is possible to use will without resistance, without judgment, and without effort. It can be used to manifest what

you want through a laserlike focusing process. Get highly intentional, focus on what you want, and there it is.

11. It takes letting go of what we know to gain access to a deeper place of wisdom and to expand our capacity. Having a broader repertoire of life skills to choose from provides less frustration, more choices, and ultimately greater ease.

12. What determines how much ease you will have is how you deal with life. If what you seek is more joy, juice, and jubilation, you have to let it in. The ideal way to experience a life of ease is to meet life open-armed, open-minded, and most important, open-hearted.

13. Don't write off these techniques as being overly simple or trite. It is how you use what you know and learn that allows you to develop yourself as a master. Transformation can happen in a day, even in a moment.

# 2

# Ease—A Simple Concept

LET'S take a look at what ease actually means, what your relationship to it is, and, most important, how you can have more of it in your life. According to Webster's dictionary, *ease* means "comfort" and "freedom from pain, worry, trouble, and difficulty." Ease is about resting, relaxing, and making life easier, even more natural.

Have you forgotten that ease can be (and actually is) a natural state of being that already resides inside of you? We can experience ease in everything we do, and guess what? We can even experience it easily.

## EASE

I'd like to introduce you to a wonderful concept. Ease is about effortlessly accessing and shifting energy. With little effort, you can tap in to energy as a resource. If life becomes too much, or not enough, you can change your relationship to the energy around you and the way you are using it. By learning to access and shift energy effortlessly, you will come to fully understand ease.

Energy is an inherent force or power efficiently applied. Energy is constantly moving and vibrating. From the smallest particle to the largest planet, everything, including you and me, is energy. We are all made of the same matter: atoms, particles, and so forth. When people say we are all one, they could be speaking spiritually, metaphorically, and physically.

Even our thoughts are made of energy and can be measured, since they are electronic waves. They affect how we feel. If you are angry, afraid, or in a state of turmoil, your heart rate increases and your breathing accelerates. You might even feel an adrenaline rush. Nervous energy makes our system work harder, while relaxing saves energy. Our thoughts and emotions can cause us to burn energy efficiently or needlessly.

Now let's look more closely at the word *ease*. To do something effortlessly means to accomplish a task using a small amount of energy or no energy at all. Results occur without strain or hardship. I'll bet you want more of this in your life. To access a thing means to make it available, while shifting something involves moving it from one place to another.

Think of ease as using a small amount of energy to get what you want effortlessly or to change a given situation. You can do less and have more when you have ease in your life. Let's explore how you can easily have more ease.

One way is to look for patterns. Everything has a pattern, which by definition repeats itself and is predictable. Recognize your patterns and engage with them by becoming aware of what happens, when, why, and how. Be in relationship with your patterns through your awareness.

Once while I was roller-skating with a friend in Colorado, the wind was blowing so strongly on our backs that it made skating effortless. But eventually we had to turn around and skate back to our car. The winds were so strong that we couldn't move. The harder we worked, the more frustrated we got, until we just started laughing. In such situations, it's easy to see you are wasting energy. We were using the wrong energy. As we relaxed more and struggled less, we began conserving energy. We skated in between the gusting winds. It was getting in synch with the wind patterns that got us back to our car.

What patterns or circumstances cause you fatigue or take you out of ease? What inspires you and what frustrates you? It's useful to know what gives you energy and what drains you. Where can you go and what can you do to have more energy? Some of my favorite energizers include: being in the sun, relaxing at the ocean or near mountains, listening to music, hanging out with friends, taking some alone time, and going on retreats. When I am tired or am low on energy, any of these things consistently recharge my battery. Knowing this gives me ease.

Become aware of where and how you waste energy. Notice when you are out of ease or feeling uneasy. When we are out of ease, we become run-down and get sick. Recent research from Ohio University suggests that having a bad attitude puts you more at risk for developing heart disease. There is a direct correlation between ease and your health. So the ideal moment to shift energy is when you begin to experience discomfort or dis-ease in your body, mind, or soul.

## FACING LIFE

Do you notice that on some days, something happens and everything seems to fall apart? It could be something as small as getting a parking ticket or something as dramatic as losing your job, or anything that catches you off-guard. When do you fall to pieces?

I once asked a computer expert to install extended memory in my computer. My computer is near and dear to my heart, since I write all my books on this little laptop. I don't let just anyone mess with it. Only people whom I trust and with proven track records get to dig into the belly of this baby.

I arrived at the predetermined time, clutching my precious machine to my bosom. His home was so dark inside I could hardly see where I was going. When he started unscrewing the wrong compartments, dropping things, and saying "oops," I became instantly distressed and out of ease. I was given a chance to practice what I preach.

I took a deep breath, walked over to a nearby couch, sat down, and opened a magazine. I effortlessly accessed and shifted energy by changing my focus. Within minutes, he proudly declared, "All done." It was complete. The job was just fine. He has a good reputation and does reliable work. That's why I used him. What I realized is that I have a different style and temperament around my computer than he does. The lesson I learned here is that I need to create physical distance, or at least a little emotional distance, when he's doing his thing. I don't need to waste energy or subject myself to unnecessary stress. Life hands us plenty of opportunities for practicing ease. Minimize your dis-ease by knowing what works for you and what doesn't. Get to know your timing and space requirements, and let others know them as well. Become aware of your rhythm and boundaries, as well as your needs and concerns. Take care of you!

What if you didn't have to be at the mercy of life? Could you imagine feeling angry and choosing not to engage or interact with your anger the way you typically do? Why waste the energy? The people involved can't even hear what you're saying if what's coming at them is venom or rage. They could hear you better from a neutral place, a place of no "charge." Getting calm and centered is going to return your power, energy, and ease.

What does it mean to be centered? It means you are calm, not out of control. You use your breath to relax and have an open mind so you see what's going on. You also have an open heart so you are compassionate, perhaps even able to see the other side's point of view. From a centered place, you are focused and fully available to engage with the situation. Learning to center offers the greatest access to ease.

If you don't engage with the anger, or whatever negative feelings may be coming at you, you often won't be affected by them. It's like when someone says something to you that you know isn't true about you. It rolls off your back. There is no charge, so you don't bother with it. This is different from just biting your tongue. If you are repressing your emotions, you are wasting energy. If you don't get angry about the situation to begin with, or refuse to let it get to you, or at least don't remain upset, you waste little or no energy and maintain ease.

Even if someone is angry with you, it doesn't have to affect or bother you. Stepping aside from your own and others' anger may take a bit of practice, but it will come. You can shift the energy coming at you by the way you meet it. If you're not engaging in a battle, others may lay their weapons down and release their anger. Fuel is needed to feed a fire. If there is no fuel or reaction coming from you, then there is no fire.

Sometimes when we have the guts and wisdom to shift first, others will follow. I love this model for leaders. The simplest technique for doing this may be to apologize. I recall a time when someone came at me spewing rage. I calmly listened. When he was done exploding, I said I was sorry about what had happened, sorry he felt that way, and sorry he was so upset. I didn't defend my position, attack him, or make him wrong. I just apologized. The most powerful thing I did was not to get sucked into his drama.

By using this technique, you remain centered and are a calm force within the chaos around you. This is a simple approach for tapping in to your power and accessing ease. It doesn't mean you won't feel or be affected by life, but if you meet life from a quiet place, you will have access to far greater resources and options for engaging with it.

## THE POWER OF ENERGY

Imagine if you could plug into life's energy. This is the energy that created oceans and continents; that moves as hurricanes or tornadoes. It is both creative and destructive. It is unbridled and awesomely powerful. It is this energy that exists in varying degrees in everything, including us.

If we were fully tapped into this force, we could instantly manifest our thoughts or desires because nothing would stand between us and everything else. We are the same energy as everything else, since we are connected to great creative forces. But on a day-to-day basis, we don't experience our power because of the blocks and defenses we have created.

Energy is always present and moving through us. We become disconnected from our natural energy because of defenses and distractions. Fears, doubts, limiting beliefs, overloading on inconsequential details, or judging and complaining rob us of our strength. The way to recharge, to get back in the flow and reconnected to a great power source, is to open. Open your mind and open your heart. You can begin to do this by using your thoughts. Our thoughts create words, which create actions. Whether you act on your thoughts or not doesn't matter. Just to have a thought activates the energy process.

Shifting energy, then, is about moving from a closed state to an open posture. The simplest technique I know for this is breathing, which I will discuss in greater detail in Chapter 3. Full, deep breathing for just one minute can help restore your equilibrium. This moves stuck energy. When we shift energy, we gain clarity and patience. We can be vulnerable rather than defensive, and can even ask for help or guidance from others.

If we can get still and reconnected to our center, ease is assured. Unfortunately, for some this will never happen. For many, it will take a lifetime to learn this skill. For you, it could occur very soon and easily, if you make it a practice and a priority.

## THE PHASES OF LIFE ENERGY

A client named Denise called me, sounding distraught. She felt that nothing was happening in her life. She felt stuck and blocked, energetically, physically, and creatively. She said her business was flat, she had gained weight, and she found everything to be a struggle.

I asked Denise what was going on in her life. She said there were two major issues. Her husband had asked for a divorce, and her only child was leaving home to begin college. "No wonder you feel the way you do," I said. "This is not the time to be initiating new projects. This is a time for *you*."

Denise was in a completion phase of her life. Many of the things she normally would be doing—things that reinforced her identity as a wife and mother—were no longer necessary. She was entering a different phase of her life, but she was hanging on to her old behaviors. Naturally, this was confusing and depleting.

At different times in our life, opportunities offer options. One of the most important things we can learn, in order to live a life of greater ease, is to recognize these times. We need to meet and match our situation or our life phase with the appropriate energy. These major phases are: 1) initiatory, 2) experiential or creative, 3) completion, 4) transitional, and 5) rest.

These phases can last days, months, or even years. When you are aware of which phase you are in, you can use the appropriate skills, and, more important, the appropriate energy associated with that phase. You can be fully present and in relationship to yourself, the circumstances, and to life. You can learn and grow, and welcome all of these phases.

When things go haywire and life turns into a major struggle, it's usually because we are in one phase of life energy, with a big preference for being someplace else. We have all experienced this pushing-a-cart-uphill syndrome. It's useful to consciously check in with yourself and see what life phase you're in and how you are doing in handling it. There are times when we should be creating, moving forward, and making things happens. There are also times when it would be silly, perhaps even dangerous, to do this.

What will give you ease is to become aware of what's happening in your life and how you are feeling about it. You can create dramatic and wonderful results in your life with small amounts of effort when the time is right. But the converse is true, too. All the effort and energy in the world are not going to help you if it's not the right time.

An Ease Master (which you are in training to become) learns to read the signs along the way, making sure to take the path of least resistance. Let's explore the five major energetic phases of life and see where you are now.

### Initiatory Phase

This is the phase of beginnings. Perhaps you are in a new relationship, home, or job. During this phase you may feel as if you have a lot of energy. You may feel happy or overwhelmed. There's often a lot of activity. This is a time of great creativity. New ideas may be flowing, and new opportunities often follow.

You may be asked to make some major decisions during this phase. You may feel alive, vibrant, and enthusiastic. During one of my biggest initiatory phases I was writing a new book, in production on a national infomercial, and preparing to launch Dream University (a weeklong curriculum in Maui). Often I don't like to have so many big things happening all at once. But during this particular phase I had a great deal of clarity and tremendous amounts of energy. The more I recognized this time as an initiatory phase, the more I was able to meet it with my own start-up energy.

Realizing that this was a phase, I understood I didn't have to—and wouldn't be able to—maintain this level of energy forever. But I used it while I had it. I was so tapped into this "birthing" process that I even got an idea for a new book. I knew it wouldn't work to write two books at once, so I outlined my idea and set it aside as a great future project.

Recognizing this energy in myself helped me offer useful guidance when I received an excited phone call from one of my readers. Charlene is in her mid-fifties and lives in Seattle. She had been a nurse for more than thirty years and today was her last day at work. For at least five years she had been developing a new dream. She wanted to be a Feng Shui consultant. Feng Shui is an ancient Chinese art for designing and creating beautiful environments. It is an intuitive practice that teaches how to use furniture arrangement, color, plants, and lighting so that your home or office becomes a source of renewed energy.

There was only one problem, Charlene told me. "All I need to do in order to become certified is complete a program offered in California. Now that I've quit my job, I'm a little afraid to spend the money."

"Charlene," I said, "if this is your dream, it is essential that you put your money where your mouth is. Invest in yourself. Invest in your dream." During initiatory phases, people often draw back, unsure or afraid. This is the most important time to take a step forward. This is the "take action" phase. Giving birth requires pushing and expelling energy.

Do I think Charlene quit her job too soon or should have planned ahead? Not necessarily. When you feel ready, or when it's time to make a change, and you are more committed to your dream than to your reality, take the leap and move ahead.

The point is that while you are in this phase, you want to learn to ride the wave. Initiatory phases can be exciting, but if you are unaware, they can also be dangerous. The rest of your life still exists. The bills need to be paid and you need to eat, sleep, and take care of yourself, so some planning ahead is useful. Initiatory phases and opportunities come often. Prepare for them by knowing what your needs are. Learn to recognize when these powerful times arrive, and use the techniques in this book to clear the space so you can take advantage of them.

### Experiential or Creative Phase

Once you are in progress on something, you are in what I call the experiential phase. Whether you are a working professional, a student, a parent, or an athlete, when you are fully experiencing what you are doing, you are truly living. This is often a very creative time, but it differs from the initiatory phase because you are entrenched in your project rather than at the beginning of it.

The creative phase can take us to many wonderful places. We feel alive and engaged with life, our process, and our projects. We can also get lost, feel overburdened, or become overly critical of our progress. This phase can either generate or sap your energy.

The questions are, While you are doing what you do, are you also aware of what you are feeling? Do you notice your level of energy? How about the environment where you are doing it? Is it comfortable and supportive? Are you in relationship with the people around you?

Do they know what you are doing and how they might help? Are you learning and growing while you are doing this? And are you loving the experience? Do you still get turned on by the little things in life?

So much of our life is spent experiencing, but often after the first time, or after a while, jobs, tasks, or relationships become stale. If you are fully present to your experience, the chances of this happening are reduced. To stay present, be aware and notice what's happening, including your thoughts and actions, while you are engaged with your tasks.

Sometimes we love what we are doing so much, we keep doing it long after we've mastered it and are ready for the next step. The more present we are, the more likely we will be to realize when this experience is nurturing, fun, and important, and when it might be time to move into the next phase. Perhaps it's still "fun" but it's no longer "important" in that it's not growing you.

Another reason to be as aware as possible during an experiential phase is to notice if you are turning into an "intensity junkie." A new personality category has been identified called the "type T" personality. The "T" stands for thrill-seeking. My friend Jeff is a type T. He had mastered boogie boards and surfing, so he moved into skydiving. Skydiving soon got old, so now it's bungee jumping. The problem is, there's no place high enough for him to jump from anymore.

By getting in touch with what he was feeling and needing, Jeff realized that what he wanted was not a physical thrill, but to feel himself and to be affected by life. He was mistaking physical intensity for emotional aliveness. He had to stop running, flying, and jumping so he could get honest with himself and connect to what he really wanted.

### Completion Phase

When we are completing, we are winding down and ending something. Sometimes we want to celebrate the completion and sometimes we need to mourn a loss. For example, when Denise realized that she was in a completion phase of her life, her priorities changed. She focused on getting her son off to college. Then she celebrated by taking good care of herself. Part of her completion plan included losing extra weight and redecorating her son's room. And there were important conversations to have with her family, especially with her husband, and with her attorney.

Concurrently, she was trying to launch a new accounting business and fill a workshop with paid clients. She clearly saw that this was not the time for this project, but rather an important time to build a support system around herself. So she put her new venture on hold.

When my friend Sandra left her job as a lawyer, it was a long time before she felt ready to initiate something new. She had spent most of her adult life building an identity and reputation as a lawyer. Although she knew she was doing the right thing, she had to face the ego death associated with leaving something that was such a big part of her. The completion time took many months. Only she could decide when she was ready to begin something new. Along the way, she did have to work and make some money, but she chose a job much less taxing than law. She got a part-time job as a salesclerk. It gave her some mental and emotional space in which to reflect on her feelings, as well as a gentle way to reenter casual relationships.

Stay finely tuned to your feelings and internal needs during the completion phase. This is a time for some to reach out and ask for help and for others to turn inward, tapping internal resources.

Later in this book, I'll take you through a process guaranteed to clear out some clutter and free up energy in your daily life. If you feel that you are in need of this right now, you can skip ahead to Chapter 12 and begin the process. It's never too soon to handle "incompletions."

Whether you choose to do this process now or later, it's essential to recognize and honor the fact that you are in a completion phase. These are necessary and important milestones in our lives. If we never completed certain aspects of our lives, we would have little or no time for initiating anything new. And although rebirth and new projects and opportunities do follow, sometimes these things don't happen right away.


## Transitional Phase

Often we are so eager to jump into what's next that we don't let ourselves enter the transitional phase. To make a transition is to pass from one stage to another or from one activity to another. Transitions can be anything from moving to a new home or city to changing a career or a major relationship. Transitions are often crossroads in our lives and usually require some time for contemplation, reflection, and introspection.

During transition, it is often unwise to make major decisions. Transition is about change, but it's a process. There are many things that you may be unsure of until the dust settles. Any decision that can be postponed should be.

When Leslie was making a move from New York to California, she was having a hard time deciding what clothes and furniture to take. Tired of thinking about it, she sold just about everything she owned. Upon hitting the West Coast, she was shocked to see how expensive everything was. By the time she paid all her moving expenses, it would be a long while before she could afford to buy a new bed. "Perhaps I overreacted a bit," she told me.

On the other hand, Leslie was thrilled that she hadn't brought her New York wardrobe to California. She knew she wanted to feel different living out here, and that included having a new look. Her budget forced her to buy slowly, but she loved every item she bought. Creating a new wardrobe became part of her transitional process. "Besides, sweaters are much cheaper than sofas," Leslie told me.

Janet, an accountant living in Boston, told me that the biggest transition she ever experienced was her father's illness and eventual death. She said it was a time of huge growth, and she wouldn't trade the experience for anything.

"On my dad's deathbed he told me things about himself that I never knew. He showed me how he had met his obligations but in the process, how he had abandoned his dreams. He'd always wanted to be a greenskeeper at a golf course, but never did it. He inspired me to live my life differently, but it wasn't until he actually died that I felt free.

"My father was a proud, dignified, intellectual, and gracious man. He was struck by cancer, and his physical decline was very hard on him and on me. But the time we spent together those last three years of his life was extraordinary. We completed our relationship with many tears and much laughter. We said all the things we needed to say, everything that was in our hearts. Without a doubt, my dad's transition was the most transformative time of my life."

I recommend moving just a bit more slowly during times of transition. Transitions may bring heightened emotional swings. This is often a great time for new ideas to incubate. While incubating, a new idea has the leisure to percolate, develop, and take form. Just keep checking in with yourself to see what you need, and honor the urgings of your heart and soul as much as possible. Personally, I love transition time. I feel it brings an element of surprise and newness to my life. Just be aware that this phase requires different energy and actions than initiating, experiencing, or completing something.

*Rest Phase*

Here's a phase that often is overlooked, yet it is one of the most powerful periods of our lives. When we are resting, which includes taking time out in between these phases, every part of us has the chance to heal and rejuvenate.

Many of us fear rest. My friend Bob's motto in life is "Do or die." He's afraid that if he slows down, he'll become complacent, lethargic, and unmotivated. He hardly ever rests, and he's often exhausted, ill, or both.

On a recent episode of *Mad About You*, Jamie is excited to have a week off from work so she can do nothing. After reading *Jane Eyre*, making new curtains for all the windows, and laying shelf paper, she realizes she can't stop and simply rest. I went on a retreat with a friend who was the same way. We were eager to do nothing but rest. For her, that translated into exercising every day, working with art supplies, photographing nature spots, writing a song and three poems, and calling the office daily. Sound like anyone you know?

It is in the quiet time that some of the most profound things happen. Do you know how to stop and really do nothing? Do you know how to just hang out? This is difficult for many of us. We have spent so much of our lives keeping busy, being productive and occupied. It is in the quiet time that we can reconnect to our true selves, our true needs, and our true desires.

Practice being with yourself. Schedule "time out" from the world, when you do nothing. Don't read or watch television or talk on the phone. Use this time to tune in to your inner self. Use this time to get to know yourself. Use this time to rest, especially when you have completed one phase but are not yet ready to initiate something new. Hanging out "in the void" or not acting on something right away is an essential part of the creative process. If it weren't for the silences between the notes, we wouldn't have music. Don't miss the sweet music of life. Remember to rest.

## SEEING THE WORLD

Ease has everything to do with how you use your energy to engage with life. This section provides three essential skills for clearly seeing the world. If you become aware of them and practice them, you can master them. Although they are not complicated in nature or form, there is some work to be done here.

We each have our habits and behaviors. You and I have our own funny little quirks and ways of dealing with things. Sometimes we respond from a conscious and centered place. Unfortunately, at some time or another, we react to life's difficulties from an immature or irresponsible place. Primarily what we do in these instances is blame and judge others.

The following three techniques—projection, perception, and point of view—will empower you to take responsibility for your own life. Maybe that sounds exciting; maybe it sounds scary. For some, taking responsibility is liberating and for others it's burdensome. This I do know: If you want a life of less effort and wasted energy, a life of ease, developing these skills is important.

### Projection

Projection is one the most life-changing skills I know. When it comes to accessing and shifting energy, this is a skill you will want to know about and understand. I had heard about projection for many years before I began to see the impact it was having on me, my relationships, and my life. I now understand it so well that I can present it to you in a simple and straightforward way.

We all have reactions—positive and negative—to people and situations that we encounter in everyday life. If you look at your relationships with family, friends, coworkers, or even with the post office, taxes, or bad weather, this basic principle is the same. It is possible to use these reactions, known as projections, to see things about ourselves that we are often blind to. The irony is, although we can often see these quirks in others and they see them in us, we don't easily see them in ourselves.

But we need to see them and should want to. How else can we begin to know ourselves? How else can we stop wasting tremendous amounts of energy blaming others for our upsets? How else can we gain peace of mind and ease, if we can't see the truth around us and about us? Here's how projection works.

*Step 1:* The next time you are having a reaction to someone, in the form of not liking something that is being said or done, begin to notice what you are thinking and feeling. Call this the "pointing finger" phase. Say to yourself, "They are so mean, controlling, and manipulative," or whatever else applies. The more you can recognize and name the adjectives that are upsetting you, the better.

*Step 2:* Ask yourself when you have felt this way before. It's important that you find a specific memory of when you actually felt this. Sometimes it takes a while, and sometimes a memory will pop right up. You can use your feelings to help you recall. Let your anger, fear, or frustration bubble up, and use it as a vehicle to help you remember a past experience.

*Step 3:* Ask yourself when *you* have acted the way you are describing. Again, find a specific memory of when you were the controlling, manipulative one. You may have to broaden out the experience. For example, if the projection you are working on has to do with your sense of outrage at a crime you saw reported on the evening news, perhaps you are angry about the violence involved. Although you may never have shot someone or been physically violent, you may remember a time when you were intrusive or verbally abusive. There is sure to be a memory, or you would not be having the reaction you're experiencing. This is how projection works.

*Step 4:* This step is essential. Ask yourself how you do this to yourself. When are you violent or invasive? When are you self-annihilating or manipulative and mean? Don't just answer, "Always." Look for specifics and let yourself feel the impact of what you do to yourself and others. This begins the process of awareness. As I see the behaviors in others that I don't like, trust, or respect, I can begin to see parts of myself that are "disowned" or unrecognizable.

As we learn to work responsibly with projections, we can begin to develop greater compassion for ourselves and others. We can learn that when we are pointing our finger at someone else, this is an amazing opportunity for us to look, listen, and learn about ourselves.

Projections are everywhere. Turn on the television, open the newspaper, go to the movies, listen to conversations, call a relative, or just look out your window. As I've said, we have positive and negative projections. The things that you like, respect, and admire in others are also true about you. Use your positive projections to learn about these parts of yourself as well.

Once you practice and understand projection, you will no longer waste energy blaming, ridiculing, or judging. In a moment, you will be able to shift your energy from making them or "it" wrong, to feeling gratitude, acceptance, and compassion, because you will see that what you are upset about and reacting to is you. A Jungian analyst once said, "What other?" We are all one. You are me and I am you and we are perfect mirrors for each other.

This idea may be hard to grasp, but as you work with your projections, you will see how true this is. Projections can be like neon signs. They are pointing out lessons to be learned and places where energy can be accessed and shifted. Use them, learn from them, own them, and, ultimately, release them.


*Perception*

As I once read in *The Daily Word*, "I no longer try to change outer things. They are simply a reflection. I change my inner perception and the outer reveals the beauty so long obscured by my own attitude. I concentrate on my inner vision and find my outer view transformed."

Where do you put your attention and energy when something upsetting happens to you? Do you need to be right, and so put energy into making other people wrong? Is your focus on "them" and what they are doing or have done to you? Are you focused on being right, rather than on resolution?

I had a disagreement with a client recently. She wrote me a harsh letter, accusing me falsely of something she felt I had done to her. I turned to a friend for guidance. To my dismay, my friend put her attention on making my client wrong. After ten minutes of hearing her trashing the client for what she said and how she was acting, I felt worse, not better. I realized we had our attention in the wrong place.

My goal was to resolve the situation amicably, ideally maintaining the relationship. First I had to get clear about what had happened and what I was feeling about it. Using the steps above, I worked with my projections. I saw how my reactions about her were, at some level, reactions to myself.

Once I had handled my reactions, I could focus on the facts — "Just the facts, ma'am." I wrote out in detail, as best I could, what had transpired. For the first time, I saw how vague my language had been regarding our agreement. This objectivity was what I needed before calling my client.

I apologized for the portions of our agreement in which I had been misleading. I told her I could see her point of view, although I didn't agree with her conclusion. I offered to have a new document drafted, at my expense. I also did something else that was important: I asked her what she needed to get our relationship back on an even keel.

Have you ever tried to have an argument with someone who is agreeing with you? It's not easy. This is a great technique for conserving energy. I'm not saying that you should abandon your beliefs or take blame for things you didn't do, but if you can at least agree that the other person's point of view is valid, she will feel heard, respected, and perhaps appreciated. Rather than meet her head-on, you are meeting her with open hands. An argument can disappear in a moment through agreement. Now, on neutral turf, you can both explore what needs to be done. You may find this process difficult if your attention is on being right rather than on reaching a resolution.

A mother of three little children shared this story with me. "I came home after a long day at the office to find that my two youngest kids had colored with crayons on the living-room wall. My first reaction was to want to scream, but I took a deep breath and just smiled at them. We went to the local drugstore, where I bought frames. Imagine their delight when I turned their scribbles into works of art by framing them. When I shift my perception, reality changes, too."

How we view the world, other people, and the messes we get ourselves into is important. How we choose to clean them up is essential. To practice ease, be responsible for your perceptions and actions.

MISPERCEPTION

As a new member of the monastery, a young monk observed many of the elders sitting around a large wooden table with pen in hand. The young monk asked, "What do they copy, Brother?"

"As they have been for centuries, they are writing word for word what is contained in the ancient writs. These will take the place of the old, and will be handed down to the next generation of monks to copy as well."

"What happens if they copy it wrong?" the young one asked.

"Throughout the centuries that has never happened. Here, follow me and I will show you," said the elder monk, leading the younger one by the hand toward a great door with many locks on it.

After unlocking the first door, the elder monk whispered, "Wait right here and I will find the first book ever written with our teachings in it and you can compare it to the newest book."

After waiting for about an hour, the young monk got curious and peeked inside the room to see the elder monk with his head bowed in his arms. Hearing sobs, the younger monk raced into the room and said, "Brother, Brother, what could be wrong?"

The elder monk looked up with tears in his eyes and said, "Celebrate! The word was celebrate, not celibate!"

Where has your perception turned into misperception? Misperceptions can lead to false beliefs that can be handed down from generation to generation. Evaluate your perceptions throughout your life. See if they are still true and accurate, and be adaptable.


*Point of View*

Sometimes just being willing to see a new point of view can completely shift the energy and resolve tension. Although seeing a new point of view doesn't mean you have to shift your former one, it does help you broaden your horizons, offering more options. When we take a fixed position, we may become self-righteous and ultimately lose what matters to us. Being flexible will always give you much more range than being rigid. Remember, it is the ocean that washes away the rocks, not the other way around.

Especially in our closest relationships, we often take a firm stand and are unwilling to bend. How many friendships has this cost you? Virginia Woolf said, "I have lost many friends. Some through death, others through the sheer inability to cross the street."

When you cross the street, you gain a new point of view. Do you meet your opponent or dig in your heels, insisting that he come to you? Everything looks different from another's point of view. During times of stress or duress, the thought of doing this can be a lot to swallow.

Here's a tip that is often taught in couples work. When you and someone else are having a dispute over an issue, see if you can get on the same side. Imagine for a moment that a piece of paper is the issue. Hold it up at arm's length in front of you, perhaps even blocking your view. Picture someone you care about or are at odds with on the other side. This issue has come between you.

Now imagine or actually have this person sit next to you. Both of you reach out and hold the paper/issue together. You are on the same side looking at ways to handle or resolve your problem. You have shifted your point of view. From this place you probably will see new ideas and alternatives. Even if you don't reach a resolution, at least you'll be sitting together. From here you can at least agree to disagree.

One evening, dining out with friends, I watched Katie and Larry fight. Neither of them was listening to the other. It sounded as if they were caught in a loop. Every time one of them said something, it was as though a bell rang in a boxing ring, and they were at each other. This created more and more frustration and mistrust. They entered couples counseling, where an impartial listener could help them sort out their behavior toward each other.

In counseling they saw that they were wasting tremendous amounts of energy trying to be heard. Each had a valid point of view, but until each could begin to make some space for the other's view, there was no chance for peace. With a little practice they learned to see each other's point of view. Katie would speak and Larry would repeat back to her what he heard her say. This required him to really listen, rather than focusing on his own point of view. They began making statements like "I hear you." And they really did begin to hear each other. Their relationship became safer, they shared deeper emotions, and they fell in love again. "Whether we are right or wrong has become secondary to our desire to understand each other. We are practicing honoring our differences and learning from each other," Larry told me.

Shifting your point of view gives you access to more options and an opportunity to grow. It takes the focus off us/them, me/you, right/wrong, and win/lose. It helps you get to the heart of the matter and stop wasting energy, which is what ease is all about.

Accept the premise that we and everything in life, in one form or another, is energy and you will appreciate that we have the opportunity to tap into a great source of power and potential. Just this will give you ease because it will open your eyes to more of life.

## FUNDAMENTALS OF EASE

1. According to Webster's dictionary, *ease* means "comfort" and "freedom from pain, worry, trouble, and difficulty." Ease is about resting, relaxing, and making life easier, even more natural.

2. With little effort, you can tap into energy as a resource. By learning to effortlessly access and shift energy, you will come to fully understand ease.

3. Our thoughts and emotions can cause us to burn energy efficiently or needlessly. Nervous energy makes our system work harder, while relaxing saves energy.

4. Think of ease as a way to use a small amount of energy to effortlessly get what you want or to change a given situation. You can do less and have more when you have ease in your life.

5. When we are out of ease, we often experience disease and get sick. It's no surprise that being out of ease causes us to become run-down and ill. There is a direct correlation between ease and your health.

6. You can shift the energy coming at you by the way you meet it. Fuel is needed to feed a fire. If there is no fuel or reaction coming from you, then there is no fire.

7. Sometimes when we have the guts and wisdom to shift first, others will follow. The simplest technique for this may be to apologize.

8. Learning to center offers the greatest access to ease. You are calm, not out of control, have an open mind, and see what's going on. You are compassionate, able to see the other points of view, focused, and available to engage with the situation.

9. One of the most important things we can learn, in order to live a life of greater ease, is to meet and match our situation or our life phase with the appropriate energy. These major phases are: 1) initiatory, 2) experiential or creative, 3) completion, 4) transitional, and 5) rest.

10. Ease has everything to do with how you use your energy to engage with life. The following three techniques will

empower you to take responsibility for your own life: pro-jection, perception, and point of view.

11. We have positive and negative projections. The things that you like, respect, and admire in others are true also about you. Use your positive projections to learn about these parts of yourself as well.

12. Once you understand projection, you will no longer waste energy blaming, ridiculing, or judging. You will shift your energy from making them or "it" wrong to feeling grati-tude, acceptance, and compassion, because you will see that what you are upset about and reacting to is yourself.

13. How we view the world, other people, and the messes we get ourselves into is important. How we choose to clean them up is essential. To practice ease, practice being re-sponsible for your perceptions and actions.

14. Willingness to see a new point of view can completely shift the energy and resolve tension. When we take a fixed position, we may ultimately lose what matters to us. Being flexible will always give you much more range than rigidity.

15. Shifting your point of view gives you access to more op-tions and an opportunity to grow. It helps you get to the heart of the matter and stop wasting energy, which is what case is all about.

## 3

# Making Life Easy

I T'S worth repeating: How you choose to interface with life is what will give you ease. Notice what's happening and what you are feeling. Become aware of how you are reacting and responding. Take a moment to breathe and check in with yourself.

There's a time to stay with your reactions and to engage with the discomfort; to access the place inside you that is out of ease. These feelings and reactions can be amazing teachers, offering great insight and growth. You need to decide "when to hold them and when to fold them."

Different situations at different times in life obviously require different responses. Practice, inquire, and experiment. Ask yourself, "Where do I need to go inside myself emotionally or physically? What will give me ease right now?"

When you are present and aware, you are able to make choices. Use some of the following techniques to make your life easier. By expanding your repertoire of responses and trying some simple new behaviors, you can become an Ease Master.

## TEN STEPS TO GREATER EASE

1. **Focusing**—Focus encompasses how you look at life and what you decide to do about any given thing. If you can clearly see where you are and know where you want to be, figuring out how to get there actually is easy. When we are focused on something, our energy is sharp. With clear sight, we see what's happening in our current situation. We are less scattered and less ambivalent. Focus is the point where everything comes together. When you focus, your efforts easily produce results. There are many skills that you can learn and use to help you focus. Meditation, contemplation, breath work, and goal setting all help develop greater focus. We'll discuss these later in this chapter.

   Pay attention to where your focus is. David had just started running as a way of keeping fit. He noticed that sometimes he had tremendous energy and could run for long periods of time, and that at other times he was dragging himself along. His energy level corresponded to where he put his focus. If he saw a big hill ahead, he would think, "This is going to be hard work." His energy would drop, making him tired and wanting to quit.

   If he came to a steep decline, he would think, "If I go that way, I'll have to run uphill on the way back." David laughed at himself, realizing he was so busy focusing on the ups and downs of the hills that he wasn't even seeing the beautiful scenery along his path. As a first step, he focused his attention on his feet and the road right in front of him. He stopped being distracted by the hills and eventually hit his stride. He started feeling that runner's high.

   Elated and really enjoying his run, David felt inspired by a divine presence. He asked, "God, if you are the reason I feel so happy, please give me a sign." David turned his eyes up toward the sky and with his next step planted his foot in a huge pile of cow dung. The moral of the story is: Life will distract you. Stay focused.

2. **Resting**—I mentioned this earlier as a phase in life. Although many of us resist resting, it is essential. Daily rest is especially useful. Resting doesn't have to mean stopping, although for some of us this would be the greatest gift we could give our-

selves. Quiet time allows us to rejuvenate, empty out, and re-
fresh ourselves. A rest period, whether it be a nap, deep sleep,
or a wonderful overdue vacation, is the ideal time and way for
us to reenergize ourselves. A little inactivity can go a long way.

How do you give yourself relief? Where do you go for peace
of mind? Do you even know how to be still? Please don't turn
your resting time into a stress period by forcing yourself to sit
or be still. Tune in to your needs by listening to your inner
wisdom. Learn how to shift gears, from go, go, go to rest.

I was kayaking in Northern California with some friends. It
was my first time out and they promised it would be restful on
the calm water, and it was. After two hours, while paddling
back to the shore, I became tired. I took my internal pulse by
simply noticing how I was feeling and what I was doing. I saw
that I was rushing back with everyone else, trying to keep up
with them. I decided in that moment to move at my own
pace, to honor my particular needs. By slowing down and relaxing, I returned last, but rested.

If you are someone who can rest only when you are away
from home, the phone, the kids, and so on, ask yourself these
questions: "When was the last time I took time out for me?
When was the last time I had a good rest—one that left me
invigorated?" If it's been more than a year (or more than a
month, depending on your tolerance and needs), I invite you
to take out your calendar and schedule an ease break. The
purpose of this break is to rest, and to access and shift your
energy. It is in this quiet time that some of the most profound
things can happen.

3. **Dreaming**—While you are sleeping, are you aware of your
dreams? Our dreams are the bridge between the world as we
know it and other realms, such as our imagination or fantasy
world. Dreams connect the unconscious to the conscious.
When you are asleep, your mind is free to roam. You can receive guidance and knowledge from these wanderings. Learning to work with your dreams gives you access to your own
unbounded creativity.

During times of stress and frustration, I often go to sleep.
Just prior to dozing off, I'll ask for a dream to offer some insight and relief. If you are someone who likes to keep a tight
rein of control in your life, the idea of surrendering a current

struggle to your dreams might be a tough one to swallow, but I am convinced that dreaming can help you tap in to great energy and shift where you are. Once I was stressed because I couldn't find my credit card. In my dream, I remembered where I put it. Another time I was unable to decide whether to go away for the weekend or stay home. In a dream, I saw myself lounging around the house, feeling quite content. Dreams can often be clear and direct in their messages.

You can choose to work your dreams consciously by learning about dream symbols or by finding someone who can help interpret your dreams. You can intuit what the images are showing you. Whether you figure out a small piece or understand the entire dream, your dream can provide insight.

Studies indicate that we may be able to program our dreams to help us solve problems or to make things happen. If you are intrigued by this concept, I recommend reading *Dream Alchemy* by Ted Andrews.

4. **Deciding**—When you are in the decision-making process regarding anything important in your life, this is not the time to act. Spend too much time deciding, however, and you may dissipate your energy or miss the opportunity to act. Much more than doers, we should be deciders. Once the decision is made, the doing is easy. And once the decision is made, all the energy around you shifts to a more relaxed state.

One of the most important things we can do to expedite decisions is to use our intention. Once we are clear about our purpose and values, we can set our mind in the right direction.

Whenever I'm faced with an important decision, I have learned to give myself a time frame. I set a specific date or time in the near future within which I *intend* to make up my mind. When the pronounced moment comes, if I'm still unsure, I have learned to say no. My self-imposed deadline requires resolution.

My friend Alan Cohen, author of *The Dragon Doesn't Live Here Anymore* and a dozen other books, offers the best way I know for making decisions. Flip a coin. Heads it's yes, tails it's no. Then see how you feel about the response. If you are disappointed by the coin toss, do the opposite. If you are delighted, then proceed as advised. In other words, sometimes you just have to follow your heart or instinct. Often there is no evidence that what you are doing is a good idea. But if you can practice believing that life is about lessons, experiences, and opportunities, then can you really ever make a wrong decision?

Be aware of the energy you may be wasting in the "worry process," or by vacillating endlessly. Make your decisions as efficiently as possible and you will experience much greater ease in life.

5. **Acting**—Once the decision is made, take some action. Show yourself and the people in your life that you are not just talking about your hopes and dreams, but are actually in action, moving them forward. Everything changes when you move forward. New resources become available, self-esteem is fueled, and powerful messages of self-confidence are sent to your psyche. It's a whole new game.

Taking action links vision and passion, because as your imaginative juices get sparked, your projects become charged and energized. This will intensify the creative process, inspiring you to keep going. If you continue to take action, both small and large steps, the fulfillment of your dreams is assured.

When I wanted to move to California and couldn't sell my condominium in Washington, D.C., people around me were telling me to forget the dream. When I finally became focused and intentional that what I wanted was to live on the West Coast, new energy and ideas took over. I decided to rent the condo. Taking this action opened the floodgates.

I picked up and moved. I found my first client. I wrote a book, and then another. I caught a wave and it took me on a fabulous and fast ride. But unless you take your board and paddle out, how is the surf ever going to pick you up? Are you looking for the wave? Are you showing up with your gear? Are you available? Are you saying yes? Are you meeting life? Are you letting it take you for a ride? Say yes to life!

I was giving a keynote speech last week at the Body, Mind and Soul Conference in Maryland. An excited woman came up to me at the end of my talk. She said, "Last year at this conference I heard Dr. Wayne Dyer speak. He offered great wisdom about believing in your dreams. Today you gave me an additional piece, and I can feel how it is going to change my life forever. It's essential to believe in your dreams and to act on them. The acting shows you that you really do believe!"

6. **Talking**—Some people think by talking. You can talk out your ideas and thoughts, your frustrations and concerns. I often feel better about something after I talk it through. What's useful, perhaps essential for most of us, is to have someone who is listening.

If you can find someone who is more than a polite listener, someone who is an empathetic listener, it will make a big difference in how you express yourself. You can spot empathetic listeners by such cues as facial expression, eye contact, and interested questions that they may ask you. Securing a committed listener and a good friend can be one of the most valuable things you do for yourself. When they wind up being one and the same, you have hit pay dirt.

Don't overlook the possibility of turning to professionals in this area. A good therapist, analyst, or support group can get your energy moving. My husband and I are currently in couples counseling. Since this is his second marriage, initially the thought of going to see a counselor was negative and discouraging to him. When I showed him how a little skill-building in communicating with each other would help us listen to and really hear each other, he became receptive to the idea. What a gift. Every week we meet with an unbiased expert who teaches us better ways to talk to each other. Sometimes we are in a session arguing and sometimes we're just conversing.

We practice "mirroring" by repeating verbatim what the other person just said. We validate and empathize with what the other is feeling (whether we agree with it or not) by saying something like "I see how you might feel that way." The process is very rich and has brought us great intimacy: Intimacy = Into Me You See. We are learning, growing, and sharing our hearts.

So much is possible just through talking. You can articulate your point of view or express an idea. You can ask for feedback or share a feeling or an experience. This is how relationships are built. This is how ideas come into being. And this is how dreams can come true.

One night I was home all alone and steeping in my "stuff." I was confused and upset about an argument I'd had with a friend. I was unable to talk to her about it because we were both distressed. In that moment, to tell anyone else what had happened felt like gossiping. I picked up my hand-held recorder and talked to myself for about twenty minutes. When I played it back, I could hear sadness and disappointment in my voice that I hadn't been aware of. I gained new clarity and was easily able to call my friend the next day. Resolution wasn't far off, since I had done some very responsible work on my own. I'm a big believer in talking as a way to gain insight and to shift energy.

7. **Feeling**—Our feelings can be powerful messengers, but often we are either cut off from them or swept away by them. If you can be in tune with what you are feeling, you will have access to a deep and wise part of yourself.

Our feelings send us clear messages if we can learn their language. The simple practice of becoming still and recognizing what you are feeling can be life-changing. Not only will it give you access to yourself, it will help others in your life understand you as well. Most evenings, when my husband and I come home from work, we'll sit down on the couch and each take about five minutes to express how we are feeling. The listener simply listens and does not interrupt or offer feedback. At the end of my five minutes, my husband may simply say, "I hear you." I feel heard, held, validated, and loved. Then we switch roles. It's simple and it's awesome.

For many years I did not know what I was feeling, much less how to express it, especially without blame or judgment. But I practiced. One of the ways I do this is called "soul work." It is an easy technique for getting in touch with your feelings. It's also a positive way to use bottled-up energy.

I bought a sketch pad and a box of pastels. Whenever I'm feeling something, whether I know what it is or not, I pull out the pad and just start putting color on the paper. I can't draw very well, and my loud critic's voice used to kill my creative expression so quickly that I once abandoned this process. Now I don't try to draw anything. I simply focus on moving my feelings, through the use of color, out of me. I smudge and get colors all over my hands. Sometimes it takes a few pages to get connected to what I'm feeling, but by the time I've finished, I have definitely shifted the energy inside of me.

When I'm really intrigued by an image, I might delve a little deeper and (metaphorically) let it speak to me. I ask the drawing, "What's going on?" or "What are you trying to show me?" Or a feeling might become so apparent, like fear or sadness or confusion, that I can then ask, "What are you so frightened or confused or sad about?" Before I began drawing, I didn't even know that fear, sadness, or confusion was what I was feeling.

This process is called soul work because by doing it you are giving the unconscious parts of yourself an avenue for expression. You are engaging with your essence. Your essence has great wisdom to teach. Open, ask, tap it, dive in, feel, and express yourself.

8. **Laughing**—Laughing is one aspect of feeling, but I love it so much I decided to give it a listing of its own. As a powerful tool for shifting energy, laughter is in a category by itself, and it is highly undercrused. When is the last time you had a great belly laugh? Recently I was at a ski resort with some friends. We were on the slopes and saw a man grab his wife and sit her between his legs on a sled. Off they went, down a gentle hill. They were laughing uproariously. "Laughing all the way ho, ho, ho." It was pretty hysterical watching them.

Thank God that laughter, the greatest medicine of all, is extremely contagious. Medical research has shown that laughter has a powerful effect on the immune system, helping to boost our ability to fight illness. It may add years to our lives by lowering blood pressure and the levels of stress hormones in the blood. Laughing promotes relaxation.

How often do you laugh? Are you still ticklish? Do you even know? What cracks you up? Do you ever laugh out loud watching a sitcom or a comedian? Most important, can you and do you laugh at life? Can you even laugh in the face of disaster?

Here is one of my disasters. We arrived at San Francisco Airport hours early for our international flight. We were on our way to Bali to get married. Twelve people were traveling with us, and we were meeting another dozen coming from Los Angeles. We stepped into SFO to find a dark terminal.

There was a blackout. No planes would be leaving that night. "Powerless and in the dark—is this any way to start a marriage?" I asked. I started to cry. I was so upset. My dear friend Lynn took us back to her home for the evening. I called my father and friends in L.A. and told them we would hope to see them the next day in Bali, if Garuda Airlines would honor our tickets.

We cried and moaned and groaned until all there was to do was laugh. We started laughing so hard, we couldn't stop. Lynn and my husband-to-be embraced me and I felt their laughter rolling over me and through me. We were caught in what I call a "giggle wave." When we finally stopped, it was almost half an hour later.

I love to laugh and pray for you to have a lifetime of laughter and giggle waves. Nothing will give you greater ease than having a good sense of humor about life. Jean Houston said, "At the height of laughter, the universe is flung open into a kaleidoscope of new possibilities."

9. **Ideating**—Isn't this is a great word? Yes, ideating or ideation is in the dictionary. It is the process of thinking or dreaming up ideas. For many of us, being involved in a creative process is very invigorating. The process of ideating can help move energy.

You can get unstuck through the use of your imagination, by trying on different options. You can visualize yourself in different scenarios. You can even create an imaginary Mastermind group of people, alive or dead, who can offer you words of wisdom and encouragement. In my mind, I have turned to people like Eleanor Roosevelt, Ted Turner, David Bowie, and Grandma Rose for advice. If you are working on a problem, seek specific advice. Ask your imaginary mentors and friends what they would do. Use your idea machine, also known as your mind, to tap creatively into new perspectives and modes of operation.

One woman I know loves to ideate. It is her favorite thing to do. Eileen's dream is to be paid to think, and she often serves on corporate boards or participates in think tanks. She has developed the wonderful ability of training her mind to act like a beam splitter, where she can effectively do two things at once. Whenever she is doing a simple or mundane task, like ironing or paying bills, she is simultaneously ideating. Her favorite pastime is gardening. While she has her hands in the soil, she gets her best ideas. Some of Eileen's ideas are geared toward problem-solving, but many are fantastic visions or business ideas. Either she shares these with colleagues and professional associates or she acts on them herself. She has an ideation manual, chock-full of amazing ideas, that is covered with dirt, since it accompanies her in the garden.

10. **Waiting**—Although it is not often a favorite practice in the Western world, there's a lot to be said for patience. A friend once said to me, "Patience is a virtue I can't wait to develop." If you are having a reaction, such as being upset or angry, if you wait awhile, your energy will shift on its own. How long it takes depends on all the typical factors: you, the subject, how important it is, and how attached to it you are. Sometimes the best thing to do is nothing. Most of us aren't very good at or comfortable with doing nothing because we never cultivated the skill. If you are interested in ease, the skill of waiting is worth pursuing.

Don't misunderstand me. Complacency or passivity is not always the ideal route. The question is, Does waiting exist in your repertoire? Give it a shot. Next time you are all tangled up in something, take a walk, take a nap, or just wait and see what happens.

## BREATHING, MOVING, AND MEDITATING

In addition to the list above, there are three important ways to have greater ease and to access more energy that deserve special recognition. They are breathing, moving, and meditating. Perhaps you already practice these, but a little more awareness of them may prove useful. Of course you breathe and move, but let's explore how you do so and how you can use these activities as transformational tools.

### Breathing

Ninety percent of our energy should come from breathing, yet most people use only 10 percent of their full breathing capacity. Improper breathing can make you tired and moody, while deep, healthy breathing will help you feel more alive and relaxed, focused and centered, positive and invigorated. You can actually transform your life through correct breathing.

Breathing is by far the best way I know to access energy and put ease in your life. It's a great way to take your internal pulse, helping you to steady yourself and see what you're feeling. Breath is a barometer and can be used as a correlation to the quality of your life. Is your breathing slow, gentle, natural, stagnant, short, rushed, or forced?

Breathing is the bridge between our body and the world, between our inner and outer worlds, between our thoughts and our actions. As you return to healthy, full breathing, you reconnect yourself to the physical world, as well as to unseen internal energetic resources that are available to assist you.

To inspire literally means to breathe and be alive. Are you breathing in life? Are you inspired? Do you remember what or who inspires you? When we have expired, we have stopped breathing.

Many of us have forgotten how to breathe. We are so busy, so on the run, that we shallowly fill our lungs with just enough air to keep ourselves from being asphyxiated. If you want to have access to ease, it is paramount that you get into "right relationship" with your breath. Breathing helps us dissolve stress, feel more alive and connected to ourselves, to others, and to life. It helps remove emotional blocks and burdensome thoughts. Breathing is guaranteed to shift your energy.

Breathing can even improve your skin and your sex life. Many dermatologists are reporting that as many as half of their patients see a 20- to 100-percent improvement when alternative therapies such as deep breathing, yoga, and meditation are added to traditional treatments. Breathing exercises for lovers have their roots in an ancient Indian tradition known as tantric sex. Couples face each other and synchronize their breathing as a great way to slow down and tune in to each other. For more tantric breathing tips, I recommend *Tantra: The Art of Conscious Living* by Charles and Caroline Muir.

Let the spirit of your breath move through you. Try some breathing practices. Here are three:

Yogi Paramahansa Yogananda teaches a simple walking and breathing exercise. While walking at a comfortable pace (which he recommends we do every day), inhale, counting from one to twelve. Hold the breath for twelve counts; then exhale, counting from one to twelve. Throughout your day, notice when you are fully breathing, fully taking in life, and when you have forgotten to breathe fully. The more you breathe, the more you will fill yourself with the life force and the more energy you will have.

Some gurus believe the awareness of our breath is the key to enlightenment. If you do the following technique, your mind will turn from its journey into the future or the past. You will find yourself very much in the present, and the point of power is in the present.

Here's the practice that Rajneesh, a spiritual master, offers. Sit still, someplace quiet. First become aware of your breath as it comes in. Then let the breath move in and enter you. Do not go ahead of it or lag behind it. Just go with it. Move in with the breath, then move out with the breath, in-out, in-out.

You can breathe anywhere and anytime. My favorite time to do this is when I am (impatiently) waiting for an elevator. I focus on deep breathing until the elevator arrives, and continue until I get off the elevator.

Our goal in practicing our breathing is not to trip off into some esoteric place, but rather to bring relaxation and ease to your daily life. The more awareness you have regarding your breath, the greater your inner resources will be. When you set the pace of your life, you have more time to think, feel, and react, so you feel more in control.

This last technique is the simplest. Lie on your back on a mat or carpeting. Bend your knees and position your feet hip-distance apart. Place a small towel under your neck so it's in line with your spine. Close your eyes and pay attention to how you breathe. Don't change the way you breathe—simply observe it. Once you've observed your normal breathing pattern, you can work on extending it. As you learn to focus and expand your breathing, the calmer you will feel and the easier life will be. With practice, you'll be able to breathe away anxiety whenever a stressful situation arises.

## Moving

Dancing or any kind of physical movement is also one of the best ways I know for accessing and shifting energy. Whether you walk, run, dance, or skate, you are doing something great for your body and soul. Moving generates energy, and energy creates more energy.

You can use movement to shift into the essence of who you really are. Use it to get unstuck, to feel, perhaps to fly. While moving, feel the energy as it vibrates around you and let it move through you. Are you dancing through life? What dances do you do? Do you twist, waltz, or full-tilt boogie? If you don't dance your dance, who will?

Moving is so natural that we often take it for granted. But movement is everywhere, and it's a sign of life. Watch the trees. Some are danced wildly by the wind, while others are more rigid. Which do you relate to? There are many natural rhythms that life is attuned to. These are universal rhythms. In nature, we can see and feel a natural flow as we watch the ocean or feel the wind. Besides flow, some of the other types of rhythm you may recognize include chaos, staccato, lyrical, and still.

These five rhythmic energies can be danced. On her video entitled *The Wave*, Gabrielle Roth offers a delightful visual and physical workout using these five rhythms. You may like some more than others. Some may make you feel free and alive. Some of the movements may make you dizzy or queasy. This is important information. For example, if you tend to prefer control or structure, feeling the energy of chaotic or of lyrical motions may initially make you uncomfortable. But as you expand your capacity through movement, you will notice that you are becoming more fluid and flexible. Expanding our movement ranges and capacities gives us more ease.

Flowing movement is fluid, continual. We each have our own flow. This is the dance or movement of tapping in to your inherent rhythm. It's an easy movement. Without thinking about it, if you follow your breath and just let your body go wherever and however it wants, that's your flow.

Chaos is a very different feeling. It may feel out of control. You can imagine it as an elemental force. It moves this way and that way. It doesn't follow a clear path. It simply moves, and it can change its direction at any moment. It needs no justification and is very free. Chaos as an energy or as a force is valuable to explore. We'll do this in more detail later.

Staccato has edges and angles. It's sharp and intense, clear and focused. It has a definite beginning and end, and a definitive beat. Through movement, staccato involves hands, elbows, knees, and feet. You can really feel the downbeat. It's firm.

Lyrical movement is at the other end of the spectrum. It's light and whimsical. There's much spinning and twirling. Often it feels playful and youthful. You might imagine a spinning top or a whirling dervish when you feel lyrical. The dervishes use whirling as a comprehensive training of the body, mind, heart, and spirit. The whirling is a meditation in motion.

Even stillness is a movement. Can you imagine moving in a way that is so still you hardly move? Picture yourself walking through honey. You can move only so quickly. One of the movements of stillness is breath. Can you get so still that all that is moving is your breath? Can you do the disappearing dance?

All of these rhythms can help you access more energy and greater ease. Start to notice how you use them in life. Where has staccato become rigidity? Where has chaos become confusion? Where has stillness become sloth? Where has lyrical become childish rather than childlike—or has it died altogether?

Movement is one of the most direct and powerful ways to get your energy moving. What I love about it is that it's not a mental process. You don't have to figure anything out. You don't need to understand how it works. You just have to bring your body and show up. The next time you are feeling low, blue, moody, or just out of sorts, try putting on some music and moving. If you feel achy, tense, uptight, scrunched up, or confused—move. It doesn't matter if it's slow or fast, whether you are alone or with friends. Just move and see where it takes you. You won't wind up in the same place you started.

Yoga is another wonderful movement discipline. It actually can incorporate all three elements of ease: breathing, moving, and meditating. For some, yoga is a path for achieving liberation and is a way of life. For many, it is a system of exercise or movement that allows for long stretching, deep breathing, and relaxation. Yoga helps you become more cognizant of the connection between mind and body, and more perceptive of the flow of your thoughts. If you are interested in finding out more about yoga, read *Yoga Journal's Yoga Basics: The Essential Beginner's Guide to Yoga for a Lifetime of Health and Fitness.*

However you choose to move, what is important is that you do it. Body shifting is mind shifting because you are moving energy. Movement is a great way to get into the flow of life. Listen and open up to the beat. Find your rhythm. Get in synch. Once you are in the stream, this is the ideal time to dream.

*Meditating*

To talk to you about ease, shifting energy, or doing less without discussing meditation is impossible. I could pretty much give up everything in my life, with the exception of meditation. I want to have your attention as I briefly touch upon what I think is one of the single most essential things we can do to have ease. I make it a practice not to start my day (no coffee, phone calls, or errands) before I sit, close my eyes, and breathe for twenty minutes.

If you already meditate, this can be a good time to check in and see if your meditative practice is giving you what you want and need. Personally, after doing it for a few years, I got a little bored and stale. So I took a refresher course, and what got refreshed was me.

If you have never meditated and the thought of sitting in a funny position or sitting still for any extended period of time leaves you flat or uninspired, hang in there. As a bumper sticker I recently saw read: "Meditation is not what you think." Meditation is actually the absence of all thought—of rambling disconnected thoughts, as well as of concentrated thoughts.

Why do we want this? When our mind is still, empty, and quiet, we can totally relax, and relaxing the mind also relaxes the body. Our minds are like engines; they need downtime. After meditating, even for just twenty minutes, you will feel refreshed.

Imagine that you could take an instant vacation and recharge your battery anyplace and anytime. Now imagine that doing this on a regular basis could make you look and feel younger and healthier. Add to this that you no longer need to be at the mercy of your reactions, and that you could actually expand your capacity for dealing with reality. Sounds good, doesn't it? That's the promise of meditation. The outcome of meditation is not only greater ease and more energy, but also more patience, compassion (for yourself and others), creativity, and generosity.

Are you intrigued yet? How about this: Medical research shows that meditating slows your heart rate and relieves pressure and stress. In his bestselling book *Ageless Body, Timeless Mind*, Deepak Chopra asserts that meditation can even reverse the aging process.

Here's a simple meditation technique to get you started. It has similarities with the breathing techniques earlier in this chapter, since breathing is the simplest and quickest way to relax, which is the first step in meditating. Sit comfortably with your back straight. Close your

eyes and breathe in through your nose. When you have filled your
lungs, slowly exhale through your mouth. After three or four breaths,
tell your body to relax. As your body releases tension, breathe normally, but inhale through your nose and exhale through your mouth.

You will notice that thoughts surface. Imagine them as clouds gently floating by. Rather than following them and activating your mind,
simply allow them to pass by. Don't force yourself not to think. When
we have a lot of stress, we may also have a lot of thoughts. When you
realize that you are following your thoughts, focus your attention on
the air coming into your nostrils and going out of your mouth.

As your body relaxes more and more, your thoughts will slow down.
You'll notice there is a gap or space between your thoughts where
nothing is happening. As you slow down more, this gap widens and
you can know peace of mind, because when the mind is not thinking,
it is totally at ease.

Eventually, focus on the space between the in and out breaths. At
the junction where the in breath meets the out breath is emptiness,
a void. This is where eternal bliss and peace live. There is no place
to get to, no goal to obtain, no result to produce. There is no resistance, only bliss and ease. Breathe the whole world into you, feel the
ebb and flow in your being, feel the ocean of your being rising and
falling like a wave. Practice gathering your energy in as you seek the
emptiness.

It is said that people have become enlightened through breathing
and meditating. At the very least, this discipline will give you a calm
feeling. With practice you will see that you can go to this quiet and
relaxed place for twenty or thirty minutes. Then you can learn to
bring this same quality of stillness into your daily life. The benefits
include more clarity, greater latitude in stressful situations, more
spontancity, and heightened intuition.

Keep in mind that what I have provided here is a simple approach
to meditation. There are many more advanced techniques and wonderful books written by people like Ram Dass, Salle Redfield, and
Jack Kornfield. Or pick up the CD by Dr. Andrew Weil, *Eight Meditations for Optimum Health*. The lessons cover everything from finding a comfortable position for meditating to focusing the mind and
unwinding. Explore what works best for you.

## NEW TOOLS

At different times in this book, I introduce you to new ways of exploring who you are and what you want. There is a smorgasbord of tools, technologies, and skills available to us. Consider looking into some of these. I invite you to be curious and see what life has to offer and teach you through new ideas. Shortcuts and greater ease become available to us as we experiment and experience new things.

One of my favorite teachers or tools is the tarot deck. A set of colorful cards filled with images and symbols, tarot can unlock creative ideas and help you tap into universal energies and fresh perspectives. There are many tarot decks that span different cultures and thousands of years. Every morning I ask for guidance about my day or I ask a specific question, such as what should I do about a given situation, or how I can best take it easy. Then I pull a card.

Do I believe in fortune-telling? Not really, but I do understand that there are patterns and symbols that offer insight and understanding, wisdom, and knowledge. I use the cards to deepen my awareness and understanding, and to feed my desire to grow and try new things.

As I wrote about moving, meditating, and breathing, one tarot image came to my mind. It is the Chariot card, which represents the universal principle of stillness and movement. "Motion or change and identity or rest are the first and second secrets of nature. Motion and Rest. The whole code of her laws may be written on the thumbnail," said Ralph Waldo Emerson.

The Chariot demonstrates this dual principle of movement and stillness. The card shows a beautiful vehicle that is grounded, yet that easily moves in different directions. It knows when to stop and rest. Imagine a chariot from the movie *Ben Hur*, but this one is not going to war. It is available, however, to take you on a ride.

In one deck, the word *Abracadabra* is written across the top of the Chariot's canopy. This magical word suggests that when we combine our emotional nature (our hopes and desires) with our life force (breath and wind) we can produce tangible results that have been stimulated by intuition, often resulting in extraordinary outcomes.

What I love most about this card is that the Chariot is on a yellow brick road, the royal road of spiritual growth and evolution. Choices made from a spiritual place or during a heartfelt time connect us to a deeper commitment to the original purpose of our life.

Finally, in most decks, the Chariot contains another powerful symbol: the Wheel of Fortune. This reminds us that through choice we have the ability to select fortunate, positive, and abundant changes for ourselves. In times of change it's important to assess which changes will assist our growth and evolution and which will be nurturing, comforting, and supportive.

All of this is available through breathing, moving, and meditation. Enjoy the combination of quietude and activity, motion and rest in these activities. Use these skills to accomplish effortlessly, to do less and have more. Practice the art of accessing and shifting energy. In any given moment, by consciously dealing with life, you will experience ease.

## FUNDAMENTALS OF EASE

1. How you choose to interface with life is what will give you ease.
2. Different situations at different times in life obviously require different responses. Practice, inquire, and experiment. Ask yourself, "Where do I need to go inside myself emotionally or physically? What will give me ease right now?"
3. If you can clearly see where you are and know where you want to be, figuring out how to get there actually is easy.
4. Schedule an ease break. The purpose of this break is to rest, and to access and shift your energy. It is in this quiet time that some of the most profound things can happen.
5. Dreams connect the unconscious to the conscious. When you are asleep, your mind is free to roam. You can receive guidance and knowledge. Learning to work with your dreams gives you access to your own unbounded creativity.
6. While you are in the decision-making process regarding anything important in your life is not the time to act. But spend too much time deciding and you may dissipate your energy or miss the opportunity.
7. Taking action links vision and passion, because as your imaginative juices get sparked, your projects get charged and energized. This will intensify the creative process, further inspiring you to keep going.

8. So much is possible through just talking. You can articulate your point of view or express an idea, you can ask for feedback, share a feeling or an experience. This is how relationships are built, how ideas come into being, and how dreams can come true.

9. Our feelings can be powerful messengers, but often we are either cut off from them or swept away by them. If you can be in tune with what you are feeling, you will have access to a deep and wise part of yourself.

10. As a powerful tool for shifting energy, laughter is in a category by itself, and it is highly underused.

11. Doing nothing is a skill that most of us aren't very good at or comfortable with because we've never cultivated the skill. If you are interested in ease, the skill of waiting is worth pursuing.

12. Breathing is by far the best way to access energy and put ease into your life. It helps us dissolve stress, feel more alive and connected to ourselves, to others, and to life. It helps remove emotional blocks and burdensome thoughts. Breathing is guaranteed to shift your energy.

13. Movement is one of the most direct and powerful ways to get your energy moving. It's not a mental process, so you don't have to figure anything out or need to understand how it works. You just have to bring your body and show up.

14. To talk about ease, shifting energy, or doing less without discussing meditation is impossible. When our mind is still, empty, and quiet, we can relax totally. After meditating, even for just twenty minutes, you will feel refreshed.

15. There are patterns and symbols that offer insight and understanding, wisdom and knowledge. Use them to deepen your awareness and understanding, and to grow and try new things.

## 4

# The Test of Ease

SINCE awareness is such an essential part of creating ease in your life, it's useful to recognize where you lose ease and become stressed. As you become more aware, you will gain greater skill at accessing ease. You may try new ways of responding to those daily occurrences that can make us all a little crazy.

What follows is a short test. Wait, don't get stressed. You can't fail this test. There are no right or wrong answers. There are only *your* answers. The purpose of this test is to help you reflect on how you deal with situations like these.

After totaling up your answers, you may begin to see a pattern and recognize your style of coping with stress. No style is better than any other. There is usually good news and bad news about them all. Different styles have different costs and payoffs.

As you come to recognize your style, you become more self-aware. The more conscious we become about how we react, the more willing and able we are to try other things to achieve ease. *Doing Less and Having More* is about options, exploring alternative behaviors and learning to see things from new perspectives.

I've presented this test to many different groups. All of the responses came from people like you and me. They came up with the scenarios and the answers. Some couldn't believe others would respond a given way, while many were excited to expand their repertoire of reactions.

So take the test of ease. See where you get stressed or don't, and begin to recognize your style of dealing with challenging situations. See what works for you about your style and perhaps what doesn't. Explore where you might like to deepen your range of response or simply try something new.

## THE TEST OF EASE

1. You are cruising in your beautiful new car. Someone runs a red light and plows into you. You aren't hurt, but your car sure is. You:
   a. get angry and rant and rave.
   b. get resentful and chastise him.
   c. make sure he's okay.
   d. obtain his insurance data and deal with what needs to be done.
   e. do not get stressed by this.

2. You are at the bank, waiting in a line that is crawling forward. You're in a hurry and notice that your teller is overly friendly and chatty. You:
   a. complain to the manager.
   b. reprimand her.
   c. patiently and quietly wait.
   d. ask for help in getting what you need.
   e. do not get stressed by this.

3. Due to circumstances beyond your control, you've missed your plane. It's the last plane of the day. You:
   a. get hysterical — either angry or sad.
   b. blame yourself for not having a backup plan.
   c. travel the next day.
   d. explore or create new options, not giving up.
   e. do not get stressed by this.

4. You've been working for weeks on a big presentation and now it's the night before it's due. As you put the finishing touches on it, the computer crashes and you can't get the data you need. You:

a. "wing" the presentation the next day.
b. swear at the machine.
c. go to sleep.
d. use every resource to get it fixed.
e. do not get stressed by this.

5. After driving around for a long time, you find a parking spot. As you prepare to back in, a little sports car steals your spot. You:
   a. tell the driver to move; you were there first.
   b. chastise yourself for not being faster or more assertive.
   c. quietly move on.
   d. physically chase the car away.
   e. do not get stressed by this.

6. Your close friend or spouse tells you he's taking a friend to a restaurant you've been dying to go to, and you're not invited. You:
   a. ask him to go with you another time.
   b. feel abandoned and hurt.
   c. don't say anything, even though you are upset.
   d. show up at the restaurant to join them.
   e. do not get stressed by this.

7. You've promised you would deliver a report or a project to someone and now see that you will not be able to meet your commitment. You:
   a. get angry or upset.
   b. make the other person wrong for asking for too much.
   c. become shut down.
   d. talk it out and renegotiate.
   e. do not get stressed by this.

8. You're on your way to an important appointment and it's clear that you're going to be late. You:
   a. get a little crazy or angry.
   b. beat yourself up for not planning well.
   c. give up and go home.
   d. call and apologize or explain.
   e. do not get stressed by this.

9. Your bank card has been swallowed by the cash machine. When you try to report it, you get hung up in "voice-mail heaven." You:
   a. become enraged, taking it out on anyone.
   b. contact a high-level manager to discuss your upset.
   c. decide never to use the cash machine again.
   d. change banks.
   e. do not get stressed by this.

10. You're out of town on business or on a long overdue vacation. You prepare to give your credit card to the hotel clerk, only to find that you've lost your wallet and credit cards. You:
    a. flip out, have an anxiety attack, or cry.
    b. punish yourself one way or another for being careless.
    c. decide it doesn't matter; you still have a checkbook.
    d. get on the phone and recruit help.
    e. do not get stressed by this.

11. You're caught in a major traffic jam, moving along at a snail's pace. You:
    a. yell and become enraged.
    b. wonder how you let this happen.
    c. pull out audiotapes or the newspaper.
    d. get off this road the moment you can.
    e. do not get stressed by this.

12. You're speeding down the highway when you hear a siren. Looking in your rearview mirror, you realize you're caught and you have left your license at home. You:
    a. sweet-talk or play dumb.
    b. blame yourself for screwing up.
    c. make up an elaborate story.
    d. confess and surrender.
    e. do not get stressed by this.

13. Someone important to you is pressuring you to do something that you don't want to do. You:
    a. just say no, honoring your own truth.
    b. feel guilty and think that you should do it.
    c. say yes to please the other person.
    d. say maybe and then never get back to the person.
    e. do not get stressed by this.

14. You arrive at the airport for one of those convenient shuttle flights, only to find out that they've oversold the plane by 40 percent and you may not have a seat. You:
    a. make a scene, explaining why you *must* be on this flight.
    b. wonder how you let this happen.
    c. decide to take a later plane.
    d. seek someone in charge.
    e. do not get stressed by this.

15. Someone is offering you an unsolicited opinion that makes you feel bad. Since this person is an authority figure or a friend, you notice that you're considering editing your response. You:
    a. blow up and tell her off.
    b. say what she wants to hear because you think you should.
    c. say nothing.
    d. honestly tell her what you think and feel.
    e. do not get stressed by this.

16. You've just paid a big bill to have your car fixed. You drive it away, only to realize that the problem is still there. You:
    a. get angry, perhaps even threatening legal action.
    b. reprimand yourself for picking and trusting a bad mechanic.
    c. find another repair shop.
    d. immediately return the car to the shop, calmly requesting that it be fixed.
    e. do not get stressed by this.

17. You've just rented a new home or office space. After moving in, you're surprised to find you didn't get what you expected and there are many problems with this place. You:
    a. initiate a lawsuit.
    b. blame yourself or the renting agent for not being more thorough.
    c. decide you can live with it.
    d. confront the landlord, making him fix the problem immediately.
    e. do not get stressed by this.

18. You're tired after a long day of travel and eager to check in to your hotel. Upon arrival, not only do they not have your reservation, but the hotel is full. You:
    a. become enraged and demand a room.
    b. blame the staff for being incompetent and never come back.
    c. quietly go find yourself another hotel.
    d. have them find and pay for a room at another hotel.
    e. do not get stressed by this.

19. You had a little too much to drink at a gathering of friends and coworkers. Your morning memory is that you publicly humiliated yourself. You:
    a. call everyone who was there and apologize.
    b. annihilate yourself for your behavior.
    c. pretend it never happened.
    d. quit or move to another city.
    e. do not get stressed by this.

20. You're on your way to an important meeting and you're so lost that you don't know which way to go. You:
    a. cry, rant, or rave.
    b. blame the person who gave you the directions.
    c. give up and go home.
    d. call and ask for help or let them know where you are.
    e. do not get stressed by this.

Total up the number of a, b, c, d, and e responses. See which is your primary response and which is your secondary mode. Then read below to learn a little more about how you tend to deal with stressful situations.

A= Expresser
B= Blamer
C= Dismisser or Avoider
D= Fixer or Doer
E= Accepter

## STYLES OF REACTING

**Expresser**—You let your feelings be known. You say what's on your mind, often in the moment. You have a range of expressions, including sad and angry. People know where they stand with you. You are clear about your needs and expectations, and when you're dissatisfied, you voice it, often loudly. You often feel better after you blow off steam, but are you leaving others wounded? You may never have an ulcer, but do you give them? Sometimes you are very effective, but people may have a negative reaction to your response.

**Blamer**—You tend to look for a place to point your finger when something happens that upsets you. You often blame yourself. This has developed your capacity to take responsibility for your actions, but are you also taking the blame for things that aren't your fault? You're very reliable and can be counted on during tough times; however, you tend to be quite hard on yourself and carry a burden longer than you need to.

**Dismisser or Avoider**—You're good at taking things in your stride, and you're masterful at avoiding unnecessary confrontations, but when something does matter to you or affects you, are you also willing to take a stand and speak up? You have a gift for seeking alternatives, although sometimes you really inconvenience yourself to do this. Do you dismiss what is important as well as what's not?

**Fixer or Doer**—You're good at making things happen. Even in the most stressful situations, you can find some action to take. But beware: Are you wasting time and energy trying to fix some things when another strategy may provide greater ease? You're skilled at taking action in crises. You have good ideas and options. You like moving things forward and find it difficult to wait or just see what happens. You do not like feeling out of control.

**Accepter**—You have a real talent for going with the flow. You're not easily ruffled; in fact, many things don't bother you at all. Are you equally aware of your personal needs and boundaries? Do you get taken care of while you are letting things roll off your back? You're a great team member and get along easily with most people. You're extremely flexible and open to new ideas. You're willing to try new things, but you don't usually initiate them.

As you can see, there are no right or wrong answers to this test of ease. Each style of reacting has its pros and cons. The secret to doing less and having more is awareness. Come to know who you are and how you deal with life's annoyances and inconveniences. Then try some new options. Experiment. Extend yourself and your repertoire.

## EXPAND AND INTEGRATE

One of the best tools I have found for self-reflection is called the enneagram. This is an ancient system that is over five thousand years old and is said to be a path toward enlightenment. The basic theory behind the enneagram is that each of us has a world view that affects how we perceive different situations. Based on our view, we make choices and decisions. The path to enlightenment, according to this model, is to reclaim all parts of ourself and become more whole.

This system is a nine-point model (*ennea* means "nine" and *gram* means "model"). It describes nine personality types and their inter-relationships. While you may recognize yourself primarily as one point in the model, we all possess aspects of every point, although one will be your prime point.

I will describe each point in brief detail. If this information is interesting to you, I highly recommend *The Enneagram in Love and Work* by Helen Palmer. You may come to find this one of the most powerful relationship tools you have ever encountered. Knowing yourself through these teachings will give you ease. They help us recognize ourselves, our issues, and how we relate to each other.

The enneagram has significantly affected my life. I've gained insight into how I deal with others and stressful situations. One place I experienced this was in my relationship with my husband. For years, when we were dating, every time we started to get close, I became afraid of being hurt or disappointed. I would handle this by picking a fight with him and driving him away. After reading about my enneagram point, I began to understand my fear. I started to express my feelings honestly and asked him for help. Since I wasn't attacking him anymore, he could offer his love, support, and compassion for what I was feeling. Now we are happily married.

This process has helped me better understand my husband, too.

He is a nine point, very free-flowing and easygoing. I am a three point—all about focus and goals. We used to drive each other crazy. Thanks to this system, we now understand that together we can make one healthy whole human being. Learning about our differences brought great ease and understanding into our lives.

Here is a "baby bite" of the nine different points. The game here is not to change who you are or to get rid of your "defective" parts. The goal is to broaden and expand, learn and integrate. Come to know all of yourself.

## The Enneagram

One point—The Perfectionist—critical of self and others, convinced there is one correct way, uses "should" and "must" a lot.

Two point—The Giver—demands affection and approval, devoted to meeting others' needs, manipulative and seductive.

Three point—The Performer—seeks to be loved for performance and achievement; competitive, type-A personality, master at appearances.

Four point—The Tragic Romantic—attracted to the unavailable, ideal is never here or now, sensitive, often sad.

Five point—The Observer—maintains emotional distance from others, protects privacy, feels drained by commitment.

Six point—The Devil's Advocate—fearful, dutiful, plagued by doubt, afraid to take action, loyal to the cause.

Seven point—The Epicure—playful, adventurous, gourmet approach to life, happy but finds it hard to commit.

Eight point—The Boss—extremely protective, openly displays anger, has to be in control, combative.

Nine point—The Mediator—obsessively ambivalent, sees all points of view, self-forgetting.

The best way to see how this system works is to view a panel. One person from each point sits on the panel and when asked the same question, they will have very different responses. I asked someone representing each point, "How do you deal with stressful situations?"

One point—The Perfectionist—"I withdraw and become really focused on everything else except what I need to do. I become very controlling, single-focused, and often will turn to a physical activity, like vigorous exercise."

Two point—The Giver—"It takes a lot for me to get stressed out because I'm so busy being nice and taking care of everyone else. But once I cross that stress line, look out. I become bossy and enraged, controlling everyone and everything. I become hard-driving and intense, blaming others and instilling guilt."

Three point—The Performer—"I fall apart in stress. I just shut down and become inadequate. I usually cry and if possible will over-eat or go to sleep. I just check out and try to disappear."

Four point—The Tragic Romantic—"Stress makes me intensely emotional. I rant and rave and cry. I see how impossible everything is. This can turn into uncertainty and depression. But there is hope. If someone will listen to me vent, I can get back on track quickly."

Five point—The Observer—"I walk from room to room in a daze. I'm unable to focus on one person or task. I literally bounce from one place to another, feeling unable to settle on anything."

Six point—The Devil's Advocate—"I like stress. It makes me feel empowered. I have a desire to overcome it, so it motivates me to become very creative. I'll tackle the problem instead of eating or sleeping. Everything else becomes secondary. Because I thrive on stress, I will sometimes induce it."

Seven point—The Epicure—"Often I don't know when I'm under stress, until it gets really bad. I become critical and judgmental, make a million lists, get demanding, and do not accept opinions from others. I can get logical but frenetic."

Eight point—The Boss—"If the stress is minimal and just feels like pressure, I'll kick into gear and handle it. If there is too much of it, I'll withdraw to escape. I'll go into hibernation through mindless entertainment. Sometimes I lie and say I'm handling the problem, when I'm actually hiding."

Nine point—The Mediator—"Stress makes me feel overloaded and overwhelmed. I get sleepy and need a nap, or I get angry, thinking that others are inadequate and to blame for the situation."

What's fascinating about the enneagram is that as we begin to see more of ourselves, we can also see and accept more of others. As we recognize and accept our differences, we can become more generous and understanding of others.

Personally, what the enneagram has taught me is compassion. I now know that I am all the bits and pieces I see in everyone else. All those nagging behaviors that I didn't like about other people are just unintegrated and disowned parts of myself. Nothing will give us greater ease than recognizing and accepting our differences. As I accept myself and all my foibles, I also become more accepting of you. It works both ways.

## CULTIVATING THE WITNESS

One skill guaranteed to give you greater ease in life is developing the witness inside you. Not only will this give you greater ease, but it will also give you more resources and options in how you respond to life.

There is a wise guide that lives in each of us. This is the part of you that can see clearly, even in the fog. It is the part of you that remains calm in chaos. It is even the part of you that can see both sides of an argument. It is your witness.

The witness, also known as the aware ego, is something you should seek to develop. As you observe your feelings and reactions, you will begin to notice patterns of behavior. You will have more access to you. You will begin to try on different responses and be more conscious of the choices you are making.

Cultivating the witness is all about awareness. Become aware of who you are and when you are not being yourself. Insight, or higher awareness, comes from being attentive. Notice what gets your goat and what doesn't matter to you.

Next time you're feeling upset, practice this: Take a breath and imagine you're outside of yourself watching or witnessing the event and your behavior. See it as an observer. Get a little distance, at least in your mind. Practice viewing this event from different perspectives. Try on other points of view.

Ask these questions: What is this showing me? What is actually happening here? What am I feeling? Why am I feeling this? When have I felt this before? What might the other person or people be thinking and feeling? Why might they be right? What can I learn about myself from this? When have I acted this way before? What insights are available?

By experiencing yourself from the perspective of the witness, you've put a little space between you, your reactions, and whatever is happening. Space is a good way to create ease. You can take a moment to reflect, to reconsider, to plan. The witness lives inside each of us.

Our responsibility is to cultivate it. Give it some attention. Put a little awareness into its development, and it will serve you well.

Use everything for your growth and development. Now, more than ever, there are wonderful resources handy. Take the test in this chapter, enroll in a personal-growth class, hire a coach, read a book. Learn about you, learn about others, and, of course, learn about life.

## FUNDAMENTALS OF EASE

1. Since awareness is such an essential part of creating ease in your life, it's useful to recognize where you lose ease and become stressed.

2. As you become more aware, you will gain greater skill at accessing ease. You may try new ways of responding to those daily occurrences that can make us all a little crazy.

3. As you come to recognize your style, you become more self-aware. The more conscious we become about how we react, the more willing and able we are to try other things to achieve ease.

4. *Doing Less and Having More* is about options, exploring alternative behaviors, and learning to see things from new perspectives.

5. Explore where you might like to expand your range or simply try something new.

6. The secret to doing less and having more is awareness. Come to know who you are and how you deal with life's annoyances and inconveniences. Then try some new options.

7. The game here is not to change who you are or to get rid of your defective parts. The goal is to broaden and expand, learn and integrate. Come to know all of yourself.

8. All those nagging behaviors you don't like about other people are just unintegrated and disowned parts of yourself. Nothing will give us greater ease than recognizing and accepting our differences.

9. There is a wise guide that lives in each of us. It is the part of you that remains calm in chaos. It is even the part of you that can see both sides of an argument. It is your witness.

10. The witness, also known as the aware ego, is something you should seek to develop. As you observe your feelings and reactions, you will begin to notice patterns of behavior. You will have more access to *you*.
11. Use everything for your growth and development.
12. Learn about you, learn about others, and, of course, learn about life.

# 5

# Ten Ways We Make

# Life Difficult

I T SEEMS that our lives are filled with ups and downs, good days and bad. If we have lots of energy, we're happy; if we're tired, we might be moody. There are days when everything seems to be effortless and other days when, no matter what we do, everything seems to go wrong.

After years of watching and interviewing many, many people, I recognize patterns. We can learn much from observing patterns. It's not that everything needs to be labeled and categorized, but we can learn shortcuts and develop skills by noticing what works and how it works. When we understand why we operate the way we do, we'll have some choice about what serves us best in any given situation.

What I consistently see is that we often make life, or a given situation, more difficult than necessary. We get caught up in the details or the drama, lose our focus or sense of self, and become overwhelmed or shut down.

Here are ten common ways we make life more difficult. If you can see these patterns or habits simply stated and demonstrated, they may provide insight into your own behaviors. Once you recognize what you do, you can then learn to pause briefly and explore other options. Ultimately, I hope you will replace energy-draining and unproductive behaviors with much greater ease.

1. **Vagueness**—If you're not clear about what you want, it's impossible for anyone else to know, either. Vagueness sends conflicting messages. If you're unsure or unclear about whether to move forward, stay where you are, or select another option, you probably feel confused. Confusion is a tough energy to engage with, both internally and interpersonally. It makes it hard for others to help you.

   Vagueness can keep you stuck, even immobilize you. I have seen many dreams and relationships die because of it. Especially if you are faced with a large or important decision, being vague about it can put a veil of confusion over everything else in your life. Vagueness and confusion start a downward spiral, often leading to self-doubt and a sense of futility.

   I'm not a big proponent of forcing choices or of just using your will to decide. I am, however, supportive of making decisions in a timely fashion. Only you can decide what that is. I urge you to put all the facts down on paper. List the pros and cons or write out all your fears and concerns. Record all the unanswered questions you have. This will help you get clear about what is preventing you from moving forward. Whenever possible, give yourself a due date for arriving at a decision. Do whatever you can to meet this date. Most important, notice what being vague is doing to your energy and to your relationship to ease. Be aware of the trappings of vagueness. To live continually with the words "I don't know" can cost you a great deal.

2. **Reacting without thinking**—How often in your life have you reacted without thinking or moved too quickly on something, only to regret it later? Reactivity is the nasty opposite of being incapacitated by vagueness. Ideally, we want to find a midpoint or center between these two extremes. As you work through the upcoming Roadmap process, you will be given powerful tools to help you say yes or no to difficult choices. The Personal Profile section in Chapter 16 will give you additional skills for decision-making.

   Enthusiasm is a powerful energy, but sometimes we get swept up by it or by our optimism. A friend of mine is very busy, but whenever the call comes asking for help, she always says yes. Her quick yeses are starting to cost her. She is ridiculously busy helping everyone else, while her health, her job, and her own well-being are suffering.

Learn to recognize your style of reacting. If I am asked to do something that will take time and energy, I often don't give a quick response. I used to say yes immediately, but eventually it caught up with me: My life was out of control. Also, as your priorities change, what you need to say yes to may change, too.

I don't want to kill your spontaneity or creativity, but notice when you are reacting without checking in and practice taking more time to evaluate your needs.

3. **Believing what you see and hear**—When I wrote my first book, *Making Your Dreams Come True*, many people said to me, "Do you have any idea how hard it is to get published?" "No," I would respond, "and I don't need to know." Everyone has an opinion. Some of these opinions or ideas will serve you and support you. Many will not.

Notice how you are listening to others, and how the information that is coming in is affecting you. We need to have a strong belief mechanism. It is essential in moving forward on our dreams and desires. We also need to have a good "bullshit meter." If you believe everything you're told, you will get confused. It's only natural. For every yes, there is a no. For every person who thinks your ideas are mad or wild, there is someone who will think you are clever and brilliant.

Every person we meet has his or her own personal projections. This includes every reporter or journalist who "objectively" presents the news. I'm probably an extremist in this area, but I have given up watching the news altogether. Not only does it not give me ease, but it gives me a tremendous amount of distress to view it at all. Do you sleep well at night after the evening news has filled you with images of death and destruction?

There is evidence presented by the London Institute Psychological Society that shows bad news on TV can make viewers see their own lives negatively. Bad news affects our outlook on our own lives: We turn external concerns into internal—and unrelated—worries.

What will give you ease is to know yourself, to determine your own belief system and to live by your own convictions. You probably know about self-fulfilling prophecies. I encourage you to have your beliefs and opinions, and to be open to input and to seeing things anew. Have the courage to disagree with something that seems invalid or to dismiss something that seems unnecessary.

4. **Automatic pilot**—Are you aware of behaviors or pursuits that perhaps have outgrown their usefulness or effectiveness? I have a friend whose automatic response was to say no anytime I asked him if he wanted to do something. I might be asking him to do the most fun thing. If I nudged him a bit, he'd say okay. After having a great time together, he'd say he couldn't believe he had almost missed out on doing it.

Eventually I got tired of coercing him. I told him I would no longer ask twice. It was up to him. He began to take responsibility for himself by not automatically saying no. He realized he wanted more fun and freedom in his life. He told me recently, "I am now a yes waiting to happen, and my life is reenergized."

Habitual behaviors are sometimes hard to spot. They become part of us. When a habit is starting to cost you something, especially your creativity or sense of play, it's time to reevaluate. If you're suspicious that some part or all of your life is in a rut, consider asking a friend or family member about it. Others often see things about us that we are blind to. If you're hearing the same feedback often—say three or more times—take a good hard look at what's being said.

Once you identify this behavior, simply try something new. Start small. Maybe you'll try Peet's Coffee instead of Starbuck's, skating instead of running, dancing instead of a movie. Get the energy moving. Trying new ways of being opens a creative flow. It gives us confidence and insight for doing less and having more.

5. **Complaining**—If we take half the energy we use to moan, groan, and complain and direct it into achieving our hopes and desires, our lives will look completely different. One man I know who often complains decided he would actually track how many complaints came out of his mouth on any given day. He called me and yelled, "I quit counting at fifty! How did this happen?"

I was grateful that he'd finally become aware of what everyone around him knew. Complaining is a waste of energy.

Why would you complain? What good does it do? What is it costing you?

There are some things in life we have control over and many that we don't. The way in which you meet life will determine the amount of ease and grace you have in your life. Change what you can, release what is not needed, accept what you are able to accept, and get into relationship with the rest of it.

Does complaining have impact? Of course it does. I assure you, if you are the nagging, negative, complaining voice at work or at home, it is affecting you and your relationships. It's fine to state your displeasure or discomfort, if you're willing to do something about it. It's often the beginning of an important alteration. But there is a way to instigate action that can be more fun and empowering than complaining. It's possible to be of service and talk about what's not working or what you would rather have—these approaches actually contribute to the solution rather than perpetuate the problem.

Complaining without taking action makes us sound and look like victims. For many, griping is easy, but having the courage to act is not. If you are finding fault out there, I hope you will do the projection exercise from Chapter 2 and get to the bottom of your complaint. To criticize with the intention of doing something about a situation is very different from just needing to be heard. Although you may not always be in a position to effect a change, there is a way to voice a concern or an idea that serves and contributes, such as offering helpful suggestions or creative solutions.

Complaining does not help. If I dump my complaints on you, I am not being of service. If I ask to share some observations with you, and you agree, then I may be able to contribute something. If the emphasis is on me and my needs, especially my need to be "right," I have moved back to complaining.

6. **No action**—Often we know what we need to do or what the next step is, but we don't take it. Inactivity keeps you stuck. The way to get unstuck is to do something.

Taking action changes everything. Making a phone call, writing a letter, or asking for help are three simple ways to jump-start a stalled project. Less obvious but equally useful ways are to take a walk, exercise, or go window shopping. Move! Don't use these as avoidance techniques but as a change of pace or atmosphere that will also help change your mind.

The best part of taking action is that it often produces new resources. By making a call or going to a networking event, you may meet someone who can help you. One thing is certain: If you do nothing, no one will help you.

On the days when you need something and can't get out of the house or office for a change of scenery, the telephone can be lifesaving. Call and ask for help, for friendly advice, or for loving support.

If one of the things that matters to you now is meeting someone new and being in a relationship, you have to go out. Often people ask if I can design a strategy for meeting a partner. My number-one shortcut technique is to "flirt" or at least be friendly. Strike up a conversation with a fellow pedestrian while crossing the street. One woman met her current beau while driving on the freeway. Smiles and waves led to pulling over. That turned into coffee, then dinner and dancing, and now a full-fledged romance. Opportunities are everywhere. Ask people to fix you up. Talk to strangers. Take action. Yes, even consider placing a personal ad.

There is a time to take no action, a time when resting or "time out" is what is most needed. Just be aware of your energy level. Feeling lethargic, lazy, or sluggish can be energy-draining. Rest can be rejuvenating. Getting remotivated and restarted can be exhausting. Monitor your energy, practice balance and centering, and continually move forward in the areas of your life that matter to you.

One last point: Dreams die when we put them on our "to do" list. It's no wonder we get depressed when year in and year out we see the same goals on our list. Whether you want to lose weight, change jobs, or take an exotic vacation, what will help keep your dreams alive is to keep them moving forward. In order to do this, it is essential that big dreams be broken down into smaller projects. Then break those projects down into simple tasks and do something every day to move your dream forward.

7. **Blind faith** — It's one thing to believe in your dream, it's quite another to be uninformed or ignorant in pursuing your

dreams. We need to do our homework. Life can become very difficult when we continue to live from a naïve place.

I love when people dream. I even like it when they fantasize, as long as they are aware that that's what they are doing. But people who live in their unfulfilled fantasies or daydreams give visionaries and big dreamers a bad name.

When life is telling us to be aware or when our gut is saying slow down, why don't we pay attention? We get swept away or seduced by our expectations. We may want something so badly that we disconnect from reality. We begin to make bad choices and decisions. Sometimes we're so sure we're right, we'll put everything we have on the line. Failure is inevitable when we take action based on illusion.

It is essential that you stay connected to the truth of what's happening. This is where a good buddy can be useful. Find someone whom you trust, who wants you to succeed, so you can trust that person's advice. Regularly check in with your buddy for honest feedback.

Do whatever you can to deepen and develop your own internal guidance system. Learn to listen to your intuition. Notice when it steers you well and when it takes you off course. There is a very wise teacher who lives inside of you. In *Your Sacred Self*, Wayne Dyer wrote, "Inside of you there is a wise guide, a part of your true self that walks with you as you progress along the path of your sacred quest." Ask your guide's advice, act on your guide's wisdom, and acknowledge when you do. Acting on your inner wisdom builds self-confidence and self-trust.

When appropriate, turn to experts. From therapists and counselors to mentors and lawyers, get expert advice early. It's exciting when your energy is saying, "Go, go, go," but it can be devastating if it takes you on a wild ride.

8. **Expecting the worst**—For most of my life I lived in fear of being disappointed. This fear was so great it kept me in a career I didn't like, in a dead-end relationship, and trapped in a life of never-ending stress. The concept of fun and freedom was alien to me.

It's part of my clan pattern. The women in my life worry. My mother believes bad things happen in threes. She waits for triple misfortunes to strike and she's always right (assuming she waits long enough). Lucky me, I inherited this skill. Now I can laugh about it, but before I became aware of it, I was unconsciously making my life much harder. Once I was booked to be on the *Today* show, my publicist suggested sending postcards to my mailing list, so fans could tune in and watch. "But what if we get preempted by a space shuttle lift-off?" I asked. I caught myself and realized I was living out of my fear again. We mailed the cards. Could the show have been canceled? Sure, but we can't not live because of something that might or might not happen.

What do you expect from life? Do you expect life to let you down or even knock you down? Do you compromise your lifestyle down to what you think is realistic? Do you abandon your dream because you've had a setback, or worse, have you stopped dreaming altogether?

Can you feel how much of a burden it is and how much energy it takes to go through life expecting the worst? If this is one of your behaviors, notice how it's affecting you. I have a friend who never plans outdoor events like bicycling or picnics. "It might rain" is his justification. I know it sounds funny, but cast this attitude across your life and you can really feel the cost involved.

What can you do about this? Just being aware of it will shift your energy. Next time you realize you're expecting the worst, try another expectation. What if you expected the best? Could you live with it if the outcome wasn't the best, but wasn't the worst? How about if it were somewhere in between? Explore new options and new expectations. A good sense of humor is also extremely useful anytime you're trying to change a behavior, habit, or belief. Laughing lightens the whole thing up.

I'm a *Seinfeld* fan. Poor George. One of his characteristics is to always expect the worst. In one episode, he was at the airport and a stranger asked him to watch his luggage. After a while, George assumed the guy wasn't returning and appropriated his clothes. Everyone now assumed George, dressed like a geek, was a tourist. So he played the role of a tourist and fell for a woman he met who worked for the visitors' center.

Continuing to play the part, he created a whole web of deceit about his apartment, job, and lifestyle. True to form, the last scene of the episode showed him on the phone in his underwear (the real tourist had caught up with him), crying to Jerry. He'd lost his job with the Yankees, his new girlfriend had dumped him, and he had no clothes. This was exactly what he was expecting. If we listen to what we're saying and notice what we're doing, we may be able to avoid unconsciously sabotaging ourselves.

9. **Searching for something that doesn't exist**—Can you imagine putting everything you have into the pursuit of something that doesn't exist? In the case of blind faith, mentioned earlier, we don't see evidence that what we want is possible, but we believe that it still may happen. Searching for something that doesn't exist is worse, because we seek the impossible, something that doesn't exist. Talk about wasting time, effort, and energy! It's essential to distinguish between dreams and fantasies. With a dream you can design a strategy or a plan to make a dream happen; with a fantasy, you cannot. Winning the lottery is a fantasy. Just because it's a fantasy doesn't mean it can't or won't happen. But there is little you can do, short of buying lots of tickets, that will make it happen.

Are fantasies important? You betcha. But what is equally important is that you keep a realistic perspective on your fantasies. Use them to help you dream and create and imagine. Then design realistic plans to achieve the aspects of your fantasy that you can. Setting yourself up for failure by embracing a fantasy is self-defeating. If you're seeking something, define what it is, where it can be found, and who can help you.

There is one caveat I'll add here. If you are a "seeker" and what you are seeking is something spiritual or esoteric, a different set of rules may apply. Perhaps there is no evidence that what you're looking for exists as we know it. In this case, I invite you to seek with open hands. This means that you may not know the form your vision may take; what you seek may be unrecognizable to you. This is a very different kind of journey. Use your energy level as your compass. If you feel energized, excited, and alive, you're probably being led to something that will fulfill you. If you feel drained or exhausted, this feedback is very telling.

10. **Withdrawing or isolating**—Although I think alone time is precious and necessary, you might want to see if you're using

it as an avoidance technique rather than as a time for rejuvenating. Self-reflection and contemplation can be nurturing, calming, and clearing, but when it comes to simplifying your life, other people are not only useful, but often are essential.

Are you sabotaging your life by declaring you are the only one who can do all the things to get the job done, while complaining that you just don't have the time to do them, so therefore nothing is happening? This is a very common pattern.

When you get stuck, where do you go? Whom do you turn to? What do you do (or not do)? What do you ask for or say? Anything? Whether you are solving a problem, creating something new, or just in need of support, will you reach out?

Of course you'll need someone to reach out to. In Chapter 11, I will show you how to build a support team. Even one friend or associate will do. At different times in our lives we need help. Since many of us were raised to be independent, you have may have negative feelings and judgments about needing help. Do you think that asking for help is a sign of weakness or vulnerability? Perhaps it makes you feel needy and you don't like that feeling. What's true for you about asking for help?

There is a whole different approach to this that I would ask you to consider. What if by your not withdrawing, people got to play with you? What if asking for help was seen as an act of generosity on your part? What if the next time you felt like isolating yourself, you tried something different, perhaps even invited a few friends over? The outcome may surprise and delight you. I know many "loners" who, once they found their "own kind"—people they could talk to who encouraged their ideas and helped them along the way—really turned on to this idea of relating to others.

## TEN MORE WAYS

The more I think about it, the more I realize that there are still more ways in which we make life harder and drive ourselves crazy. See if any of these resonate with you.

1. **Trying**—If you're using lots of effort, energy, and will to make something happen, maybe your approach needs to be reconsidered. What does it mean to try, anyway? Remember what Yoda said in *Star Wars*: "Try not. Do or do not."

2. **Resisting**—There's an old saying: "What you resist persists." If you've been pushing against something or someone, stop. If you're not resisting, there is no energy being wasted. Yield and see what happens.

3. **Attaching**—When something attaches to you, it feels sticky, icky, gooey, and clingy. It is impossible to move with ease when you are attached to an outcome or to another person. If you are being drained of vitality, an attachment (or two) probably isn't far off. One *Star Trek* movie features the Borg, a race that attaches to others and assimilates them, causing all life force to cease. Check your life force. Is it yours? Is it clean? Is it detached?

4. **Forcing**—Since it is possible to tap into an energetic stream and go with a natural flow, using force is a waste of energy. There are times when it's useful to use force, such as when opening jars and stuck doors, but more often than not, forcing something is a waste of energy and will put you in an uneasy state.

    I am a master at trying too hard. I have screwed up many opportunities by doing this. If I am lusting after an outcome and am really attached to making something happen, usually it goes awry. The difference between unhealthy attachment and holding on to your dream is subtle, but trying too hard throws things out of balance. I'm not saying you should not prepare or not give your all. Do your work and then, if you can, let it go.

5. **Judging**—It takes a great deal of energy to stand in judgment of something. There's nothing wrong with having an opinion, but if we become overly positional about something, we can deplete all our energy. Read the section about projection in Chapter 2, and see what you can learn about yourself through what you judge.

6. **Struggling**—To struggle implies difficulty. The more effort we use, the more energy we waste. When we force something, we're pushing from the inside out, or against something. Struggle is more of an internal battle. The opposite of struggle is surrender, and the finest magic in the world happens when

we do. Steve Sisgold, a wonderful author, teacher, and friend, just returned from India. While he was there, rather than seeking something, he was wide open for life to give him gifts. As he wandered through a small village, a young man motioned to him. Normally Steve doesn't go walking down alleys, but it felt right. This man said to Steve, "Dalai Lama." "Dalai Lama?" Steve repeated. The young man nodded and pointed to his motor scooter. Off they rode.

A few blocks away, Steve joined a small group of about twenty locals and was blessed by His Holiness the Dalai Lama. Steve said the moment was nothing short of a miracle, a dream come true. All the internal struggle in the world wouldn't have made this happen. Willingness and surrender, the antithesis of struggling, are what provide ease.

7. **Analyzing** — It's wonderful to know how things work, but after a while, all you have is more information. Especially when you're in the process of getting to know yourself, the best advice I can offer is to release the need to understand. I'm not saying not to look and learn, but if you can be curious rather than certain, you are being spacious with life. Life will return the favor.

8. **Forgetting** — How much time and energy do you waste looking for your keys or glasses? By bringing mindfulness or awareness into your life, this can disappear. You can read about mindfulness in detail in Jon Kabat-Zinn's book *Wherever You Go, There You Are.*

Practice noticing where you put things. Be mindful, or present, when you do or say something, and remembering what you did and said will become easier. Although you may still have lapses and some of us will always need to write things down, we don't have to be at the mercy of our half-asleep minds. For most of us, remembering little things can make a big difference.

If I'm continually digging through my piles to find stuff, leaving things behind or losing them, it is a loud message that I'm out of sorts and need to take time for myself. This means taking a nap, meditating, or cleaning my desk. I know I will not have peace of mind until I do something good for myself.

9. **Nagging** — Who are you "on"? Nagging has a bothersome quality unique unto itself. Scolding, constant fault-finding, and

complaining are all behaviors that ask you to look at yourself.
I'm not kidding. If you don't like it out there, at some level
you can't stand it in you. Once again, visit the section on projection, practice the exercise, and "quitcher bitchin'." You're
wasting precious energy.

10. **Ignoring**—Not to pay attention to what you are doing, to what
people are saying, and to the signs of life is a disservice to
yourself. Another variation of this is not listening or only hearing what you want to hear. Pay attention to what life and people are handing you. Notice what you are ignoring and
whether it's going away or growing.

## TRY IT ON

Trying it on is what this whole chapter is about. What if you tried
one new behavior? What if you gave it a shot? We know that if you
keep doing what you have been doing you'll get more of the same. I
assume you bought this book because you are ready for a change. So
here's a great place to start.

Here are three important lessons of *Doing Less and Having More:*
1. Notice how you are expending your energy.
2. See where you are draining yourself unnecessarily.
3. Create some new energizing behaviors.

Listed throughout this chapter are the ways we make life harder
and drain our energy. Some of them may apply to you and some may
not. As you become aware of the ways in which you are making life
difficult and as you begin to try a new, easier way, you will see pro-
gression in your life.

Make small changes at first. By altering your behavior, you're
changing your life. Awareness is the first step. Willingness helps. Taking action is transformational. A sense of humor eases the way.

### FUNDAMENTALS OF EASE

1. We can learn shortcuts and develop skills by seeing and
understanding what works.
2. When we understand why we operate the way we do, we'll
have some choice about what serves us best in any given
situation.

3. If you're not clear about what you want, it's impossible for anyone else to know either. Vagueness sends conflicting messages and makes it hard for others to help you. Vagueness and confusion start a downward spiral, often leading to self-doubt and a sense of futility.

4. Make decisions in a timely fashion. Only you can decide what that is. Put all the facts down on paper, listing the pros and cons or writing out all your concerns and fears.

5. Notice when you are reacting without checking in and practice taking more time to evaluate your needs.

6. If you believe everything you're told, you will get confused. For every yes, there is a no. For everyone who thinks your ideas are mad or wild, there is someone who will think you are clever and brilliant.

7. What will give you ease is to know yourself, to determine your own belief system, and to live by your own convictions. Have your beliefs and opinions, be open to input and see things anew. Have the courage to disagree with something that seems invalid or to dismiss something that seems unnecessary.

8. Be aware of behaviors or pursuits that perhaps have outgrown their usefulness or effectiveness.

9. Habitual behaviors are sometimes hard to spot. When a habit is starting to cost you something, especially your creativity or sense of play, it's time to reevaluate.

10. If you're suspicious that some part or all of your life is now in a rut, consider asking a friend or family member about it. Others often see things about us that we are blind to.

11. If you're hearing the same feedback often—say, three times or more—take a good hard look at what's being said.

12. If we take half the energy we use to moan, groan, and complain and direct it into achieving our hopes and desires, our lives will look completely different.

13. There are some things in life we have control over and many that we don't. The way in which you meet life will determine the amount of ease and grace you have in your

life. Change what you can, release what is not needed, accept what you are able to accept, and get into relationship with the rest of it.

14. Often we know what we need to do or what the next step is, but we don't take it. Inactivity keeps you stuck. The way to get unstuck is to do something. Taking action changes everything.

15. With a dream you can design a strategy or a plan to make a dream happen; with a fantasy, you cannot. Just because it's a fantasy doesn't mean it can't or won't happen. But there is little you can do that will make it happen.

16. Setting yourself up for failure by embracing a fantasy is self-defeating. If you are seeking something, define what it is, where it can be found, and who can help you.

17. Self-reflection and contemplation can be nurturing, calming, and clearing, but when it comes to simplifying your life, other people are not only useful, but often are essential.

# PART II

# THE
# ROADMAP
# TO
# EASE

# THE ROADMAP TO EASE©

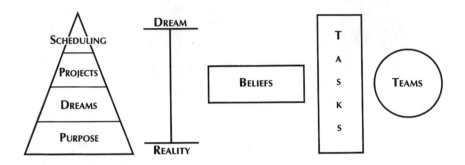

# 6

# The Process

Y OU are about to embark upon a journey. This voyage will take
you to a most wonderful place. It will take you home to yourself. Let's call this the journey of your soul. By following the process
outlined in these chapters, you will reconnect to whatever matters to
you most, and you will have a clear idea of how to create it.

Think of this process as a Roadmap, because it will give you a clear
direction and destination. Along the way you will be given rest stops
and assistance in making decisions.

This Roadmap provides five elements of core technology for simplifying your life and getting what you want. I believe you will find
this process enjoyable and exciting. It will help pump up your inven-
tive muscles and unleash your brainpower in pursuit of your dreams.
Some of us are good at dreaming and being creative, but perhaps are
lacking in the implementation phase. For others, the opposite may
be true: Perhaps you need some practice or work in the dreaming or
imagining aspects of life, but are quite skilled at planning to meet
your goals. Regardless of where your strengths are (which may change
on any given day), this process will provide a whole-brained approach.
We need to be able to dream and implement.

At the end of each of the next five chapters, pause at the rest stops
and complete the simple exercises. By the time you reach the end of

this part of the book you will know your purpose, have a clear picture of your dream, and see where you are in relation to achieving it. You will also create a positive new belief to assist you in moving forward on your dream, a short-term project to start the process now, and the beginnings of a new team, so you are continually supported in living your dream. You can proceed at your own pace; just keep heading forward.

## SWIMMING IN THE SOUP

When it comes to ease, one of the most common problems is that we treat our life as though it were a big pot of soup. We make a big pot of soup and then we swim in it. This soup can be so thick that we can't tell what the ingredients are. We throw everything into one big pot and then wonder why it tastes so bland or awful. We wonder why we're not clear about what we want, why we feel so confused, and how it got this way. Do you remember what you put in the soup? Are you aware of some of the seasonings that others dumped in when you weren't looking?

After a thorough investigation, here's what I have found: In any given pot are our passions, dreams, and limiting beliefs. Our parents' limiting beliefs, our worst fears, doubts, and our sense (proven or not) of reality may also be in there. If you have a big pot, you might include some disappointments from the past, concerns for the future, and such a long list of "to dos" that you may even be thinking that you need a bigger pot!

If you want greater ease in your life, if you want to do less and have more, you need to see what's in your soup. Begin to recognize the ingredients and consciously decide which spices to add and which to get rid of. Sense when you have added too much of one thing or not enough of another. Most important, see when you have more than one pot cooking. When have you put the ingredients from one recipe into the wrong pot?

Here's how your soup-pot experience translates into everyday life: Perhaps you have started to identify what you love and what you want. For a moment you feel alive, even elated. Then, in an instant, you feel awful, or maybe afraid. You wonder what you were thinking. You must have been mad to have such a notion. You then invalidate the entire thought and your feelings of hope and joy. If they surface again, you have a cadre of logical reasons telling you why you shouldn't feel this way and encouraging you to dismiss these flights of fancy immediately and "get real."

Then you wonder why your dreams don't materialize or why you feel stuck and unfulfilled in life. As you connect with your purpose and passion, old programming surfaces. As you start to feel your dreams and desires, your limiting beliefs will show up. And as you start to act on what you truly want, reality will test you.

This is good news. You have well-developed protection systems and internal mechanisms. They have served you effectively in life. You probably have much to be thankful for. But at a certain point in life, it's time to expand your repertoire. Rather than feel as though you are swimming in the soup, you can take a higher road. You have already decided to create a new path. I will give you a detailed map that will provide you with such clarity, definition, and ease that the only thing you'll want to do with your soup is dump it.

The key to this process will be your passion. The purpose of the Roadmap is to connect you to what you love, inspire you, and encourage you to live the life of your dreams.

## THE ROADMAP

The following process is the best and most succinct of all my work to date. It is a system that has been used successfully by thousands of people and companies. It is tried and true. It is also simple. Upon completion of this process you will know your passion and how to use it as a motivating force. Many people refer to their passion as their life's purpose. You will understand the importance of having dreams in all areas of your life. You will learn how to create a belief system that will help you dream big and make those dreams a reality, as well as learn how to create powerful teams that will make your life easier.

The process begins with the Passion Pyramid in Chapter 7. The Passion Pyramid will show you how to live more from your passion than from your calendar. It will introduce you to a new way of living that is life-changing, yet simple. You'll love it so much that I'll bet you'll be inspired to share it with others.

Whether you know where your passion lies or not, whether you are passionate about making money, helping others, or simplifying your life, I will show you how to raise your passion level to new heights. Then you will be delighted to see how you can create and design a life that is aligned with your purpose. Until we know who we are and what really moves us, it is impossible to truly know our deepest dreams and desires.

Chapter 8, on dreams, may very well redefine how you look at and live your life. A dream is defined as a hope or desire. I will work with you to encourage dreams in all the important areas of your life, at work, and at home. We'll even consider your fun dreams. Fun often gets left out of our lives, but not in this process.

I'll demonstrate a simple three-step process useful for making any dream come true. Whether you are launching a multimillion-dollar idea or streamlining or revamping your life, this dream process is guaranteed to give you a quick result.

Often we are so wrapped up in reality that we have forgotten our dreams. Perhaps you've been disappointed by a dream, so you abandoned it or stopped dreaming altogether. Without our dreams, all we have is reality. Although reality isn't a bad thing, you're living a different kind of life when you're focused only on reality than if you were also pursuing your dreams. I'll show you how to create a dream that you are more committed to than your reality. The evidence of your commitment will be in the action you take.

The Beliefs section of the Roadmap, discussed in Chapter 9, is worth its weight in gold. Our beliefs determine the choices and decisions we make each day of our lives. Your beliefs are either moving you forward or holding you back. I'll show you how to create a powerful belief that will support you and your dreams. Believing in yourself and your dream can mean the difference between the life and death of that vision.

Once you are clear about your passion, purpose, and dream, and armed with a strong belief, we will move into the Strategies and Tasks portion of the Roadmap in Chapter 10. This is where it all becomes real. I'll show you how dreams die, how we sabotage them, and a guaranteed way to keep yours alive and moving forward.

Of course there are times when we hit walls or experience setbacks. But they don't have to mean the demise of our dreams. Defeat or disappointment can be used to revisit and reformulate aspects of your dream. Having a team in place to support you will help you do this. Even one other person is sometimes all that is needed. In Chapter 11, I will show you a simple method for building an Ease Team: people who will make your life easier.

At the end of this process you will feel your passion, be clear about your dreams, have recognized and removed the obstacles to your dream, and begun to live the life of your dreams.

Not only will your outlook on life change, but the way in which you deal with life will be different.

## REAL PEOPLE

Armed with simple but effective techniques, people do magnificent and exciting things. From dramatic financial success to substantial weight loss, from career changes to starting their own businesses, by tapping into ease we can change and improve the overall quality of life. Here are a few examples of how the ease process helped some people do less and still have more of what they wanted.

Michael was a one-man commodities brokerage for eight years. From his seven-hundred-square-foot office, he booked about a million dollars a year in business. By connecting to his passion, he transformed his business in less than one year. He now has thirty-two brokers working in a four-thousand-square-foot office, doing a million dollars *a month* in business. He found a way to enjoy tremendous success, while still having time to enjoy his wife and newborn son. His secret? He used his passion to build an awesome team.

Sally transformed her life by creating a dream that mattered more to her than her reality. She was overweight and terribly unhappy when I met her. In just six months of committing herself to a program of steady weight loss, she went from a size fourteen to a size four, and completely changed her career and lifestyle. Sally told me that once she got clear about what mattered to her, losing the weight was one of the easiest things she ever did. Five years later, she is still a size four.

Cheryl wanted to have more time to be a quality mom. By following the Roadmap to Ease, she started a very successful in-home business representing business trainers and speakers. She lives by her own schedule. Her life does not run her. Cheryl cherishes her child above all else, and has created a lifestyle of ease that supports her priorities.

Steve decided to become a motivational speaker. Since he had a stable job in computers and a good income, Steve's friends and family thought quitting was a bad idea. We thought it was a great idea and devised a plan not only to make the transition a reality, but to make the shift with ease. Within three months, he landed a sixty-thousand-dollar contract.

For eleven years, Ilene was miserable as a corporate manager for a utilities company, working far too many hours. She created a clear vision of what she wanted and got what mattered to her most: a quiet town house with a deck, creek, and trees. Besides quitting her job and finding a fun new position, she now has balance and peace of mind every single day.

Bessie became a world-famous photographer at the age of seventy. Everyone she knew told her she was too old to pursue this dream, and to be realistic. By creating a simple short-term project and equipped with a powerful belief, she entered and won a national photographic contest sponsored by Kodak. The prize was ten thousand dollars, and in 1997 her award-winning photo toured around the world with the "Journey into Imagination" exhibit. This exposure catapulted her into her new career.

These are just a few of the inspirational stories I've gathered about everyday people like you and me who got clear about their priorities and made things happen. By following this Roadmap to Ease, and using passion, dreams, beliefs, tasks, and teams, you too will experience a shift in your world.

## LIFE RENEWED

A few years ago, I gave a speech in Southern California to a Young Presidents' Organization chapter. After the meeting, a very attractive woman named Cathy introduced herself to me. I could not believe it when she told she was almost sixty years old.

"The reason I look so great," she said, "is because I love my life. My husband and I live in La Jolla on the beach. We ski and skate for fun and to stay in shape. We work hard and we play harder. But it wasn't always like this.

"Ten years ago we lived in Canada and we were freezing and miserable. We decided we would follow our hearts. We knew we wanted to live someplace warm and sunny, that we wanted wonderful friends, and that we wanted to live someplace where we could thrive. We got in our car and drove south. We just kept driving until it felt right. We were committed to finding and making a beautiful new home and community for ourselves. Everyone we knew thought we had lost our minds. We landed here and created a dream-come-true life for ourselves."

Cathy's story illustrates the power of what's possible when you connect to your heart's desire. With the right tools, you too can live a free and abundant life filled with good health, good friends, a beautiful environment, and the time to enjoy it all.

## TIPS FOR SUCCESS

This system is simple, simple, simple and will yield extraordinary results. It is designed to walk you through a process, just as if you were working one-on-one with me. I invite you to imagine that I am sitting with you and together we are designing exactly how you want your life to be.

Since I am not physically with you, there will be one difference. You can work at your own pace. It is not necessary for you to race through this. However, I do recommend that you keep moving forward. Each step you take in creating your dream life will move you closer to that life. A great hint for success is to try to do something, at least one tip, technique, or exercise, each day. These are not cumbersome, and they will keep you motivated

On any given day you might recognize where you are wasting time and energy. Maybe you will catch yourself saying yes when you want to say no. You'll begin to notice when you are sabotaging your dreams. Daily progress will keep you inspired, optimistic, and moving ahead. Here are some additional tips for success:

Try something new. It's been said that if you can use or implement something newly learned within twenty-four hours, it has the highest chance for retention. After you've read about an idea or suggestion in this book, give it a shot. Go out in the world, into your family, into your job, and into your relationships willing to try some new things.

Taking action on a daily or regular basis helps build confidence. Seeing yourself practicing new skills and behaviors sends a very positive message to yourself and others. Small steps are usually easier to take than big leaps. The steps suggested here are designed to yield big results.

Recap your day. Review your actions, results, or lack of action. Check in with your feelings. What felt right? What was awkward? When or where did you feel at ease? Consider keeping a journal of your observations.The practice of reflecting and writing can be fun and informative. If this feels like a big chore, skip it. If it works for you, do it; if it doesn't, don't. This is a good rule of thumb.

Look for success. Find one thing you did today that made you feel positive. Notice where you did less. See where you had more. Acknowledge your successes and modify your behaviors as you go.

In Chapter 11, I'll discuss the power of teams. Be a buddy to others and find one for yourself. Many people have told me they have had amazing results and great fun doing this entire process with a buddy, spouse, or friend. Whom do you know who would love your support in transforming his or her life or in creating something new or different?

You can meet on a weekly basis by phone or face-to-face, and do the exercises together. You then have a week to implement, explore, and practice. When you next meet, share your ups and downs, your wins and your obstacles, and brainstorm ideas. It can be a life-changing practice to be accountable to another person. Imagine having someone who is on your team, on your side, cheering you on to success. It works!

Review the Fundamentals of Ease at the end of each chapter. No matter where you are in the book, even if you have finished reading the book, the Fundamentals are a great refresher. If you feel confused at any point, these will prove useful. They offer an overview. Sometimes when we are steeped in something, we may lose our way, perhaps even wonder what we're doing here in the first place. The Fundamentals take the pearls from each chapter and spell them out in a concise manner. They are designed to keep you clearly focused and moving forward.

Most important, enjoy the process. Remember why you're doing this. Commit to doing less and having more. Let your desire and passion lead the way.

## FUNDAMENTALS OF EASE

1. Some of us are good at dreaming and being creative, but perhaps are lacking in the implementation phase. Perhaps you need some practice or work in the dreaming or imagining aspects of life, but are quite skilled at planning to meet your goals.

2. When it comes to ease, one of the most common problems is that we treat our life as though it were a big pot of soup. We throw everything into one big pot and then wonder why it tastes so bland or awful.

3. In any given pot are our passions, dreams, and limiting beliefs. If you want greater ease in your life, if you want to do less and have more, you need to see what's in your soup.

4. As you start to feel your dreams and desires, your limiting beliefs will show up. And as you start to act on what you truly want, reality will test you.

5. The key to this process will be your passion. The purpose of the Roadmap is to connect you to what you love, inspire you, and encourage you to live the life of your dreams.

6. Upon completion of this process you will know your passion and how to use it as a motivating force. Many people refer to their passion as their life's purpose.

7. Until we know who we are and what really moves us, it is impossible to truly know our deepest dreams and desires.

8. I'll demonstrate a simple three-step process, useful for making any dream come true and guaranteed to give you quick results.

9. Often we are so wrapped up in reality that we have forgotten our dreams. Without our dreams, all we have is reality. Although reality is not a bad thing, you're living a different kind of life when you're focused only on reality than if you were also pursuing your dreams.

10. Once you're clear about your passion, purpose, and dream, and armed with a strong belief, we will move into the Strategies and Tasks portion of the Roadmap, where it all becomes real.

11. Defeat or disappointment can be used to revisit and reformulate aspects of your dream.

12. Armed with simple but effective techniques, people do magnificent and exciting things. By following the Roadmap to Ease and using passion, dreams, beliefs, tasks, and teams, you too will experience a shift in your world.

13. Each step you take in creating your dream life will move you closer to that life. A great hint for success is to try to do something, at least one tip, technique, or exercise, each day. These are not cumbersome and they will keep you motivated.

14. Look for success. Find one thing that you did today that made you feel positive. Notice where you did less. See where you had more. Acknowledge your successes and modify your behaviors as you go.
15. Review the Fundamentals of Ease at the end of each chapter. No matter where you are in the book, even if you have finished reading the book, the Fundamentals are a great refresher.

# 7

# Passion—The Juice

WHAT do Tony Robbins, Tom Peters, Stephen Covey, and I have in common? We are all talking about passion. Passion is defined as "being compelled to action." Being passionate means being excited enough about an idea or project that you will actually do something about it. In this day and age, a good sign that you are passionate about something is when you schedule it into your life.

Since we live primarily according to our clocks and calendars, the secret to having a more passionate life is to schedule more things you love and fewer things you don't. As you gain more precious moments by saying no (when you can) and by scheduling more things that you love (that also get done faster), the end result is more quality time in your life. Passion is the ultimate time-management tool and will give you great ease. This idea is discussed in detail in Chapter 13, where I talk about time.

During a workshop in Boulder, Colorado, one man told me that he considered passion to be a bad thing, because he associated it with the suffering of Jesus during the Crucifixion, or with sexual passion. But there are other definitions, and in my book passion is not a dirty word. The objects of any strong desire, enthusiasm, strong love, or affection are good things. Passion's close companion, enthusiasm, comes from the root *entheos,* meaning "inspired by God."

This chapter is designed to connect or reconnect you to your passion. Connecting with your passion is essential for creating the kind of life you want. Until we know what your passion is, how can we answer the question "How do you want your life to be?" We can't. If you want to do less and have more, identifying your passion is important.

Do you know what you are passionate about? For many, passion is something that existed before the kids were born or before life became overwhelming. But guess what? Passion can give us energy to handle the things that overwhelm us. It's an expression of life. When you are in touch with your passion, you have more energy, vitality, and creativity. In business, passion sells. Wouldn't you rather do business with someone who enjoys what he is doing rather than with someone who is just doing a job?

Recently I met Marty Shih, the president of a company called 800-777-Club Inc. In 1989, Marty came to America from Taiwan with five hundred dollars in his pocket and limited English, but with a belief in the American Dream. Now with one thousand employees, his company serves over a million members of the Asian-American community. He told me, "I am the least educated person in my company. Everyone else has college degrees and M.B.A.'s. But I have passion, unlimited amounts of passion. If I had to attribute my success to one thing, it would be to my passion." His slogan is "Think big, aim high, have passion, and have dreams."

In my travels, I've interviewed hundreds of people from all walks of life. These were businesspeople, housewives, husbands, kids, even people from different countries. Most of them were pretty content and would say that they were satisfied with life. What they had in common was passion. Whether they described it as something still and quiet that lived deep in their heart or as a burning fire that resided in their gut, these people all spoke about passion as a powerful force.

The happiest people all seemed to share a special knowledge. They knew that passion lived inside them and that the secret to a fulfilling life is to find conscious ways to design more of what they love into their everyday existence. They sought ways to express their passion, rather than complaining about not having any or not having enough.

One man told me, "Knowing what I'm passionate about has put

real power in my hands. It's as though I'm walking around holding a plug, seeking outlets where I can connect to it and express more." I often refer to passion as the "juice" because we can plug into it and get energized.

## YOUR PASSION QUEST

What if you're not passionate, or if you have lost your passion? Maybe, like many, you're passionate about some things, but not about others, like your job or a particular relationship. Let's first discuss where you can find your passion and then how you can reignite it.

I owned a marketing company for more than ten years. Although it was successful, I was burnt out and knew I needed to make a major lifestyle change. I had passion when I started the company, but many years later, with a big staff and huge overhead, I lost it.

When you lose your passion, I recommend that you take yourself on a Passion Quest. Start to do the little things in life that you love. If you love to cook, take a class or have a small dinner party. If you love adventure but time or money (or both) won't allow you a major vacation, consider a day hike or a weekend adventure.

Do the things you love, but make them part of the research phase of a project called "finding my passion." When I am in Passion Quest mode, I pay extra attention to how life affects me: what makes me laugh or cry and what upsets or excites me. I notice what I am drawn to, even the movies I'm watching.

It was a Passion Quest that led me to a new life and the path I am on now. I was driving home from work when I heard an announcement on the radio that the Make-A-Wish Foundation needed volunteers. I noticed I was intrigued. Rather than driving home, I went to the meeting.

Around ten years ago, a young boy in Phoenix, Arizona, who was terminally ill, had a dream to be a state trooper. Someone sewed him a uniform and made him a hat. A trooper took the boy out for a day and fulfilled his wish. Soon after that the boy died, but the boy's family said that day had been the most joyous of his life. Since then, the Make-A-Wish Foundation has granted more than ten thousand wishes to children all over the world.

That night, about a dozen of us gathered in a small room, where we discussed how we could raise money for puppy dogs and trips to Disneyland. After the meeting ended, I went out to my car and was about to start the ignition when I began to cry. I sobbed for a long time, not even sure why. For the next few days, as part of my Passion Quest, I allowed myself to feel how deeply I had been affected by that meeting.

I realized I had found my passion. I wanted to use everything I had and everything I knew, including all my personal successes and failures, to help make wishes and dreams come true. I wanted to do it for all kinds of people, from all walks of life, all over the world.

It's years later, and I'm now considered a dream achievement expert. I give speeches on visionary thinking to corporations. I speak also in prisons, at conventions, and to kids. I speak all over the world about hopes and desires. I feel extremely blessed that I have integrated my passion into all areas of my life, especially my work.

I'm often asked if I believe that every passion can be turned into a business. I believe it can be, but it doesn't have to be. For some, taking what you love and turning it into a vocation would kill the passion. For others, being paid for doing what you love would be the ultimate dream come true.

When I was a guest on *The Oprah Winfrey Show*, Oprah walked into the audience and asked people to name their passion. My job was to suggest, on the spot, a business idea that would allow them to turn their passion into a profession. One woman said, "I love to cook and to travel." I inquired if she would consider being a traveling chef. She now cooks aboard a cruise ship.

Kathleen was a real-estate agent whose passion was Italy. She lived, breathed, and dreamed about moving to Italy. I asked her if she could do anything at all, what would that be? She replied, "Marcia, the truth is I have two great loves. I love to walk and wander and I love to cook and eat." Next time you're in Tuscany, look her up. She leads walking tours and picnics in one of the most beautiful places in the world. Often the unexpected becomes obvious and available when you connect to your passion.

You can use your passion to become focused, intentional, and determined. Think creatively and new avenues open. In his book *The Bridge Across Forever*, Richard Bach says, "Passionately obsessed by anything we love, sailboats, airplanes, ideas, an avalanche of magic flattens the way ahead, levels rules, reasons, deserts, bears us with it over chasms, fears, doubts."

## REIGNITING PASSION

My passion is "to inspire." It's so simple and allows for so much. For many years I stood in front of audiences inspiring people to dream. Once I began to notice my energy was getting stale and with it, my speeches. I started to think about my next career.

"Oh, no! Not that again," I thought. I decided to explore what had happened.

I asked myself, "What am I passionate about?" Inspiration was the answer.

"So, Marcia, what inspires you?" Taking risks, trying new things, accomplishing something that I didn't know I could do.

"How can you bring these qualities to your work?" I decided that the next speech I gave would be done with a wireless hand-held microphone, in the audience. Rather than stand up on the stage, I'd get out there with folks and rap. I'd be willing to let the talk go wherever it needed to go.

It was pretty risky business. People would ask questions and I would teach what I knew. My worst fear was, What if I didn't know the answer?

When that happened I would say, "Gee, I don't know. Who in this room can help this person?" Someone always could. My talks became alive, organic, exciting, and filled with unknowns.

The best thing that happened was that I got inspired. I got inspired by the courage of my audiences and they got inspired by my genuineness. My passion was reignited and I was taught an amazing lesson. We can relight our pilot light. We have the resources to turn up the flame and really burn brightly.

When you have a sense of your passion and purpose, you have the ability to be responsible for your own happiness and satisfaction, both at home and on the job. The great economist E. F. Schumacher said, "If your body gets hurt at work, you're covered, but if your soul is hurt at work, you're on your own."

## THE PASSION PYRAMID

Once you know your passion, you can use the Passion Pyramid, the first stop on the Roadmap to Ease, to actively design the life you want. The Passion Pyramid is a tool for putting more passion and vitality into your life, every single day, regardless of what you're doing, where you're doing it, or whom you're doing it with. I have used this model in companies such as AT&T, American Express, and Kwik Kopy, as well as with individuals, to fulfill all kinds of dreams and needs.

Look at the pyramid first as a universal shape. In the study of symbols, it is the most ancient and widely known symbol used to represent manifestation. With a wide foundation or base, it is firmly grounded. Only from a firm base can it reach amazing heights, coming together with precision and perfection at one singular point. This is the point of realization and where dreams are attained.

From my home in San Francisco, I can see the Transamerica Building, often referred to as "the pyramid." It's an amazing structure that towers high above all the other buildings, and its presence can be seen or felt all over the city. It is sound and solid, reaches for great heights, and houses many successful companies and people. The pyramid is awesome.

What's important about the Passion Pyramid is that your focus starts at the base. You read it from the bottom up. Once you know what your purpose is, then you can create dreams that truly express your passion. Dreams, which are our hopes and desires (discussed in detail in the next chapter), are often vague at this point. They need to be turned into projects or goals that are specific and measurable. We then reach the apex of the Passion Pyramid: scheduling. This includes strategizing, breaking your projects down into simple tasks, identifying resources that will help you achieve your dreams, and scheduling all of this into your life.

The Passion Pyramid will help you get from where you are to where you want to be, while keeping you balanced in all the areas of your life. When used properly, it can help you design a blueprint for achieving what you want, streamlining the process of reaching your dreams. Let's look more closely at how the sections of the Pyramid work.

*Purpose.* Your purpose is the foundation of your Passion Pyramid. It answers the question "Who am I?" Some people think they've known the answer to this question for years. Then they're surprised to discover a "different" truth. Later in this chapter, we'll complete an exercise to answer the question "Who am I?" or "What's my purpose?"

*Dreams.* With clarity of purpose, your dreams develop a deeper meaning. Once you have established your foundation and know who you are, you can start to look at how you want your life to be. For example, if your purpose is to live life as an adventure, your dreams might include bringing adventure into everything you do, or into a specific aspect of your life, like your business or your marriage.

*Projects.* Standing in your purpose, connected to your dreams, you will be able to develop projects that will take your dreams out of your imagination and make them part of your reality. Not only will your projects be "real," but they will further the journey toward realizing your dreams. You can think of projects as goals or dreams with due dates.

*Scheduling.* Scheduling, at the top of the Pyramid, actually puts your projects onto the calendar, giving you dates for meeting your objectives and making your insights usable and real. The good news is that most of your time will be spent doing things you love, not just more busywork.

Don't sabotage yourself by trying to deal with the Pyramid from the top down. Often we have a negative reaction to "Scheduling," because we feel anxious about finding time to take on additional tasks. Starting at the top of the Pyramid rarely if ever allows you to build a life you can live on purpose. Work this process from the bottom up. Start with your purpose and rest assured that you will accomplish things faster and more easily when you are passionate and "on purpose."

When I first started doing this work some years ago, I used to say, "Every day I'm doing something I love." Now I can say, "I'm *always* doing things I love." My office is devoid of files, except for project files. Since the projects come from my dreams, which come in turn from my purpose, I am living a life that I love, one filled with passion. Whenever I have extra time, which I often do, I reach for one of my project files. I love working on them because I know that doing so puts me constantly in action on the life I intentionally created for myself. This is called "Life by Design."

## A CRUISE STORY

For many years I described my purpose as "to use my creativity to make things happen." I love to be creative and to produce results. One without the other was unfulfilling. Using this purpose as my Passion Pyramid foundation, I asked myself how I wanted my life to be and what some of my dreams were.

One of my dreams was to travel the world in style and elegance. My project was to go on a free cruise speaking to people about how to make their lives easier. I put together a bio, a short blurb on my talk, and a photo of myself and sent them all off to Cunard Cruise Lines, the company that owns the QE2.

A few weeks later, they called and booked me (and a friend) for two weeks, all expenses paid, to cruise around the Hawaiian Islands, in exchange for giving three twenty-minute talks. Ann Miller (still with great legs) was the other guest lecturer. It was one of the easiest dreams I ever realized—and if I can do it, so can you!

If you're thinking that you have nothing like this to offer, listen up. Every day at sea I saw an elderly gentleman smiling and relaxing on deck. I introduced myself to him and asked why he seemed so happy.

He said, "I'm a retired dentist. My wife and I cruise all over the world. I hang out on board in case anyone loses a filling."

The average age of the guests on board was seventy years old. I noticed that the people who still had dreams for themselves, their children, and grandchildren had passion and were spunky. Those who thought they were too old to have dreams were like zombies, a little like the walking dead. No passion, no dreams, no sense of purpose, perhaps no reason to live.

## PURPOSE

Let's examine this notion of purpose more closely. It is impossible to talk about passion in depth without also exploring your purpose. Purpose answers the question "Who am I?" This simple question throws many people into a tizzy. It can be so simple, yet so profound, to explore the richness of purpose. Coco Chanel wrote, "How many cares one loses when one decides not to be something, but to be someone."

If what you want is to live life fully, have fun and wonderful relationships at work and at home, and ultimately make your dreams come true, it is essential that you explore your purpose.

Sanskrit, the oldest language known to mankind, speaks about dharma. Dharma is defined as the unfolding of your life's purpose. To have a fulfilling life, one must have purpose. To live on purpose requires three things: Have a spiritual practice, know what is unique about you, and find a way to be of service with your gifts and talents.

A spiritual practice could be anything from listening to music or taking walks in nature to prayer or meditation. Knowing what is unique about you can be expressed through your passion. What you choose to do with it remains to be seen.

When Susan came to work with me she said, "I have lots of dreams, but they keep winding up as dead ends. I have a strong sense that I'm missing something." She was right. She was missing her purpose. That's why her fondest memories felt incidental when she thought about them. I asked her to share one.

"I remember being in Cape Cod. It was a rainy, blustery morning. I was sitting in my bed, wrapped in a blanket with the window cracked open. I could feel the rain and wind on my face and I felt so moved. I felt so touched by life. But what can I do with this?" she asked.

As Susan let herself feel the memory, her whole body and being transformed right before my eyes. She had arrived at my office wounded and collapsed. As she told the story, her voice enlivened and her posture straightened. She became animated and alive.

"Susan, this is what yearning feels like. You are a perfect example of someone who is passionate about life's expression."

Keep in mind what the noted author and speaker Marianne Williamson said: "Our insecurity is inevitable in the absence of personal meaning." What Susan couldn't see was how her memories had anything to do with who she was. When she pictured them, they felt insignificant. She dismissed them, feeling lost and invalidated.

When she shared her Cape Cod experience with me, I said, "It sounds like you were being kissed by God. Your purpose feels like it has to do with expressing yourself or with the expression of life."

She began to cry and said, "That's me!"

Susan's assignment for the next thirty days was to reconnect to her love for expression. She danced, wrote, worked with pastels, and spent time with a therapist. She wrote letters to old friends and made fun phone calls. She also sat quietly and began to hear the nagging voices inside herself that invalidated who she was and who she was becoming.

She called me recently and said, "I have found my voice. I am fully expressing myself. Now that I have *me* back, everything looks better, tastes sweeter. I feel alive."

Passion is your access route to ease, and the way to tap your passion is through your life's purpose. Your purpose is who you are or what gets you excited. I might even say that your purpose is remembering why you're here.

## REMEMBERING YOUR PURPOSE

If you're like a lot of readers, you might say, "I picked up this book because I wanted to make my life easier, but, between you and me, I don't think I have a purpose."

Yes, you do. Your purpose is not a big, burdensome, heavy weight that you "must" accomplish in your life; rather, it's an expression of who you are. If you're busy running, doing, and accomplishing, perhaps you've forgotten your purpose. You can spend a long time trying to remember. Or you can reconnect to it in a moment by getting still and reflecting on what you love.

Some people do remember and are living their lives with purpose. History has recorded some of them as the most mission-oriented individuals in the world—Mahatma Gandhi, Mother Teresa, Martin Luther King, Jr. At some point they remembered. But everyday people like you and me are remembering, too. People like Carol Penn, who decided to use her passion to create an inner-city dance company in Washington, D.C., or thirty-year-old Steve Moroski, who teaches kids in Atlanta to be "dream warriors" rather than street fighters.

Or Brugh Joy, a surgeon who found that alternative healing could do things that medicine couldn't, and who left the medical field to become a healer and teacher of body energetics. Or Laura Henderson, a champion for change, whose company Prospect Associates did the research that led to the ruling that eliminated smoking from airplanes. Or Jay Hair, who, when his young daughter Whitney was dying from a strange disease, found a rare plant in the rain forest that saved her life, and who is now president of the National Wildlife Federation. (The Rosie Periwinkle plant, which saved Whitney's life, is now extinct.) Jay's purpose is to sustain life.

Remembrance of your purpose can occur when you're young or old. Many people never remember, and some don't even know that they don't know. But how many of us have suddenly stopped what we're doing and said, "Wait a minute, this is not what my life is about." In that moment, with that realization, you start to remember. Wake up. It's time to remember and start living your life on purpose.

## QUICK STARTS

Begin to recognize who you are passionate about *being* rather than just what are you passionate about *doing*. Why? Because the broader your area of passion, the more places you can express it. For example, if you tell me that you love mountain-biking or hiking and that you want to bring more passion to your work, those might be difficult things to do around the office. But underneath the activities, I can hear that you are someone who loves adventure or risk-taking.

Let's explore your passion. What do you love? Here's a simple exercise to get the ball rolling:

Think of a time in your life when you were doing something you loved. Perhaps you were excited or joyful or perhaps you were quiet and moved. Think of a specific memory. Perhaps you won an award, and that was a special moment. Maybe a passionate memory for you was getting a new job or buying your first home. Maybe a highlight was having your kids. Be specific. Were you passionate about having your kids or about getting them out of the house?

After working with many people, I recognize commonalities. Listed below are some of the most frequent areas that tend to express people's passions. These are designed to be quick starts for you, places to begin. Don't let them limit you. Let them assist you and provide ease as you start to explore.

Close your eyes and picture yourself in a time in your life when you were doing something you loved. Feel the passion. Notice if you have the tendency to dismiss your memories as not being big enough. Based on your memory of passion, which of these best describes you?

Are you passionate about learning or teaching?
Do you love being of service or making a contribution?
Are you turned on by risk-taking or adventure?
Do you enjoy being creative or solving problems?
Are you jazzed about inspiring others or expressing yourself?

These general categories will help you begin to find your purpose. You may find that you have a combination of passions, such as learning and risk-taking or teaching and making a contribution. Good. Find *you*. To know your passion is to have access to your purpose.

The more you express your passion, the more you are living on purpose. Living on purpose is key to ease.

## DEFINING YOUR PURPOSE

Your purpose is anything that touches your heart and makes a difference to you. If you're working at a job just for the money, and what you're doing doesn't fulfill you, perhaps you've lost your sense of purpose. The test is, how do you feel? Are you turned on? Considering that most of us will work about a hundred thousand hours before we retire, if you don't love what you're doing, something is wrong. Matthew Fox, the founding director of the Institute in Culture and Creation Spirituality, says, "For many of us, our soul, which includes our dreams, passions and values, is too big for the office."

Most of us are so busy reacting to the needs of daily life that we're happy just to be getting through the day. It's hard to live on purpose when life revolves around daily crises or you're always feeling overwhelmed. By taking the time to define your purpose, you'll open up more time and space, have more energy, and be more focused. Life becomes richer and has personal meaning.

You don't have to know exactly what your purpose is at this point, but I will give you an easy exercise to help move you ahead. If you have a sense of what turns you on or already know what your purpose is, great. I invite you to do the exercise anyway and see if anything new or different shows up.

This five-minute exercise will help you begin to get in touch with your life's purpose by looking for additional past memories. Then we will deepen this process by looking for a pattern and seeing what your memories have in common.

Remember to be as specific about your memories as possible. Details will make a difference in helping you pinpoint your purpose. Small, precious memories work well here.

## EXERCISE: GETTING IN TOUCH WITH YOUR LIFE'S PURPOSE

On a piece of paper, list three times in your life when you felt joyful, passionate, inspired, or moved. Look for three memories about which you can say, "I did that; it felt good." It could be something you did on your own or with others, or something you did for someone else.

Perhaps it was having your first child, a speech you gave in high school or college, a project at work, skiing intermediate runs. Write them down quickly. As you write the first one, the other two will come.

When the exercise is completed, take a deep breath and relax; the hard part is over. Now look for the pattern. What was present for you in all three examples? Look for the big picture. If you think at first that there's nothing consistent about your experiences, reflect on the details of each situation. Remember the time and place. Get in touch with what you were feeling then, about the events and about yourself. Perhaps all the items listed were fun, or perhaps all had a partnership component, or perhaps they all made you feel uneasy at first, but you did them anyway. Perhaps they all went beyond what you thought was possible, or they led to other things that you hadn't even considered. Maybe there was a quality of creativity connected to them, or they were things you made happen against all odds. The broader the common thread is, the better.

The commonality need not be factual — for example, that all the events happened in the same season of the year. What you're looking for is the consistency of how you felt in each case — *who you were being* — not what was happening externally. If you're having difficulty finding the common thread in all three memories, but you were excited by two of them, you're probably on the right track. Once you find the commonality, jot down a phrase or a few adjectives on page 111 after the words "My purpose is:"

## SOUND BITES

Using language that expresses your newly defined purpose and allows you to introduce it into your daily speech will affirm your passion, keep you connected to it, and move you toward having greater ease. Christine, a woman I know, created a great little sound bite to describe her purpose: "To Make a Difference by Being Different." A sound bite is a short, pithy phrase. We live in the age of information overload where such phrases can carry great power. According to an article in *USA Today*, in the 1980s a politician had seventy-five seconds to deliver a message and have it be heard and remembered. Now we have about eight seconds. How will you use your eight seconds? You can use them to express your passion, demonstrate your purpose, and have people make your life easier.

The most important reason to turn your passion into a sound bite is so you can remember what it is. Next time you're stuck in a traffic jam, you can say, "What's my purpose again? Oh yeah, To be a student of Life." Then you can dig out a language tape, pop it in your tape player, and practice *being* a true student. Instant access to your passion is a key factor for creating ease in your life.

A sound bite can be formed by stringing together a few nouns, verbs, and adjectives. For example, fun and achievement can be turned into "Having Fun While Achieving." Adventure and experience could become "To Experience the Adventure of Life."

Or you could create a statement, a short phrase that expresses you. Going for the Gold, Doing It My Way, A Champion for Change, and The Voice of a Visionary are some fun examples.

Tina was preparing to take early retirement as dean of a woman's college. She knew she wanted to start a business of her own. Businesses that excel are usually an expression of someone's vision and passion. Out of our work together, she saw clearly that her life is about inspiring people into action. She now owns The Inspiraction Company, where she inspires entrepreneurs to take risks. Her purpose and sound bite became her company name. As I said earlier, passion sells.

## A WORK IN PROGRESS

Your sound bite, statement, or adjective doesn't have to last forever. After you determine your purpose, if it leaves you feeling a bit flat, disappointed, or anything less than turned on, I have two suggestions. First, see what's missing. For example, if you have spent much time helping others and your purpose statement—"To Help Others"— leaves you feeling tired, perhaps adding the word *easily* would be useful. To easily help others.

Second, notice what limiting beliefs surface as you contemplate your passion and purpose. If you're someone who loves variety and trying new things, maybe your sound bite is "To Experience Life Fully" or "To Dance with Life" or "To Taste the Spices of Life." Do you immediately hear a booming parental voice saying, "When are you going to settle down and figure out what you want to do?"

Or perhaps your purpose in life is all about having fun. Can you imagine the beliefs *that* might dredge up? Can you hear someone—

perhaps even you — saying, "How do you expect to pay the rent doing that?" This takes us back to the soup theory discussed in the previous chapter. If, the moment you start to feel the essence of who you are and what you love, your limiting beliefs start to kick in, you are swimming in the soup. Separate out some of the ingredients. See what's in the pot and where you got lost.

Do this by writing out the negative thoughts surrounding what you love most. I promise we will revisit these in detail in the chapter on beliefs.

Many people are afraid to determine their purpose. They think this will somehow be limiting or they'll have to live it for the rest of their life. Questions and doubts may surface.

"What if it's too big or too small?"

"What if I change or don't like it?"

"What if it's wrong?"

The good news about purpose is that it can grow and change with you. But if you have an overly elaborate purpose statement, you won't remember it or use it on a regular basis. Simple. Simple. Simple. Purpose can be one word. Fun. Inspire. Learn. Share. Several words are okay, too: To be of service, to help others, to express myself.

Earlier I mentioned Christine's sound bite. It didn't come to her all at once. It evolved. During my workshop, she realized that her passion was about being different and unique.

Weeks later she called me and said, "Hey, I got the rest of my purpose. To Make a Difference by Being Different." Months later she called again and said, "You can get a lot of mileage out of these purpose statements. I ran mine as part of a personal ad and met my soon-to-be husband." Amazing things happen when people connect to their passion and begin to live on purpose.

Roadmap Stop #1 — Purpose

My purpose is:_____

_____

_____

_____

## FUNDAMENTALS OF EASE

1. If you want to do less and have more, identifying your passion provides important information.
2. Passion can give us energy to handle the things that overwhelm us. When you are in touch with your passion, you have more energy, vitality, and creativity.
3. The happiest people know that passion lives inside them and that the secret to a fulfilling life is to find conscious ways to design more of what they love into their everyday existence.
4. For some, taking what you love and turning it into a vocation would kill the passion. For others, being paid for doing what you love would be the ultimate dream come true.
5. When you have a sense of your passion and purpose, you have the ability to be responsible for your own happiness and satisfaction, both at home and on the job.
6. Once you know your passion, you can use the Passion Pyramid to actively design the life you want and put more passion and vitality into your life, regardless of what you're doing, where you're doing it, or whom you're doing it with.
7. When used properly, the Pyramid can help you design a blueprint for achieving what you want, streamlining the process of reaching your dreams.
8. Once you have established your foundation and know who you are, you can start to look at how you want your life to be.
9. Standing in your purpose, you will be able to develop projects that will take your dreams out of your imagination and make them part of your reality. Not only will your projects be "real," but they will further the journey toward realizing your dreams.
10. Scheduling, at the top of the Pyramid, actually puts your projects onto the calendar, giving you dates for meeting your objectives and making your insights usable and real.

11. Start with your purpose and rest assured that you will accomplish things faster and easier when you are passionate and "on purpose."

12. If what you want is to live life fully, have fun and wonderful relationships at work and at home, and ultimately make your dreams come true, it is essential that you explore your purpose.

13. Passion is the access to ease, and the way to tap your passion is through your life's purpose. Your purpose is who you are or what gets you excited. I might even say that your purpose is remembering why you're here.

14. Begin to recognize who you are passionate about *being* rather than just what you are passionate about *doing*. Why? Because the broader your area of passion, the more places you can express it.

15. By taking the time to define your purpose, you'll open up more time and space, have more energy, and be more focused. Life becomes richer and has personal meaning.

# 8

# Dreams—The Focus

A DREAM is defined as a fervent hope or desire. The dictionary states that part of the definition also includes "to devise a plan." Making your dreams come true means getting clear about what you want and figuring out how to obtain it. I will provide you with a simple formula for doing this.

The prime dream we are working to achieve here is doing less and having more. Are you starting to imagine what this would look like and how it will feel? Another of my all-time favorite dreams is to make great money doing what you love. Both can give you ease.

Have you ever noticed that sometimes you are all excited about an idea or dream, and the people around you aren't? When I announced to my family and friends that I was closing my marketing business to become a dreams-come-true consultant, they thought I was nuts.

"Oh, Marcia, you used to be so sensible. Can't you call this goal-setting? Do you have to use the word *dreams?*" they asked.

I think goal-setting is important, but there's a different kind of energy released around dreams. Our dreams are spacious and creative. You don't need to know how to make a dream happen. You don't have to believe it's possible (this is useful, but not necessary, and will be addressed in detail in the next chapter). Also, you never actually have to do anything about your dreams. The dreaming process *itself* gets us to swing outside of "being realistic," which opens new doors and creates fresh opportunities.

There are two important components for realizing your dreams. First I will provide you with a simple formula for getting what you want. Then I will show the importance of creating a dream that you are more committed to than your reality.

## THE FORMULA

I've used this formula to assist multimillion-dollar companies in launching new products and to help a woman who was earning less than twenty dollars an hour produce a one-woman off-Broadway show. It has helped people lose hundreds of pounds, double and triple their income, meet their soul mates, start new businesses, and move to new cities. The point is, it works, and it works on all kinds of dreams.

In three simple steps, here it is:

1. Get clear about your dream.
2. Remove the obstacles to your dream, especially the limiting beliefs.
3. Design the strategies for achieving your dream, including building a team.

1. Get clear about your dream.

Being clear about your dream means being able to articulate it easily, so people understand what it is and you can remember it. There is one essential key here: Get your dreams out of your head. In your head they don't have much chance for survival. They are in there with all that other stuff that comprises your "soup": your agenda for the board meeting, your shopping list, and your schedule for tomorrow, next week, or next month. Your new sound bite from the previous chapter will assist you in remembering what matters to you, in the midst of all your busyness.

Write down your dream. Don't omit this step. Don't fool yourself by saying you know what it is without having to write it down. Write it down so it is out of your head and you can see it. Reading it regularly is useful, but just the act of writing it down can set it into motion.

Second, talk about your dreams. We'll discuss this in much

greater detail in a moment and again in the chapter on Teams. By talking about your dreams with other people, you are usually less likely to easily dismiss them.

The talking process is useful because it can help your dream grow and crystallize. You can experiment with describing different components. You can embellish the dream by brainstorming with others. It is in the expression of what we love that we actually begin to see it and create it. Talk your heart out.

I know there are some people who don't agree with this approach. They think you are dissipating energy by talking about it. I am not one of those people. I firmly believe that the greatest magic happens when we share our dreams with others. It is essential that the people in your life know you are committed to greater ease. You need them on board. Their help will make a big difference. And if they don't support your dream, you definitely need to know that, and find someone who does.

2. Remove the obstacles.

Contrary to what you might believe, the biggest obstacles to our dreams are not time and money. The biggest blocks are our limiting beliefs, and fear and doubt are the worst of all. The entire next chapter (and one of the stops on our Roadmap to Ease) is dedicated to this one point. Your attitudes and beliefs determine the choices and decisions you make. If you don't believe that you can do less and have more, you're probably right.

Don't give up here. I'll show you how to change your limiting beliefs and how to create an empowering belief that will support you in achieving your dreams. For right now, just being aware that your beliefs are your biggest obstacles and trusting that you can do something about this should be very liberating.

Here's my most basic and essential theory about obstacles: Wherever there is an obstacle, design a strategy to manage it. Uncovering our internal objections is a good thing. Find out what you (or others) are concerned about regarding your dream and then explore options and alternatives. Obstacles and objections can lead to extraordinary brainstorming and whole new approaches to a problem.

3. Design the strategies.

Designing the strategies involves creating a clear dream, breaking it down into small steps, identifying the resources that can help achieve it, and taking action every day.

The number-one way to experience shortcuts and ease in pursuing any dream is to share your dream with others so they can help make it happen. Build an Ease Team, even if it's just one other person who believes in you and what you are trying to create. Find someone who shares the dream. Trust me. There are plenty of people around who are either working on this same dream or who want to have ease.

As we've already noted, if you are committed to having your dream come true, it is necessary for you to share it with others. Ideally, you'll share it with someone who will hold you accountable, someone who will check in and ask, "What are you doing to move that dream forward?"

Imagine the magic that can happen when you apply this simple formula to something you want. (By the way, magic is defined as producing extraordinary results. It's when A plus B equals something other than C. Think of it as an access to shortcuts and a big win.)

A woman I know makes great brownies. She told me her dream was to quit her corporate job and become the Brownie Queen.

"What are you doing about this? I asked.

"Nothing," she replied. "I'm afraid no one will actually buy them."

"How many cafés would you be willing to take them to in the next week, with the intention of taking orders?"

She looked me square in the eye, folded her arms firmly across her chest and said, "I can't believe you're doing this to me."

I said, "You ought to be grateful. I'm supportively holding you accountable to your dream. I'm on your team."

"Okay, I'll take them to three cafés, but that's it and don't push me."

A year later, her brownies are being sold in cafés all around the country and she has just met with a national distributor. In the face of her fear (her limiting belief), the dream was too big. By breaking it down into small tasks (designing the strategies) and getting help (building a team), she took action, built up her confidence, and is off and running on realizing her big dream.

## DREAMING UP YOUR DREAM

When a dream first enters your mind, you may not be able to see with clarity what it looks like. Often a dream starts in the subconscious and remains a nebulous idea floating around in the back of our head. Then it simply stays a dream or a nice idea. It's when we clarify it and take action on it that it becomes a real possibility.

There are many different ways to gain access to the details of your dream, which is needed before you can move forward. What follows are six different ways or places where you can access dreams. They are: 1) expression, 2) inspiration, 3) real-life desires, 4) active imagination, 5) sleeping, and 6) exploration. Whatever means you use for creating or discovering your dream, remember this simple and powerful point about where dreams come from: We make them up.

1. Expression

Some people find their dream by writing; some carry on conversations with others about their dream; you can even talk into a tape recorder. One client told me she actually thinks by talking. Whether you use a journal, a note pad, or a tape recorder, create a place where you can express all the aspects of your dream. Use the Dream Big exercise later in this chapter as a way to get the dream out of your head and allow it to live as part of reality. Get a clear image of what you want, define the details, and picture all the resources that can help you. Notice whether you believe it's possible to have your dream, but for right now, don't let your beliefs limit you.

Many people I know have found a vehicle of expression through the wonderful book *The Artist's Way* by Julia Cameron. The practice of morning pages, introduced in that book, encourages quiet time to write about whatever is on your mind or in your heart. This is an ideal time and process for exploring your desires. See what comes up and out. As Carl Jung said, "The creative mind plays with objects it loves."

If you aren't happy with what you write down at first, you don't have to leave it at that. Keep writing and let your dream evolve. Allow more wild and fun bits and pieces to emerge. As you start to gain clarity, what gets committed to paper will begin to feel right. But for now, let your stream of consciousness take you on a magic-carpet ride, where dreams can and do come true.

2. Inspiration

The specifics of your dream may not come all at one sitting; perhaps it will take a few days, even a few weeks. You may need to seek inspiration to complete the exercise: Go to the library, to plays or movies; rent children's videos or foreign films; or go away on a retreat, even just for a day. This is where Passion Quests, described in Chapter 7, can be useful.

Inspiration can happen anywhere. While in Hawaii recently, I met John. Years ago he came to Hawaii with his parents and dreamed of someday returning to open his own business. He has a huge passion for the water and for meeting new people. He got this great idea to buy an old boat and give it a funky paint job, covering it with black-and-white zebra stripes. He opened his own company called Sea-fari Cruises and now takes people out on snorkeling and whale-watching trips. His new dream is to have a fleet of twelve zebra boats.

John took his passion and turned it into a business. Notice that his dream includes cruising in beautiful water, meeting people from all over the world, and having a great time.

"All this fun and they pay me, too. Doesn't get much better," he told me with a big smile.

3. Real-life desires

If there's something simple that can be brought into your life right now that will make you feel good and give you ease, do it. Make an investment in yourself and bring part of your dream into reality. You will be that much closer to having it all.

I love New York cabbies. They have a unique and fresh perspective on life that I rarely hear elsewhere. During my last visit, the cabdriver didn't stop to pay the toll coming across the Verrazano Narrows Bridge into the city.

"Don't worry, lady. I have E-Z Pass. There's an electronic eye that reads this thing I have hanging from my mirror. At the end of the month they send me a bill, based on how many times I've passed through here. My theory is, I'm willing to spend my money on anything that will save me time." Bravo.

Look around your life. See what you see. Feel what you feel. Explore what you have and what you want. Notice the little things that move you and the big things that inspire you. Perhaps you admire somebody's beautiful office, somebody's lovely home, or aspects of someone else's job. When you're building your dream and delineating its details, feel free to borrow from dreams you like and respect.

Necessity is the mother of invention. What do you need? Albert Einstein said, "In the middle of difficulty lies opportunity." Use all of your life to serve your goal for dreaming. As you view your life, what do you wish, what do you desire? Dream from here and for now, release your need to have to do anything about it. Your only job here is to dream.

4. Active imagination

Some people stimulate their dreams by using photographs. That cabdriver had a photo of a younger, healthier him on his visor. He said it keeps him away from late-night pizza. A salesman friend of mine carries a picture of his dream car in his briefcase. It keeps him inspired, and he often shares it with clients. It's amazing to watch him get orders because people want to support his dream. It beats the old "the kids need new shoes" line.

Perhaps you want to live near the ocean and have a view of the mountains. Find a picture of what you want, put it into your reality by posting it on the bathroom mirror, and start connecting to it. If you begin to think about it as existing now, it will become real.

Whatever you do to stimulate your mind, pay attention and notice what works. Relax and have a good time. You are creating a design for your life by letting your dream come forward and elaborating on its urgings. Remember, this is your dream. You don't have to do things you don't want to do, or have what you think you should have, or what you've always had, or what your mother wanted you to have.

Start by thinking about your dream as being real, by visualizing it and expanding on your image. Learn to speak about it clearly: The more you speak about it, the more detailed it will become.

Use your active imagination to take it to the limit. This is a good time to dream up an extraordinary Mastermind group of people, living or dead, and see what wisdom they might offer you. Use a notebook or tape recorder to document their wisdom. What might Abraham Lincoln, Helen Keller, or Nelson Mandela have to say to you? Access the experts or people you admire. Whom would you like to hear from? Have fun with this. Remain open and receptive and see what happens.

5. Sleeping

Another great source for finding or creating your dream are the dreams you have while sleeping. No doubt you've heard this recommendation before, but it's worth repeating. Place a pad or a cassette recorder next to your bed. Tell yourself before you fall asleep to remember your nocturnal dreams, and eventually you will. In fact, you can plant a question in your subconscious before going to sleep — "I want more information about my life," for example — and see what comes up during the night.

Pay attention to your dreams. They can give you much valuable information and expand your perceptions. Your mind and mouth may be saying you don't know what you want, but your nocturnal dreams may be painting a very clear picture. Learn to work with the symbols. Consider painting or drawing the images. Use your curiosity to take you deeper into the mysterious and rich dreamworld.

Hypnosis, regression, or working with a dream expert may prove valuable and provide ease and assistance in understanding your dream messages. Dream alchemy is the process of learning to control and direct the dream state and all of its energies so that we can come to know ourselves better on all levels. Some believe we can even program our dreams to bring us what we want. How's that for the ultimate in ease?

Your dreams offer exceptional communications and deserve special time for closer examination. Treat them with respect and reverence, honor them as teachers, and they will reward you justly.

6. Exploration

My friend Peter's purpose is to live life as an adventure. This was embodied by his dream to bring adventure into every facet of his life. However, Peter was having trouble finding a way to accomplish one of his dreams, which was to take a lengthy, luxurious fishing trip to a tropical location.

When Peter first started to speak about his dream, there were many "reasons" he believed he couldn't have it. The more he spoke about it, however, the more committed to his dream he became. As he explored his dream, it stopped living as a fuzzy thing in the back of his mind. He began to get clear about what the dream would look like.

Peter became an explorer by asking himself questions and putting into writing exactly what his dream would look like. The first question Peter asked was how long he wanted the dream trip to be. He was surprised to discover that he wanted it to last at least a month. Who else was with him? He was alone. Where was he living? In a tropical paradise.

As he wrote, Peter came up with more and more questions, and as he answered them he became clearer and clearer about his dream. For instance, he decided to forsake his alarm clock and sleep until he awakened naturally.

Then Peter started to ask more about how he spent his dream day. He visualized owning a small fishing boat; he saw himself using the boat to take fishing trips, both for fun and for the opportunity to meet other people. He kept designing into his dream all the details that he wanted.

Peter also expressed some concern about being away for an extended period of time. He wondered what impact his trip would have on the people and the business he was leaving be-hind. He tempered his anxiety by speaking openly to his family about his dream. They verified that they would function well in his absence, and that his business would continue to generate profits.

Once he was clear about his dream, Peter resolved to try it out on a short-term basis. He determined that within three months, he would take a two-week fishing trip to an exotic place. He chose Costa Rica, scheduled it, and went.

Peter had a wonderful time, and he learned a few important things. The first lesson was that two weeks was long enough. The fishing was great and so was the adventure, but he missed his family, and, after two weeks, he'd had enough of doing the same thing every day.

He also observed that bringing adventure into his life deepened his relationship with his family. There's renewed romance in his marriage, and now, anytime he chooses to do so, he's able to bring adventure into many different areas of his life. Peter discovered — and you will, too — that one adventure can lead to many more, if we stop holding back and go for what we want.

## WHERE ARE YOU NOW?

How can you create a strategy for where you want to go if you don't know where you are? If you are trying to get to Florida from New York, you would use a different map than if you were coming from Texas.

I can't stress enough the importance of making an honest assessment of where you are now. Starting with inaccurate information will lead to erroneous decisions about what has to be done and how far you have to go to reach your dream. Often when we assess our reality we either inflate or deflate it. Don't deny any part of your present existence. Get everything out on the table. List where you are with respect to each of the facets of your dream.

An honest assessment of your current situation may lead to the disappointing discovery that you're not even close to where you want to be. Your challenge is to use whatever your existing position is, no matter how far it is from the dream, as a starting point.

No doubt you will find that you're at a different place within each aspect of your life — closer to your dream in some and farther away from it in others. That's a typical pattern. Ask yourself where you are not only with respect to your dream, but with regard to your relationships, your finances, your feelings.

Where are you currently with respect to your personal health, professional health, and family dreams? What concerns do you have in these areas? Do you worry that going for your dream will take more time than is available? Perhaps you don't believe it's possible to make your dream come true.

## DREAMS VERSUS REALITY

In order to create a life of ease, where you are doing less and having more, it is essential that you be more committed to your dream than to your reality. Is this true for you? The evidence is in the action you are taking or not taking to achieve your dream. It is very black and white. You need to have a clearly defined dream written out, that you are obviously in action on, ideally every day.

And if your dream truly is doing less and having more, you need to be demonstrating your intention to achieve it more than once a day. Don't you want to have clear evidence that you are living your dream and be able to recognize when and where you are not?

Without your dreams, all you have is reality, and although this is not a bad thing, there is a very different kind of energy attained from your dreams than from going through life checking things off your "to do" list. The way most of us deal with reality can be referred to as conflict manipulation. We take action to get rid of or to get away from something, like a problem.

A different kind of energy is involved when you're moving toward what you want than when you're moving away from what you don't want. A common example of this is weight loss. "I've gained ten pounds again." This is the conflict. We take action, including exercising and dieting, but as soon as we lose a few pounds, we stop exercising and go looking for chocolate. The weight returns and we have come full circle back to the conflict. To avoid just manipulating the conflict, set up your life so that you're always moving toward what you want. If your dream is to be healthy and vibrant, to feel and look good, a different kind of energy will be applied than to the drudgery of getting rid of the weight by diet and exercise.

Another popular example of conflict manipulation is in how most people handle debt. When we spend more than we earn, we decide to work overtime, perhaps take a second job and resolve to stop spending. But as soon as the balance on our credit card goes down, we go shopping! Taking action for the sole purpose of getting rid of a problem usually leads us back to the problem. A more powerful model is to be clear about our dream, honest about our reality, and more focused on the former than the latter.


## EXERCISE: DREAM BIG

The critical question always boils down to this: Are you more committed to remaining where you are or to getting where you want to be? Only the latter will propel you forward. To complete this piece of the Roadmap, you need to do three important things.

So far you've been thinking about the bits and pieces of your dream. Now, first, you will write out your dream in detail (see page 128). Go for the whole enchilada. Dream big. Put in everything that you want and leave out everything you don't want. Define your dream clearly. This is the first step.

Here's a powerful, helpful hint: Imagine how you would want your life to be if you were unencumbered. What would you do and how would you live if you had plenty of time, money, and support from the people around you? This should free you up to dream.

Answering these questions will get the ball rolling. Then tap into your stream of consciousness. Let your creative mind wonder and wander. Explore your dream world.

What would you do?

Where would you do it?

With whom?

What would you create or accomplish?

Be sure to remember your passion. A dream without passion often dies young. What does doing less and having more look like to you? Don't worry if you don't know how to accomplish what you're writing. Don't even fret if you don't believe it's possible. That's why we call it dreaming. Just imagine and explore.

Second, write out your current reality about the dream. Don't minimize or exaggerate the situation, but include all the positive and negative aspects. Simply write what's so. You can take it line by line, comparing each aspect of your dream to your reality. If your dream is to live at the beach, where do you live now? Is your house on the market, have you begun the search, or hired a real estate agent? Have you told anyone of your intentions? All of this is part of the reality section.

Finally, ask yourself this, "Which of these scenarios am I more committed to? Am I more committed to my dream or to my reality?" As you confront this question, your fears, doubts, and concerns probably will surface. If you are unsure whether you prefer your dream or your reality, it's probably because you have put your fears into your dream. They don't belong here. The next chapter will show you how to set aside limiting beliefs and sabotaging behaviors.

The number-one way we sabotage our dreams is by projecting our concerns into our dreams. Fears, doubts, and concerns are part of your reality, not your dreams. Why? Because you can't have feelings in the future. You can only have feelings here and now. Part of your reality is how you feel about your dream. How do you currently feel about your dream? On your reality list, be sure to include your feelings about your dream. They are real, and they do matter. We will address them in detail during our third stop on the Roadmap. For now, just be sure to put them where they belong. They are part of your reality, not part of your dream. This is an essential point.

*An Example*

My dream: I want a life I can call my own, a life filled with ease! This includes fun and play, creativity, passion, laughter, and love. It also includes abundance, appreciation, and plenty of time to enjoy it all.

My dream includes living in a cosmopolitan city, near the water, where it doesn't snow. (Two tips here on dreaming: Be specific and mention everything you don't want).

My dream includes working less—a great deal less—and being paid well for doing work that I love. I want my work not to feel like work, but actually to be a joyous expression of who I am and why I am here. I wake up naturally with the sunlight (I hate being jolted out of bed with an alarm clock).

I look and feel healthier at forty than I did at thirty. I don't have to drag myself to the gym, but easily stay healthy and fit. I want flamboyance and fire and juice and passion back in my life. And from this place of looking and feeling hot, I want to meet and marry the man of my dreams. This partner will be strong, sensitive, spiritual, and totally in love with me and life. Basically, I want it all.

My reality (then): I lived in Washington, D.C., where the view from my home and office was of other buildings. My home was small and cramped. I felt like a caged animal. Sometimes I would leave for the office before dawn and not see daylight at all. I was a workaholic who built a marketing and media company. I walked to work and that was nice. Unfortunately, that was the closest I came to any physical activity. I even smoked. Successful by some people's standards, I was overstressed, overweight, and undernourished.

On weekends I would head for the beach or a river and was happy to be near the water. I was so busy that I would often take work with me. I rarely had time to date. When I did, I was so tired it was no fun at all. I felt sad and heavy-hearted and wondered whose life I was living, how it got this way, and how long I could keep it up. I started to imagine how I wanted my life to be.

My reality (now): I live in San Francisco with a beautiful panoramic view of the water. Although everyone in my life thought I was crazy to do this, I make a great living as a dream-achievement expert. I go into Fortune 500 companies and talk to them about passion in the workplace. I work when I want to and do what I love.

I've lost lots of pounds and body fat, mostly because I walk all over the city and now Rollerblade and ski. I wasn't the athletic type, but by connecting to my passion and redesigning my life by my standards, everything changed.

With newfound time and energy, I have wonderful friends in my life. And I just got married. You'll hear more about this later, because it demonstrates many lessons in case. I can honestly say I'm living the life of my dreams.

## YOUR TURN

If you're willing to slow down long enough to reflect on what matters to you — what *really* matters to you — and explore what you're willing to do about it, anything is possible.

You *can* live a joyful life filled with passion, purpose, and meaning. It is absolutely possible that you can have the life you dream of by actually doing less.

Yes, by doing less, you can have more. It will require some courage, but I'll show you the way. I've helped thousands of people take control of their lives, and you can do it, too. It doesn't require lots of effort, struggle, compromise, or loss. It simply requires your desire and willingness.

Are you ready to live your life? Are you tired of living by other people's standards and rules? Are you ready for more ease, play, and joy in your life? If you answered yes to any or all of these questions, then let's begin this journey of the ultimate dream. Here's how to do less and have more. Work less, stress less, worry less, run yourself around less, and live more.

Here and now, in as much detail as possible, write out what your dream looks like. Go for the gold. Express your passion and your most heartfelt desires.

Roadmap Stop #2 — Dreams

My dream for a life of ease is:_____

_____

My reality about this is:_____

_____

What am I more committed to?
  My Dream or My Reality?

### FUNDAMENTALS OF EASE

1. A dream is defined as a fervent hope or desire. Making your dreams come true means getting clear about what you want and figuring out how to obtain it. The prime dream we are working to achieve here is doing less and having more.
2. Goal-setting is important, but there's a different kind of energy released around dreams. Our dreams are spacious and creative. You don't need to know how to make a dream happen, you don't have to believe it's possible, and you never actually have to do anything about your dreams.
3. The formula for getting what you want is: Get clear about your dream, remove the obstacles to your dream — especially your limiting beliefs — and design the strategies for achieving your dream, including building a team.
4. Write down your dream. Don't omit this step. Don't fool yourself by saying you know what it is. Write it down so it is out of your head and you can see it.
5. The talking process is useful because it can help your dream grow and crystallize. It is in the expression of what we love that we actually begin to see it and create it. Talk your heart out.
6. The greatest magic happens when we share our dreams with others. It is essential that the people in your life know you are committed to greater ease. And if they don't

support your dream, you definitely need to know that, and find someone who does.

7. Designing the strategies involves creating a clear dream, breaking it down into small steps, identifying the resources that can help, and taking action every day.

8. Here are six different ways or places where you can access dreams: expression, inspiration, real-life desires, active imagination, sleeping, and exploration.

9. Whatever means you use for creating or discovering your dream, remember this simple and powerful point about where dreams come from: We make them up.

10. If there's something simple that can be brought into your life right now that will make you feel good and give you ease, do it. Make an investment in yourself and bring part of your dream into reality. You will be that much closer to having it all.

11. Start by thinking about your dream as being real, by visualizing it and expanding on your image. Learn to speak about it clearly; the more you speak about it, the more detailed it will become.

12. Your nocturnal dreams offer exceptional communications and deserve special time for closer examination. Treat them with respect and reverence, honor them as teachers, and they will reward you justly.

13. I can't stress enough the importance of making an honest assessment of where you are now. Starting with inaccurate information will lead to erroneous decisions about what has to be done and how far you have to go to reach your dream.

14. In order to create a life of ease, in which you are doing less and having more, it is essential that you are more committed to your dream than to your reality.

15. Without your dreams, all you have is reality, and although this is not a bad thing, there is a very different kind of energy attained from your dreams than from going through life checking things off your "to do" list. Taking action for the sole purpose of getting rid of a problem usually leads us back to the problem.

# 9

# Beliefs—The Foundation

BEFORE we move forward to the process of turning your dreams into projects and scheduling them, let's create a powerful tool to assist you: a positive belief. This will give you much greater ease in both developing and implementing what you want.

In the early stages of creating a dream, there isn't always evidence that your idea is a good one, or that this is the right time to launch it. The same is true about a big dream like doing less and having more.

During this time, what is essential is that you believe in your vision. At the very least, you'll need to have a belief that will support you in moving from where you are to where you want to be. Ninety-nine percent of more than 250 family physicians nationwide said they thought a patient's beliefs can aid in healing. In other words, having a strong belief system is much more than just a nice idea. A strong belief is essential.

Your beliefs become the necessary foundation to support you in moving forward in your new life. Since our attitudes and beliefs determine the choices and decisions we make, your beliefs will either empower you or impede you.

## NEVER NEUTRAL

This is important, so I'll say it again. Your beliefs are never neutral. They either move you forward or hold you back. If you dream of a life of ease but you don't believe it's possible, watch how quickly you'll prove yourself right. But if you take the same dream — to have a life of ease — and act as though you believe in it, you will take different actions. If we don't believe in our dreams, we either abandon or sabotage them. If we do believe in our dreams, we'll at least begin the process of seeing where the dream will take us.

Often we kill off our dreams before we ever explore their possibilities. Perhaps our past defeats or disappointments rear their ugly heads. We may think, "I failed at this before, so why should I try it now?" Do you use your past failures to deny your dreams? Or worse, do you use past memories as the justification for not dreaming at all? If we're not aware of our limiting beliefs, they can be deadly. They kill our dreams.

Our attitudes and beliefs determine our thoughts and feelings. These shape our choices and decisions. So if my dream is to change careers, but my belief is that this will be very hard, if not impossible, here's what happens: My belief tells me this will be difficult, and my thoughts and feelings follow suit. I might think, "This is going to be way too trying" and I'll feel overwhelmed. My choices and decisions will be to forget the whole idea.

Here's the same dream, with a new belief. Believing that the dream can happen leads to a thought like "I believe I can handle this." My choices and decisions are to go for it, or at least to move the process forward.

When you imagine your dream life, what beliefs come up? Do you believe your dream is possible? Do you believe it will be easy or difficult? Do you believe you can make it happen or that it will never materialize? What do you believe the people in your life will think? Whether you realize it or not, these beliefs are influencing us all the time.

Being aware of your beliefs is the first step toward changing them. When we can hear the subtle conversations in our head, we gain some power over them. It's the unconscious limiting beliefs that often sabotage us or catch us off guard. If we don't manage our minds through a process of awareness, we are often at the mercy of an unconscious process that undermines us.

## THE BIG THREE

At a most basic level, there are at least three core beliefs that you need to be aware of. I call these the human-being beliefs, since most of us seem to be born with them or acquire them at a very early age.

If you recognize that one of these human-being beliefs is playing a big part in your life, don't despair. Recognition is the first step. Later in this chapter, when I show you how to change a belief, you can use my simple technique to change even one of these big human-being beliefs. For now, just notice if any or all of these might be running your life and affecting the choices that you are making (or not making).

Human-Being Belief #1 — Inadequacy — I'm not (blank) enough. You can fill in the blank. I'm not good enough, smart enough, fast enough, rich enough, thin enough, young enough, old enough, etc.

At a workshop I gave in Baltimore, one young woman had written out over three pages of limiting beliefs that she recognized herself as having. After a discussion, she saw that the majority of them fit into one category called inadequacy. By noticing this theme, she was able to make a huge attitude shift, with a little bit of work.

Human-Being Belief #2 — Scarcity — There's not enough (blank) to go around. This could be money, time, resources, love, energy, support, or you.

In the movie *Out of Africa*, Karen, played by Meryl Streep, finally has her best coffee crop ever, when a raging fire burns it away. She has exhausted herself, her beloved has died in a plane crash, and now, she has even lost her farm. She shares with us her belief that her life in this exotic country is not right, and that there was never "enough" to make it right.

Human-Being Belief #3 — Trust — I don't trust you, me, the weather, the timing, the process, or God. I just don't trust anything or, for that matter, anyone. Can you imagine how challenging it must be to have dreams, much less to act on them, if you don't trust? Let's look at this belief in detail.

Many people live in an evidence-based reality. "I'll believe it when I see it" is a comment I often hear. But what if the opposite is true? What if you won't see it until you believe it?

Marie asked if she could use my car while I was out of the country for a few weeks. "Yes, as long as you're there to pick me up at the airport when I return," I said. She promised she would be, but she's so unreliable, I didn't trust her.

I returned from my long trip exhausted. I looked around and wasn't one bit surprised that there was no sign of Marie. I jumped into a cab in a huff, and headed home. Once there I found four messages on my answering machine from Marie. She had arrived at the airport one hour early to make sure she didn't miss me. The truth was, I was so sure she wouldn't be around that I had hardly looked for her. She had been there, but I couldn't see her because of my limiting belief.

If we don't trust, life can hand us ease and opportunities and we will miss them.

## THE BUT THEORY

How often do you hear yourself or others say, "Yeah, but . . . ?" *But* is one of those words that can alert us to our negative beliefs. Or it can be used to sabotage our hopes and dreams.

We can change the way we use this word. Rather than have it be our reason for stopping, we can use it as a tool for accessing greater ease. Consider my acronym for BUT: Believe, Understand, Trust.

*Believe* that your dream is worthwhile, that it matters to you, and that you deserve to manifest greater ease. Believe in the power of your dreams, hopes, and desires, and that you deserve to have what you want.

*Understand* that there are greater forces than you involved in life, and that if you clearly maintain your dream and take action on it, you will see results. Also, understand that we don't always see immediate results. Sometimes there are lags or setbacks, yet everything happens for a reason, whether we understand it or not.

*Trust* that it is happening, that your dream will come true. Demonstrate that you trust yourself and your ability to create what you want by continually moving forward. Take action.

This process of reframing how you deal with "Yeah, but . . ." can change your outlook on life and support you in taking risks. If we believe in our dreams, we tend to move forward; if we don't, we tend to become stagnant or complacent. Use the BUT theory to keep your beliefs optimistic and your dreams alive and well.

Carol said she wanted to attend my Dream University in Hawaii, BUT she had no idea where the money would come from. Rather than kill this dream, she tried a new tack. She declared that she was committed to attending, and trusted that the money would show up. She created a Dream Board, a visual tool on which she could post her dream in plain sight. In big letters she wrote, "I will easily attend Dream University." She tacked up the flyer for additional motivation.

That evening, before she had a chance to share her dream with her husband, he told her that they had an investment that wasn't doing well, and he thought they should sell it. He suggested she take the profits and pay off her credit-card debt.

Carol called me the next day. "I paid off all my debt and have exactly enough money to pay for my tuition and airfare to Hawaii. This experience changed the way I look at life. I will no longer kill off my dreams just because I don't see how they can happen. I'll commit to what I want and find a way to make it happen." She believed in her dream, understood that it could happen, and trusted that the resources would become available. Practicing this will not only give you ease, but great rewards as well.

## DEALING WITH DOUBT

Carlos Castaneda said, "In order to experience the magic of life, we must banish the doubt." William Shakespeare said, "Our doubts are traitors." My favorite quotation about doubt comes from *The Prophet* by Kahlil Gibran: "Doubt is a feeling too lonely to know that faith is its twin brother."

Worry fits into this category as well. It's one thing to be concerned; quite another to worry needlessly. Yet worry is our national pastime. While I was walking with a friend recently I asked, "What are you thinking about?"

"I'm worrying."

"About what?" I asked.

"I'm not sure, but give me a moment and I'll find something."

One of my favorite books of all time is *The Mists of Avalon*. The story relates the King Arthur legend as seen through the eyes of King Arthur's sister, Morgaine. The isle of Avalon has drifted away from the mainland, into the mists. The only way to get there is to lift the mists and sail in by boat.

Morgaine, now the Queen of Avalon, has been in Camelot for many years, visiting her brother the King. The time has come for her to return to her beloved home. She comes to the riverbank and prepares to use her magic to summon her barge. She stops and has this thought: "I wonder if I still have what it takes." She stops the thought abruptly and says, "I will not entertain that thought, because where one drop of doubt lives, no magic can survive."

On a bad day, don't you feel as though you're carrying buckets of doubt? You have plenty of opportunities to practice accessing your new belief, shifting the downward spiral of doubt, and putting yourself back in touch with what you want.

## WILLINGNESS HELPS

Where are your beliefs getting in the way and stopping you? In what ways do you not trust yourself? Trust is a skill that can be developed. Here's how:

When you say you are going to do something, do it. Acknowledge when you do what you said you would do. Then do it again. Start small and build on this. Confidence means to confide in yourself. Can you trust yourself enough to confide in yourself? For most of us, the honest answer is, sometimes. Self-trust comes from practice. It is a skill that can be honed and it is essential for creating greater ease.

You can begin to take bigger risks. Trust yourself to try new things and notice when you don't follow through or feel as if you just can't. Next time you think you "can't" do something, change "can't" to "won't." "I won't" puts the power back in your hands and is usually more honest than "I can't." You can now move from "I won't" to "I will," by using willpower. Small steps here are best. Practice moving from "I can't" to "I won't" to "I will."

I mentioned earlier that I just got married. Did I mention that I'm forty and that it's my first marriage? Did I inform you that it took me fifteen years to say "I will"? Here's the story.

I always loved Kevin, and he was my best friend. I believed that I just wasn't in love with him. When I told a girlfriend that I wanted my relationship with the man I would marry to be passionate, she suggested I try thigh-highs and a bottle of wine. Okay, so I was a bit idealistic, but I'm a dreamer and I believe you can have it all.

The truth was that I was afraid—afraid of being hurt, disappointed, or worse. Energetically, I kept my hands up to protect me, and kept our love at arm's length. Although my heart was longing, I was guarded. I was unwilling to fall in love, even though it was what I wanted more than anything.

One day I said to myself, "What if I got willing?" Was I willing to fall in love? It required that I lower my hands and move them from a defensive posture to open-handed surrender. This took all the will-power I had.

Then I had to demonstrate that I really was willing. This is the "acting on the belief" part. I called my honey and asked if I could move in with him in Colorado for a few months. I told him I was willing and wanting to fall in love.

Within a few short weeks, I fell. A couple of months later we moved back to San Francisco and were married. Out of our love, the passion was ignited. Our fire burns brightly and our love is wonderful.

If you want more love or passion in your life, check the position of your hands. Are you open and willing? Can life touch you, much less change you? What is your body language saying? Are you an open invitation for relationships, experiences, and ease?

Awareness of your posture toward life is important if you truly want greater luxury in your life. Are you making life hard by being un-willing or resistant to what life has to offer? Take a minute here and do a body scan. Are you opened or closed? Are you guarded and defended or accessible and available? What you send out is what you get back. If you want to have more, open yourself up and let life in.

## IT'S A CHOICE

Remember this old tale? A husband and wife were recently married. He walks into the kitchen to see his wife cutting the tips off the roast and throwing them away.

"Honey, meat is expensive. Why are you doing that?"

She stopped for a moment, thought about it and said, "Because this is how my mother did it." So they went off to ask Mom why.

"Mom, why do you cut the tips off the roast before you cook it?"

She answered quickly, "Because that's how my mother did it."

They went off to see their wise grandma. "Grandma," asked the new bride, "why do you cut the tips off the roast and throw them away before you cook it?"

Grandma looked at them all-knowingly and said, "Because I don't have a pot big enough for the roast."

For the most part, we inherit our beliefs. Our parents' beliefs become ours. Sometimes they're outdated, outmoded, and no longer the truth. When my grandparents moved here from Hungary, scarcity was not just a belief, it was a reality. They relished their one or two lightbulbs. In my home, with our energy-saving devices, it takes more electricity to turn the lights off and on than simply to leave them on. I just bought a hundred-year lightbulb that's supposed to provide up to 135,000 hours of light. This solid-state diode converts AC voltage into DC, so the coiled tungsten filament burns cooler, significantly increasing its life-span. I think this concept works for humans, too. Burn cooler and more efficiently, live longer.

Don't burn out before changing your beliefs. You don't need to wait for the *right* moment to change a limiting belief. I will provide you with a simple exercise at the end of this chapter so you can do it now. Although most of us are in agreement that many of our beliefs don't serve us, we have forgotten one extremely essential point. We *choose* what we believe, every moment of every day.

Our beliefs are our own opinions and judgments, but for some strange reason we seem to forget that we can choose them. In any given moment and in any given circumstance, we choose what we believe. Just keep in mind that if you choose a positive belief, you will move forward on your dreams. If you choose a limiting belief, you won't. You'll probably get stuck or sabotage your goals.

When you're not consciously choosing to believe an empowering belief, what you get by default is your old limiting beliefs. We are deeply programmed. If you're not thinking yes, some part of you is already acting on no. Learn to manage your mind by noticing the choices you are and are not making. Ask yourself, "Why am I doing this? What am I believing?" The answers may astound you.

What does it take to change a limiting belief to a positive belief? It takes willingness, choice, and practice. Be willing to choose a new belief and practice believing it by acting on it. Of course, the most essential time to practice believing your new belief is when you don't believe it. It always comes down to a self-motivated choice. What will you choose to believe today?

Shifting a new belief requires courage, like selecting the blank rune. The runes are an ancient oracle, comprised of twenty-one stones, each stone etched with a symbol. Like the tarot, they are designed to point you toward hidden fears and motivations that shape your future. The runes can direct your attention to inner choices and can mirror your subconscious process. They are a tool for contemplation.

The blank rune is "the unknowable." It is the end and the beginning. It is the rune of total trust and puts you in touch with your own true destiny. The blank rune calls for no less an act of courage than the empty-handed leap into the void. Selecting it is a direct test of faith. Know that the obstacles of your past can become the gateways that lead to new beginnings. Know that the work of self-change is progressing.

By having the courage to choose a belief that will empower you and to act on this new belief, you are claiming a powerful new level of ease and confidence.

## FEAR

Why would we ever choose a limiting belief if we knew it would hold us back? The number-one reason is fear. We fear the risks, the potential disappointment and loss. Last year my company surveyed more than a thousand people. We asked, "What are the biggest obstacles to having the life you want?" Although you might think the top answers would be not enough time and not enough money, one answer won hands down. The most common killer of dreams is lack of confidence or fear.

Years ago, Zig Ziglar coined the perfect acronym for FEAR: *False Evidence Appearing Real.* We fear that we might fail or be disappointed, so we don't take any action. Then we get to be "right" about our letdown or failed dreams.

Initially, people often tell me they can't make a dream happen because they don't have enough money.

"How much do you need?" I always ask.

The answer, nine out of ten times, is, "I don't know. But I know I don't have enough."

The same thing is true about time. We often complain that we don't have the time to get what we want, but we rarely schedule even an hour of planning or dream time. During this single hour, we could break our dream into a series of smaller projects and take action on it.

At the bottom of all our excuses, the fear of failing keeps us immobilized. Our fear is natural and understandable. But if we don't learn to use it or interface with it, it will keep us stuck.

After I downsized my company, the next phase of creating my new life was evident. It was time to move to California. I was no dummy. I knew I needed to have a chunk of change, big-time cash in my pocket, to start my new life. As someone who often seeks the easiest route, I knew what I had to do. By selling my condominium, I would have the necessary money to start my new life. Although this was a logical idea, it wasn't easy to accomplish. I put my home on the market. Three months went by and it didn't sell.

In its fourth month on the market, no one was even looking at units in my building. By the sixth month, units were selling for $20,000 less than I had paid for mine. Everyone was telling me to forget my dream of living a life of ease. They said I was asking for too much and that I should be more realistic.

When there is something I really want and nothing is happening to move it forward, I have learned to become suspicious of *me*. What was I doing or not doing, what was I thinking or believing that was standing in my way? I took some time to reflect.

My reality was that I lived in a nice city, in a furnished home, where I had clients who wanted to pay me money for a service I provided. My world existed in a five-block radius, where I could walk to work, to the health club, to several restaurants, and to see many friends.

My dream was to live near the water and to slow down. It included being paid great money for work that I loved: to inspire people to dream and express their passion. And I wanted to wear whatever I wanted, including my red cowboy boots, to business meetings.

I was terrified, full of "buts." But what if my dream didn't work? But what if no one hired me? But what if I failed? But, but, but. How would I eat? Where would I live? How would I survive? You get the picture.

Once I got crystal clear that what was stopping me was my fear, not the lack of money, my situation became very black and white. I asked myself, "Marcia, what are you more committed to, your dream or your reality?" Another way to say this is, What matters more: your dream or your fear? I was definitely more committed to my dream, and I took one bold step forward to prove it. A new strategy had become instantly available when I saw it was my fear stopping me, not the money: Rent the condo. Can you see how this was not an option when I thought I had to have a large amount of money to start my new life? I was holding on to the very thing I needed to release in order to have my dream.

Within one week, I rented my home. During that next year I trusted myself and followed my heart. I created a completely new life of ease and joy. My fear did not stop me. I had a new experience that challenged my beliefs about inadequacy, scarcity, and trust and now have new beliefs to replace those old limiting thoughts. There's nothing like taking a risk and experiencing a win (of any size) to build self-confidence.

In case you're wondering how I financed my trip west, I'll tell you. I sold all my business clothes. I invited all my petite women friends over, and they had a field day. Once out west, I did whatever it took to make my new career take off. I had to. I had no clothes or home to go back to. I had closed that door. I was relentless about making my dream come true.

I hope this demonstrates that even fear can serve a purpose. We do not need to be stopped by it. In fact, we can even be motivated by it. I wasn't going to go hungry or turn around and go back.

To begin the process of working with your fear, get clear about it. Exactly what are you afraid of? Saying "I'm just afraid" is too general. There is little you can do with that.

## THE CHALLENGE OF CHANGE

Our ego and identity have a lot at stake when we start talking about transformation. The very job of your ego is to keep things status quo. Fear is our ego's way of doing this. Every time you start to move toward your dream, you will also move toward your fears. If this dream includes your fears and I ask, "Are you more committed to your dream or to your reality?" you'll probably say, "I'm more committed to my reality because at least it's safe." But fear is simply an obstacle. Once again, my theory about obstacles is this: Wherever there is an obstacle, including fear, design a strategy to manage it. Step one: Identify what you're afraid of. Step two: Get into relationship with the specifics, by taking action. Step three: Get help or support wherever needed. Be more committed to your dream than you are to your fear.

Going back to my dream of moving out west, imagine that I'm

driving my car from D.C. to San Francisco. Let's call this my reality. Headed west for my dream city, along the way I get a flat tire. What do I do?

If I'm more committed to my dream (going to San Francisco) than to my reality (the flat tire), I will fix my car and continue on my way. However, if I'm more committed to my fear or my reality, I'll use this flat as a sign from God, turn around, and head home. When you're more committed to your reality than to your dreams, everything becomes a sign for giving up on the dream.

Don't do your dream in. Don't let your ego sabotage your goals with doubts, fears, and concerns. When these come up, ask yourself this ever-empowering question: "What am I more committed to, my dream or my reality?" The evidence will be in the action you are or are not taking. It's very simple. If you're not acting on your dream, you're acting on your fears and beliefs. Although change always brings up all sorts of doubts and concerns, it's how you deal with them that matters. When all else fails, remember this bit of coffee-shop wisdom: A small note on a tip jar said, "If you fear change, leave it here."

## THE IMPOSSIBLE DREAM

I was giving a lecture at Unity Church in Eugene, Oregon, when I met Wilson. A bright-eyed eighteen-year-old, he told me this was the first Sunday of his life that he was outside his country; actually, it was the first time he had ever been away from his tribe. Wilson was a Masai warrior from Africa and was a very long way from his home and family.

When Wilson was four, his mother took him to a medical clinic near his home. Ever since that day, he knew he wanted to become a doctor. However, it was impossible because no training was available where he lived and no one had ever left the tribal village.

Years went by and Wilson kept his desire alive in his heart and believed it would happen someday. He spoke about it to anyone who would listen. Eventually he had the chance to verbalize his wish to a visiting American. It turned out this visitor was a writer for *The Washington Post*. Upon returning home, he wrote a story about Wilson's dream.

While visiting friends in D.C., a couple read Wilson's touching anecdote and were inspired to help. They called people they knew in their hometown who worked for the University of Oregon. Within three weeks, Wilson had applied for undergraduate study, and a few weeks later, he was accepted.

But where would he live and how would he survive so far from his home? This is where the magic really kicked in. Four families stepped forward, each extending their hands and their homes. Each agreed to house, feed, and even help buy books for this young man. The logistics were easily handled. What had seemed like an impossible feat was now a done deal, and within a very short time.

Wilson said to me, "Interesting that my first Sunday in America would be spent listening to you speak so passionately about dreams. I now realize what I must do. I must become a doctor and then return to my village. When they see I have become a doctor, they will believe in their own dreams. I can inspire others to dream, even when it seems impossible."

## EXERCISE: CREATING A NEW BELIEF

When there's no proof that your dream might materialize, or no support from the people around you, what do you do? What dream are you thinking or saying is impossible? If what matters to you is having a joyful, rich, and fulfilling life, create an awesome belief that will provide the foundation for this to manifest.

In any given moment, you can choose. Choose a belief that will empower your dreams for having greater ease, for doing less and having more. Then act on your belief. This sends a powerful message to your brain and being that you are serious about your dreams. It's one thing to say you believe, it's another to actually do something about it.

Here is the simplest process I know for creating a positive belief: Write down one negative and limiting belief that you have. Go for a big one, one that gets in your way. Consider what is stopping you from having a life of ease and living the way you want. All you need to do is write one short, concise statement.

Now write the opposite of this statement. What positive and empowering phrase, if you believed it, would make your life easier? For example, change "I'm not good enough" to "I am good enough." Notice if you are judging your new belief as "not being good enough." Don't get caught in a negative feedback loop. To shift from a limiting belief to an empowering belief requires practice. Act as though you believe it. Fake it until you make it. Choose your new belief, and practice believing it by acting on it.

This essential tool will carry you far. Use it daily and on a regular basis. You will feel a new surge of power and confidence, as well as more support and ease. With this empowering belief, you are now ready to create the projects and tasks to move your dream forward.

Roadmap Stop #3 — Beliefs

My limiting belief that gets in my way is:_____

_____

My new empowering belief is:_____

_____

## FUNDAMENTALS OF EASE

1. In the early stages of creating a dream, there isn't always evidence that your idea is a good one, or that this is the right time to launch it. The same is true about a big dream, like doing less and having more.
2. Your beliefs become the necessary foundation to support you in moving forward in your new life. Since our attitudes and beliefs determine the choices and decisions we make, your beliefs will either empower you or impede you.
3. Your beliefs are never neutral. They either move you forward or hold you back. Our attitudes and beliefs determine our thoughts and feelings. These shape our choices and decisions.
4. Being aware of your beliefs is the first step toward changing them. When we can hear the subtle conversations in our head, we have some power over them. It's the unconscious limiting beliefs that often sabotage us or catch us off guard.
5. Consider my acronym for the word BUT: Believe, Understand, Trust. Use the BUT theory to keep your beliefs optimistic and your dreams alive and well.

6. This process of reframing how you deal with objections can change your outlook on life and support you in taking risks. If we believe in our dreams, we tend to move forward; if we don't, we tend to be stagnant or complacent.

7. You have plenty of opportunities to practice accessing your new belief, shifting the downward spiral of doubt and putting you back in touch with what you want.

8. Confidence means to confide in yourself. Self-trust comes from practice. It is a skill that can be honed, and it is essential for creating greater ease.

9. Our beliefs are our own opinions and judgments, but for some strange reason we seem to forget that we can choose them. In any given moment and in any given circumstance, we choose what we believe.

10. When you are not consciously choosing to believe an empowering belief, what you get by default is your old limiting beliefs. Choose a belief that will empower your dreams for having greater ease, for doing less and having more.

11. What does it take to change a limiting belief to a positive belief? It takes willingness, choice, and practice. Be willing to choose a new belief and practice believing it by acting on it.

12. At the bottom of all our excuses, the fear of failing keeps us immobilized. Our fear is natural and understandable. But if we don't learn to use it or interface with it, it will keep us stuck.

13. Even fear can serve a purpose. We do not need to be stopped by it. In fact, we can even be motivated by it.

14. Don't do your dream in. Don't let your ego sabotage your goals with doubts, fears, and concerns. When these come up, ask yourself this ever-empowering question: "What am I more committed to, my dream or my reality?"

15. If you are not acting on your dream, you are acting on your fears and beliefs. Although change always brings up all sorts of doubts and concerns, it's how you deal with them that matters.

# 10

# Tasks—The Momentum

F YOU cringe at the idea of tasks, we need to redefine your relationship to them. Tasks are the essential tools needed to create what you want. Although at first you may consider tasks to be arduous work and more responsibility, the proper use of them can be transformational. Yes, tasks can be your friends.

In this chapter, I'll provide you with a simple blueprint for recreating and restructuring your life. The result will absolutely be greater ease. If I were to sum up this process, I would say that the three most important elements are as follows: First, break down your dream into small projects. Second, identify those who can help you and make it easy for them to say yes. Third, every day, do something to move your dream forward. And since your dream is to do less and have more, ideally you want everything you do to make your life easier.

The key to this whole process is the tasks. The single steps that you take every day toward your dream determine the quality of your life. Our goal is to have these tasks, as much as possible, be things that you enjoy and that move you toward your dream.

Let's review the last few chapters briefly. Doing so will help you become motivated about tasks. Rather than swim in the chaos and confusion of life, known as the soup, you have chosen a higher road.

You now have a sense of your passion and purpose. From that, you have created a clear vision of ease that you are excited about. You are more committed to this dream than to your current reality.

You have also explored your limiting beliefs about this dream and have created a new empowering belief that you are practicing believing. The evidence that you are doing this will be in the action you take to make your dream happen. With these powerful tools—your purpose, your dream, and your belief—you are now ready to implement your action plan.

Dreams die when we put them on our "to do" list. You can't put traveling around the world, starting a new business, or even simplifying your life on your daily action list. These dreams are too big, too overwhelming, too unmanageable. The way to achieve big dreams is to create small projects. A project or goal is often defined as a dream with a deadline. Projects make our dreams real. My theory is: Dream first, then set goals for the dreams you want to move forward.

## PROJECTS

The power to develop a viable project depends on your ability to define your dream in a way that inspires you. Your projects make your dreams attainable. As you move forward, new possibilities open up and you start to launch yourself into a different dimension of living. Accomplishing our projects helps build self-confidence and self-trust. The very action of moving your dreams into projects will make them exist in your life, not just in your head or on paper.

Think of turning dreams into projects as a way to "pro-ject" yourself into the future. I recommend that you create a project, or several projects, that can easily be accomplished in three months or less, since short-term projects help us see quick results. Each project should be specific, measurable, and have a due date. Each should be designed to move your dream forward and, ideally, you should be passionate about it.

Since your dream is to do less and have more, begin by asking yourself this: What is one project I could create and easily accomplish that would make my life richer and easier? Or, what's a project that would really be fun or rewarding? Or restful and rejuvenating?

For instance, if your dream is to travel, your project might be to go on a vacation this year. If you don't yet know where you want to go, but you know you want it to be someplace exotic, open an atlas, pick a specific place, and begin to arrange your trip. In short, schedule the date.

If you want more luxury or elegance in your life, some projects might be to travel first-class, to attend at least three formal events in cities outside your hometown, to fly in a private jet at least once during the next three months, or to spend a week in a beautiful place on the ocean.

If your dream is about working less, maybe your project will be to shorten your workday to six hours, or not to work on weekends anymore, or to hire an assistant. If your dream is about appreciating your family and friends, some projects might include fun activities with them, like a barbecue or community gathering. Keep in mind that a project must be *specific*. Quantify how many hours you will work, or pick the date for the event.

You don't have to limit yourself to one project; all you need to do is make sure that all these projects are part of your dream. When I develop projects for one of my professional dreams — integrating more playtime into my work — I can pursue several projects or revise a project, so long as everything remains aligned with my purpose and my professional dream. I might create a project that would allow me to write on the road, while taking in the California scenery. You only have to create the project at this point. Don't limit the possibilities by figuring out how you're going to do it. We'll get to that soon enough.

Ellen, whose purpose was to have a life filled with fun and adventure, had a well-being goal called "To Live a Spa Life." She created a project called "Go to an Elegant Spa at Least Four Times a Year, for at Least One Week's Duration Each Time." She didn't yet have any of it planned — financially, logistically, or timewise — but once she created the project, it took on life and became part of her reality.

Some projects are easy; you merely have to schedule them into your calendar. To get into action on her dream, Ellen developed a simple project to get two facials and two massages each month. This jump-started her project, giving her a quick win and inspiring her to the next step.

A project can deal with any aspect of your life. When you pursue projects, you are mastering the techniques of consciously designing your entire life. You can learn these only by practicing. Once they've been learned, you'll find it easy to map them into all the other areas of your life.

Create projects that will bring ease into your life in the following areas: personal, professional, relationships, finance, fun, and well-being. Here are some examples of projects based on the dream of doing less and having more. Since the criterion for a project is that it must have a due date, assume each one starts with "By March 1 (an arbitrary date for the purpose of this example) I will:"

Personal — Be getting two massages a week regularly.
        Finish the novel I started to read.
        Redecorate my/our bedroom.

Professional — Decide how much longer I will stay in this job.
        Set the date for opening my own business.
        Cut my hours to thirty per week.

Relationships — Have five fun dates.
        Schedule a romantic getaway with my partner.
        Have an intimate conversation with someone important.

Finance — Open an IRA.
        Buy that car.
        Figure out how much money I earn and how much I spend.

Fun — Schedule my dream vacation.
        Register for a class, just for the fun of it.
        Have lunch or dinner with friends at least weekly.

Well-being — Take a meditation class.
        Spend at least an hour a day in quiet time.
        Walk in the park twice weekly.

Since all these are projects, you'll be able to see how you did in accomplishing them and how you are progressing on your vision. Are you making your life a priority? If not, are you willing to? What's important about these projects is that they should give you what you want. You do not need more tasks in your life, just for the sake of having more to do. The motivation for achieving these is they will give you greater ease.

With all these new projects, you may start to feel a little over-whelmed. "Where am I going to fit more stuff into my already full life? I don't have time for more projects." If thoughts like these are bubbling up, take a breather and remember this: As you are doing what you love, it will get done faster and you'll find extra energy.

When you use your passion as your guide in saying "No, thank you" to the tasks you can decline, you open more time and space in your life. As you lessen what you don't want and don't need, and increase what you love and want, your life will be transformed. Don't sabotage this process by projecting your doubts and concerns into your dream. Hang in there. Use your new belief as the foundation to support yourself in taking the next step. Act on your projects and keep your dreams alive.

## STRATEGIES AND TASKS

Now that you know what your project is, all you have to do is figure out how you're going to make it happen! To make your project part of your reality, you will need strategies and tasks to guide you toward accomplishing your dream.

A strategy is the approach you take to achieve your dream. Some common strategies include: financing or budgeting, training or edu-cation, research, communicating (especially when your project in-volves others), creating space or room for the dream, and taking care of yourself throughout the process.

Tasks are the specific steps needed to accomplish the strategy. An entire project may include several strategies, each comprised of sev-eral tasks. If the separate tasks aren't listed individually, the project usually doesn't happen. When you get clear about the project, you can explore the tasks needed to accomplish it.

Here's a formula for getting into action on any project:

1. Outline the strategies needed for this project by writing them down.
2. Break each strategy into tasks. Each strategy may have several tasks.
3. Identify where you need help and who your resources may be.
4. Add dates and then put them in chronological order. You now have a three-month (or less) plan for accomplishing your project.
5. See where you have overscheduled and where you can

reschedule. Is this actually a four-month project? Set yourself up for success.

6. Every day, accomplish at least one task. Stay connected to your passion, dream, and empowering belief.
7. Acknowledge when you complete a project and celebrate your success!

Remember my cruise dream and how easily it happened? From a project perspective, here's what it looked like. I created a project called "Go on a Free and Fun Cruise to an Exotic Place Within the Next Three Months." Then I listed the ways I could make it happen. In this case, I couldn't have chosen to purchase a ticket for a cruise, because my project was to go on a free cruise. It's important to be clear about what you want. One set of strategies might be needed to go on a fun cruise, while a different set is required to go on a free and fun cruise.

Strategies I could have chosen include finding someone who would pay for my trip or entering a contest to win a free cruise. I chose to create a bartering relationship by booking my workshop on a cruise ship in return for a free trip.

## SCHEDULING YOUR TASKS

The tasks to accomplish the project were clear: list and describe some topics about which I could speak, prepare a biography about myself, and get the names and numbers of several cruise-ship lines that might be interested in such an arrangement. Rather than mass-mailing my proposal, I decided to focus my energy on the best cruise I could find.

Because I was passionate about what I was doing, I was living in a world of possibility, and I was feeling powerful about accomplishing the results. I was definitely in action. In a period of three short weeks, I developed simple but classy promotional materials, had a photo taken, sent out a package, and scheduled a date by which I wanted to set sail. Before I had a chance to make a follow-up call to see if they were interested, they called me. I was booked to go on the cruise two months ahead of my project schedule.

Which brings us to the next step: Once you know what the necessary tasks are, schedule them into your calendar. Doing this may be the only hope you have for completing these projects and ultimately realizing your dreams — at least until you learn to live more from your passion and a little less obsessively from your calendar. More often than not, you'll begin to follow your heart.

A woman I know said half-jokingly, "Oh, my God, I forgot to get married. It was never scheduled in and somehow I just let it slip by." Point well taken. Schedule the simple and single tasks into your life and soon you will find yourself living a dream-come-true life. Forget to schedule what matters most and you may have big regrets.

## USING YOUR RESOURCES

A crucial component of creating a successful strategy for any project, especially one related to ease, is making use of the resources in all the areas of your life. Think about the people you know in the different aspects of your life; consider what's available to you in the way of technology and information.

Consider friends, teachers (past and present), family members (close and distant), business associates, organizations, the library, the Internet, and more. There's nothing or no one that's not a potential resource. Even if your list isn't long, it's a way for you to leverage what you already have.

I'm an advocate of simplification and shortcuts. If you can find a faster way of getting something done, do it. There is no more potent shortcut I know than using your resources. We'll explore this in great detail in Chapter 11, on Ease Teams.

One of your strategies might be to accomplish something you don't know how to do, and one of your tasks might be to learn it. However, another might be to hire or partner with somebody who already has that knowledge. By getting clear about your resources, you can dovetail them with your dreams and projects, and determine how they might work together.

## SIMPLIFYING YOUR LIFE

When you look at the whole picture of your dream, you will see that some of the areas overlap. The overlap will enable you to handle something in one area of your life that automatically takes care of something in another area. When things start to happen at the right time, when they flow together easily and work interchangeably, life gets easier.

As new possibilities become available, and as you develop projects and get into action on them, opportunities that you could never have foreseen will appear within reach. Of course, you might be stymied by an old attitude or belief. If you are, ask yourself whether you're still committed to your dream. If the answer is yes, stay committed and in action.

You have no idea what kind of magic could be waiting for you right around the bend, on the other side of the place where you got stuck. As long as your projects come from your purpose and are aligned with your dreams, as long as you still feel the passion, stay in action.

The only files I maintain in my office relate to my projects. As my project files grow, they open onto more projects, and sometimes new projects develop within an existing one. There's a great deal of overlap, because one of my dreams is to integrate my personal and professional lives. That doesn't mean I'm a workaholic; it means I've created work that expresses who I am in the world, and I can combine my work with the rest of my life easily and joyfully. One college student I know told me, "My goals are so interwoven that the substance of many of my courses overlaps. There are times that I can write one term paper and, with slight modifications, use it for three different classes." We can learn from her approach. It's a fine example of putting out less effort! Just beware that you're not selling out in one situation (perhaps learning less) in order to have something else.

As you create a project, if you find inconsistencies or contradictions, check to see whether your "concern" is real, or whether it's a negative attitude or belief. For example, if the hours you've designated for your project add up to more than twenty-four each day, you have an inconsistency. On the other hand, if they add up to two or three hours and you're still troubled about having enough time for everything, acknowledge that the issue comes from an old belief. Then make a commitment that you will use your time in support of having what you want.

Look at your life holistically; all of its components, including the dreams, are — or need to be — working parts of your life. Get a picture of it as a whole; perhaps there's a piece that's missing that would tie things together to give you more time and flexibility and make your life easier. What is your imagination telling you? What's missing from your life that, if it were in place, would make your life easier? Ask yourself, "What would make my life easier? What would give me more energy? What would give me more time, more fun, more excitement?"

Life does not have to be an either/or situation. You don't have to be torn between your personal and professional lives. For example, I like to give myself plenty of time to relax and play, so I often arrange vacations by bartering work, perhaps offering a workshop in exchange for a week at a health spa. Trading my services incorporates many of my dreams: my professional dream of having work that I love and that expresses who I am in the world; and my well-being dream of being emotionally, mentally, spiritually, and physically balanced. The bartering opportunities never existed before I became clear about what I wanted and what I was committed to. Now they exist regularly, and they unify many of the aspects of my life.

This is not an exercise in creating more work for yourself. By asking yourself what you may not have seen before as a possibility, you will simplify your life and allow yourself to see anew. Some people find that what's missing is not necessarily tangible; they need more space, more time, or some other personal resource.

Perhaps you can save yourself time and energy by linking two or more of the projects you've already identified. Think positively; you're designing a new life for yourself. Rather than formulating a dream that's stated in the negative, such as "Remove some of the clutter from my life," develop instead a dream that supports your having more space or time, freedom or flexibility.

When I discovered that what was missing for me was having work that I loved, just plugging that one piece into my dream enabled me to begin developing projects that I savor. For example, it had never occurred to me before that going on a cruise or to a spa could be a way of making money or of being successful in business. That possibility showed up only when I tied the dream of having work that I love together with my other dreams. I realized that I could work *and* take better care of myself while spending less time and energy than I had before.

## LEAVING A LEGACY

If you want to live every day with passion, design a project that's bigger than your life, one that you don't know how to accomplish.

This project may not even be completed in your lifetime. Perhaps you will create a legacy, a gift that will outlive you, affecting future generations. Leave your mark.

Rob, a successful businessman, told me he's flown in many private jets with executives worth over $100 million each.

"Marcia, many of them were empty inside. Amid all the money and glamour, they were lost because they didn't have generous dreams. The true joy and richness in life comes from helping others."

Rob's bigger-than-life project includes feeding hungry people in Africa and India. He and his wife, Judy, travel to remote parts of the world and use their personal resources to help those who can't help themselves.

One of my all-time favorite people is Ted Turner. He's an outspoken renegade spirit who is also very generous. He donated one billion dollars to the United Nations. "It's a nice round number," said Ted. Although most of us don't have this kind of resources, we can make priceless contributions in the areas that matter to us.

Roger Lozano is an example of a man with a big vision and a heart to match. After attending dozens of funerals in one year, of people of all ages, especially kids, Roger decided to do something about the gang problems in Texas. He started Safe Concepts & Communication, where through counseling and heartfelt talks and tough love, he has saved at least fifty lives. He believes that kids from all walks of life deserve a fair chance. He turned his passion into a business that affects thousands of people.

The Cosmetic, Toiletry, and Fragrance Association Foundation offers a great example of people using their passion to be of service to others. The cosmetic industry's trade association created a free program called Look Good . . . Feel Better, to help the self-image and self-esteem of women experiencing appearance-related side effects from cancer treatment. By calling the American Cancer Society at 1-800-395-LOOK, patients are connected to salons that provide a twelve-step makeup guide, complimentary makeup kits, as well as suggestions on wigs, turbans, scarves, and nail care.

When you can take your purpose and passion and create a big dream, amazing things happen. Many little annoyances disappear, or at least how you perceive them. You take some attention off yourself and your needs and put it into something else. When we do this, we realize that we can be generous and abundant. Our sense of self-worth and self-confidence increases, and with this comes more joy and energy.

Is there a project in your heart or mind that you would like to explore or pursue? Don't create a project "out of the blue"; develop it from your purpose, from what really matters to you. My bigger-than-life project is to ensure that, by the time I die, people will be speaking about dreams in a completely new way, as something that they absolutely can have. When you speak to me about your dreams, be prepared to pull out your calendar. I'm interested in getting you moving.

I'm not yet certain how to fulfill my bigger-than-life project, but it turns me on and gets me into conversations with extraordinary people. One of my personal dreams is to partner with creative visionaries to produce powerful results. Speaking with people about their dreams allows everyone to be a visionary, to be turned on and excited about life's possibilities.

I don't allow myself to be stopped by the fact that I haven't figured out how to accomplish my bigger-than-life project. I act on it by developing strategies and tasks and by scheduling them into my life. Every day I do something, no matter how small, to express my dream.

Last week I attended a luncheon with more than fifteen hundred people during which four Women of Achievement, Vision and Excellence received the WAVE award from Alumnae Resources, an organization that helps people make career transitions. All the winners were seventy years old or older. A two-minute slide show was shown of each woman's life. It was extraordinary to see what a lifetime looks like in hindsight. What would your two minutes look like? What will be the images that will matter to you most when you look back on your life? What will be your proudest moments, the experiences you cherish and the contributions you made? What projects will you create or participate in that will make your life fulfilled?

Projects come in all sizes and shapes. Begin with a project that will fulfill your dream of having greater ease in your life. When you're ready, perhaps now or sometime in the future, design other projects that excite and have meaning for you. No project is too small. The only criterion is that you be passionate about it.

The secret to success with any project is to break the project into small tasks, seek assistance, and do something, every day, even one single task, to move your project ahead. Jack Canfield, coauthor of the bestselling *Chicken Soup for the Soul* and other books in this series, told me that he does five tasks every day to move his project forward. His project or goal is to sell fifty million copies of his books by the end of the decade. As of this writing, he has three books on *The New York Times* bestseller list. Do you think he's doing something right? Are five tasks too much to ask? How about one?

If this starts to feel like a burden or too much work, reconnect to your passion and your larger dream. Remember why you are doing this and use your empowering belief to recommit. Turn your dreams into simple projects and move forward on them daily. Ideas without action are worthless, or just nice ideas.

A short-term result will get the ball rolling right now. Decide on your first project.

Roadmap Stop #4 — Tasks

Within three months from now, what's a project that you will complete that will allow you to do less and have more?

By_____(date) I will do the following project:_____

_____

_____

_____

_____

Within one week from today, what's a single task that you will perform to initiate this project?

By_____(date) I will do the following task:_____

_____

_____

_____

_____

## FUNDAMENTALS OF EASE

1. Tasks are the essential tools needed to create what you want. Although at first you may consider tasks to be arduous work and more responsibility, the proper use of them can be transformational.

2. Break down your dream into small steps or projects, identify those who can help you and make it easy for them to say yes, and every day, do something to move your dream forward.

3. The single steps that you take every day toward your dream determine the quality of your life. Your goal is to have these tasks, as much as possible, be things that you enjoy and that move you toward your dream.

4. Dreams die when we put them on our "to do" list. They are too big, overwhelming, and unmanageable. The way to achieve big dreams is to create small projects.

5. A project or goal is often defined as a dream with a deadline. Projects make our dreams real. Dream first, then set goals for the dreams you want to move forward.

6. The power to develop a viable project depends on your ability to define your dream in a way that inspires you. Your projects make your dreams attainable.

7. Create a project, or several projects, that can easily be accomplished in three months or less, since short-term projects help us see quick results. Each project should be specific, measurable, and have a due date.

8. A project can deal with any aspect of your life. When you pursue projects, you are mastering the techniques of consciously designing your entire life. You can learn these only by practicing.

9. Use your passion as your guide in saying "No, thank you" to the tasks you can decline, and you will have more time and space in your life. As you lessen what you don't want and don't need, and increase what you love and want, your life will be changed.

10. To make your project part of your reality, you will need strategies and tasks to guide you toward your dream. A strategy is the approach you take to achieve your dream.

11. Tasks are the specific steps needed to accomplish the strategy. An entire project may include several strategies, each comprised of several tasks. If the separate tasks aren't listed individually, the project usually doesn't happen.

12. As long as your projects come from your purpose and are aligned with your dreams, as long as you still feel the passion, stay in action.

13. As you create a project, if you find inconsistencies or contradictions, check to see whether your "concern" is real, or whether it's a negative attitude or belief.

14. Projects come in all sizes and shapes. Begin with a project that will fulfill your dream of having greater ease in your life. When you're ready, perhaps now or sometime in the future, design other projects that excite and have meaning for you.

15. No project is too small. The only criterion is that you be passionate about it.

# 11

# Ease Teams—

# The Support

F YOU come away from this book with nothing else, I do believe that this chapter contains the ultimate pearl of wisdom that I have to offer. The number-one way to experience ease in your life is to share your dreams with others and ask for help. The best way I know to do this is to build teams.

But if you're anything like the hundreds of thousands of people I give speeches to, I know what you're thinking. "I will not share my dream because people might laugh at me, think I'm lazy or crazy, steal my idea, or (*here's the biggie*) they might expect me to do something about it."

Imagine that! If you start to tell your friends, family, coworkers, and clients that you're committed to a life of ease, what will they think? Let's hear your worst thoughts and imaginings.

A doctor I know was fed up with the medical profession. Although he was still committed to healing and helping people, the fear of malpractice, the demands of HMOs, and many other concerns soured him on medicine. He told me his dream was to start a wellness center, offering alternative healing and preventive education. When I asked what was stopping him, he said he was extremely concerned about what his colleagues, friends, and family would think. His concerns about their judgments kept him stuck and suffering for a long time.

I supported him in putting down his dream on paper. In doing so, he discovered that not only did he have a clear vision for his wellness center, but he saw how this new position would give him greater ease, more freedom, and—to his delight—more quality time. He's now in the early stages of making a huge career shift, and very happy about it.

The reason we have fears and concerns about how we will be seen is that it's not a popular conversation to talk about doing less and having more. There's not a lot of agreement in our society on pursuing this. But notice that there is a great deal of complaining, exhaustion, ill health, broken marriages, and wounded spirits. More than 300,000 people in America have bypass heart surgery every year. What are our hearts saying to us?

But what if the world, or at least our little personal world, were just waiting for some brave soul to speak up and question the norm? What if all your friends or family members are thinking about ease, dreaming about it, and even longing for it? And what if you were the one who said, "Life has gotten way out of control and I would like to change this. I want to change the way we live, the way we relate to each other, how we work and how we play."

## POWER TALK

What are you saying? Are you speaking your truth? Are you inspiring others? Are you singing and expressing yourself? How are you using your voice? Our voice comes from our throat, which is situated in an interesting location: halfway between our head and our heart.

Passionate living can be defined as aligning our head and heart through action. The voice is often the launching pad, since our thoughts turn into words, and our words then become actions.

As you feel in your heart what matters to you most, it then gets formulated into ideas, in the form of thoughts, goals, and projects. But it's when we start to speak about them that the vibration changes. When we give voice to our dreams, they begin to live. They come alive as language shapes consciousness. Sometimes the speaking of the dream is the very thing that initiates it. The gift of communication is a resource to be developed and used.

Where can we go to practice articulating our dreams? When we feel unsure or awkward about discussing something, often we keep it deep inside our souls. The problem is that unless you are sharing your dreams, they remain a secret. And an unspoken dream is frequently forgotten. There is power in speaking your dreams.

There's also power in taking a stand. Florence "Flo-Jo" Griffith Joyner may be best known for her running speed, but she has a fast tongue, too. When the President's Council on Physical Fitness and Sports tried to dump the Olympic sprinter from her current position as cochair of the Council, to make room for Jake "Body by Jake" Steinfeld after he gave a hundred thousand dollars to the Democratic National Committee, she wouldn't budge.

The plan changed after Flo-Jo said that she wouldn't step down as cochair until she heard from Clinton himself. White House spokesman Mike McCurry said, "The energy and enthusiasm that Florence showed in wanting to remain a member is compelling enough for her to remain." She used her voice to be heard.

Congressman Richard Gephardt from Missouri said, "Your voice, your vote is priceless. Let your voice be heard." Be willing to rally for your cause.

Our voice and our words are two of the most awesome tools we have. What often sets us apart is how and when we use our voice. We can use our voice to make things happen or to make things disappear, like a magician. The Jungian archetype of the magician teaches that this power is not only in what we say, but in when we say it and in how we say it.

Confused communication lacks appropriate content. It may be well timed in delivery but poorly organized. Blunt communication lacks correct timing. The only way I know to become proficient in content and timing is through practice, and the safest place I know to practice is with a good friend, a loving supporter, or with your team.

Patrizia moved from Italy to California to pursue her dream of working with the San Francisco Opera. "It seems hopeless," she told me. "I sent them my résumé but they did not respond."

"In this country, it takes more than that. Call again, try to get an appointment, even just stop by," I encouraged.

"Isn't that being rude or pushy? Won't they think I'm impolite?"

"Patrizia, you have to let them know who you are. You are fluent in five languages and you're afraid to let your voice be heard. What do you have to lose?"

More sensitive to what she was saying, whom she was saying it to and when, she persisted. This past fall Patrizia's dream was fulfilled as she was hired to serve as the interpreter for a visiting Russian conductor to the San Francisco Opera!

## RALLYING THE TROOPS

One voice is often all that is needed to rally a group, and what better cause to rally around than to create a team committed to living an extraordinary life? Imagine if you took a stand on how you wanted your life to be and built a team that would help you, support you, and even hold you accountable to this vision. This could be your Ease Team.

Whom do you know who wants to do less and have more? Whom do you know who doesn't? Keep in mind, it takes only two to create a team, but there is power in numbers. What's essential in the beginning of this process is that you find at least one other person who believes in the dream and is willing to support you. The strength of the team grows exponentially if the interest is mutual.

Seek like-minded or, more important, like-valued people. Don't overlook your closest friends and family, including parents and kids. Take a look at coworkers, even bosses. Who are your teachers, or who could be? Find someone who will be there to talk to you about your dreams and projects and will ask you these two very valuable questions: "What are you doing to move your dream forward?" and "What's stopping you?"

## YOUR EASE TEAM

Barbara Sher, author of *Wishcraft* and *I Could Do Anything If I Only Knew What It Was*, wrote, "Nothing kills dreams faster than isolation. We evolved as social creatures, and we need allies to encourage our efforts."

There are two possible types of Ease Teams you might want to consider building. One is optional, the other is not. The optional team is a group of people, or a person, who, like you, want to simplify their life. You may meet on a regular basis, share your creative ideas, support each other's dreams, and exchange resources. It's wonderful to have this kind of backing.

But it's your prime Ease Team that will truly make the difference in your daily life. These are the people whom you know you can count on. These people are the resources you need to make your life easier. When I employed a large staff, my number-one criterion for hiring new people was that they had to make my life easier. If they didn't meet that need, the interview usually didn't continue.

The quality of these relationships will directly affect your life. So let's take a brief inventory of your Ease Team. Who is on your team, what is your relationship to them, and are they making your life easier? Let's explore a few basics. How's your relationship with your mail carrier, doorman, garbage collector, travel agent, local pharmacist?

How about your neighborhood supermarket? Do they deliver groceries? Will they order special items for you? If you need to throw together an emergency meal, or worse, a dinner party, are they ready to help? Do they cash your checks and give you quarters for the laundry machines?

Is your car pool reliable? Can you count on the other members to be on time and to help out if needed? How about your doctors? Are they reachable on weekends? Can you get a prescription if you are out of town and after office hours?

Do you get the idea? Wherever and whenever possible, build an arsenal of people who are on board to make your life easier. There are plenty of people available to give you grief and headaches. But if you make a point to create the best imaginable Ease Team, you'll see the results daily in your life. A snag or a snafu will be the exception rather than the norm.

Create a robust Rolodex. In a feature story in *Time* magazine, President Bush told his interviewer that he was the Rolodex kid. He keeps notes on everyone he's met. So does Bill Clinton. For more than twenty years, Bush kept three-by-five cards of all his contacts and still looks for clever ways to stay in touch.

Make sure your own fabulous resources are only a phone call away. Know who delivers (not just food) and who picks up. Oregon-based gourmet food company Harry and David sells whole smoked turkeys and hams, and you can order the night before you need them (1-800 547-3033).

Find a hairdresser that is open on Monday and a dry cleaner that stays open late, perhaps even delivers. Need new contact lenses? Lens Express will ship a new supply of contacts to you on a regular basis (1-800 USA-LENS). Find a personal trainer and masseuse who make house calls.

Have a list of baby-sitters that your kids like. America Online (AOL) offers a service called Moms Online. You can get advice from Miss Frugal on how to stretch your budget or talk to a pediatrician about your kid's allergy. The point is, limitless resources and information are just a keystroke away.

Ask friends to share their Ease Team members with you. Consider hiring a personal assistant. If you have no room in your home, you can now hire a virtual assistant: someone who will help you, but out of his or her house, not yours. With the use of technology, this is easy. Stacy Brice, in Cockeysville, Maryland, recently started Assist U, an on-line training program (at www.assistu.com) that offers a course for aspiring virtual assistants.

Andrew Tobias, author of *The Only Investment Guide You'll Ever Need*, wrote, "You learn that logic and facts really don't mean as much as personal long-standing relationships." I think anyone who makes my life easier deserves to be successful, so I'm always eager to share my favorite assets. Once you have these great people lined up, you will be better prepared to deal with unsupportive people.


## NEGATIVE PEOPLE

We all know them and have some of them in our life. I call them dream killers. You have a great idea, something you're excited about, and someone in your life—unfortunately often someone close to you—says, "Are you crazy? You're going to do *what?*"

There are several approaches for dealing with these folks. One is to ignore them. This is challenging to do, if you happen to live with them or see them daily. But you don't have to share your fondest dreams with them if they're continually shooting you down.

Another approach is to enlist them in your dream or vision. This often requires some work and a real commitment to them, to yourself, and to your project. If they are firmly rooted in their belief that your idea is bad, you may have to build a really good case. This is why I say that communication is an essential strategy for any project.

Talk to them. Find out what they're thinking and feeling. Give them some space to have their concerns and reactions. Don't try to convert them all at once. Hang in there with their disagreeing voices and concerns, and sometimes they will shift to a more supportive position.

If you can't get the support you need from them, go find it elsewhere. Sometimes when our dreams are big, they scare the people who are closest to us. Create a team or join a group, or find one other person who will serve on your team, at least for now.

But here's my favorite approach for dealing with negative people: If you consider that everything in life serves a function, you might ask, "What purpose does this negative person, or her point of view, serve?"

My mother is a pure doubting Thomas. She always imagines the worst. Because of this, I stopped sharing my dreams with her. Then I got smart. Whenever I'm preparing to launch a new product or service, I call Mom. She tells me everything that could possibly go wrong with it. Remember, my theory is that wherever there's an obstacle, design a strategy to manage it. I have my own built-in devil's advocate, who now sits on my Ease Team advisory board. Her insight has proven very useful in my pursuit of ease. Everything and everyone serves a sacred function.

It's taken me awhile to realize this, but everyone has something to bring to the party. With this type of attitude, you may find yourself more receptive to meeting and being with all kinds of people. The more open we are to each other's uniqueness, the more compassion, acceptance, understanding, and ease we will have. Who are we to judge who or what is better or more important? Some opportunities might never materialize if we only saw what we saw, or believed what we believed.

## BUILDING BRIDGES

Bridges are often used as metaphors, but imagine actually witnessing human beings coming together as a team and building a bridge with their bare hands. That's what the Incas in Peru do. It is an amazing example of how, with human strength and team effort, anything is possible.

The process begins as each woman from the village hand-twists blades of grass, making a 250-yard-long single strand. This can't be done in advance, because the grass must be moist and pliable. The next day everyone gathers at the bridge site. The single strand is woven with two other strands, creating a half-inch-thick rope, then combined with six other half-inch-thick strands to form a three-inch-thick rope. Finally, this rope is interwoven with two more strands to form the final nine-inch rope. This whole process is done twice.

The builders take the two grass ropes and string them across vast chasms. Knot experts secure vertical strands to hold the bridge in place. The entire process takes only three days and is designed to last ten years. The completed project can support the weight of hundreds of people.

Every single able person plays a part, whether a weaver, a builder, or a cook. This process would never happen without the whole team. The entire community participates in the ritual, and bridge-building is considered as much a party as it is work. When the bridge is completed, they walk or run across it and celebrate. Keep in mind this bridge began with a single blade of grass.

## A DREAM TEAM

This gathering of tribe, community, and team happens in our own society as well. When my friends Bob and Hilary decided to pay for their own wedding, they didn't want to compromise on their dream of an extraordinary celebration.

They decided to create a food registry. They made a list of every delicious morsel they wanted to serve at their reception. They imagined a seafood bar, dinner buffet, turkey station, garnishes, and decadent desserts. They called it "The Altar to the Gods Buffet."

Their letter to their guests said, "Our prayer is that you will help us create this feast in the manner of community, renewing ritual traditions from throughout the ages and bringing your contribution to the food we will all share. The gift of a joyously shared communal celebration is our most precious wish."

A few friends volunteered to manage all the logistics and convenient drop-off points were arranged, so we didn't have to carry food to the event. On the day of their wedding we feasted on salmon and oysters, antipasto and pasta, turkey and truffles. But what was most wonderful was that every bite had been prepared by Bob and Hilary's team—by the community of friends and family who loved them. And it didn't cost them a penny.

Bob and Hilary dreamed the dream and sent their clear vision out. They made very specific requests and made it easy for people to participate. They did very little and received much more than they could have imagined.

## BUILDING YOUR TEAM

Here is an eight-step process for building your team. Modify it to your liking and tailor it to your needs. The only essential secret to success in building your team is this: SHARE YOUR DREAM.

1. Clearly define your dream and find a powerful way to speak about it. This is essential. Sometimes you have one brief moment in which to invite someone to join your team. You want to give it your best shot. How you sound and your ability to articulate your vision clearly can mean the difference between success and failure.

   Practice, practice, practice. First share and declare what you want with friends and loved ones. Ask them how you sound, what they think you said, and what they think you meant. Are you being as clear as possible? Are you being succinct, and, most important, are you being convincing? You're going for clarity and credibility. When you feel and sound ready, it's time to go recruiting.

2. Break down your dream into projects with due dates. This will help you identify exactly what you need and where you can use some assistance. It will also make step one easier, since it may not be necessary to share the entire dream with everyone you talk to.

   It may be easier to ask for specific favors or to make smaller requests of people, especially in the early phases of your dream. This way, when people see how simple it is to support you, they may be willing to do it again.

3. Identify people who share your dream of having greater ease and who can help you. Whether it be people in your family, at work, in your community, or even strangers, when you team up with other like-minded people, you can find ways to share resources, as well as inspire each other. Two or more people committed to a common goal of doing less and having more can produce exponential results, which translates into even greater ease!

   Once you recognize your needs, open your phone book and see whom you know who can help you. And when you run out of names, ask the people you know whom *they* know who can help you accomplish the tasks on your project.

Then you can open the Yellow Pages or a gazillion other resource books. Stay focused on each task you need to accomplish and on who can help you get that particular task done. In your search, be open to finding new resources that can help you accomplish other aspects of your project and dream. I recommend you file those names so you have them at hand, but don't get sidetracked in pursuing resources unless doing so provides a shortcut for you.

As you identify what you need and who can help you, don't play small. Be willing to go find and recruit great members for your team. Should your senator or congressperson be on board? The local school principal or newspaper? The Surgeon General? Your family and friends (we hope so)? Do you need a professional organizer or event planner?

You never know until you ask. Be a confident caller. Speak powerfully and clearly and expect them to say yes. If they say no, find out why.

4. Make specific requests. Remember the example of the food registry: Hilary and Bob were very clear about what they wanted and how we could help. This is a critical point. Be very specific. If people want to offer more, great. Be open to that, too.

Be responsible about making agreements that you can honor and live with. If a concern pops up, graciously ask for help. What could pose a real obstacle for you might for someone else simply be solved by a phone call. See whom else they know who might help you on other specific tasks. New people can open new doors and avenues, and this is often where shortcuts happen.

5. Identify who will be ongoing members of your team. Some people may perform a single task or connect you to other resources. Some people will be involved ongoingly. See how people choose to play. Keep them informed of your progress and let them know how their assistance, no matter how small, made a difference.

If referrals really paid off, be sure to call the sources, let them know what happened, and thank them. Then ask graciously if there is some other request you have for them.

6. Set up a system for continual support and accountability. Decide what will work best for you and the dream or project

you're working on. Establish a tight and strong system that will keep you moving forward. If you work best with structure, design a team that will give you what you need. Will weekly or monthly meetings suffice? Do you need one or two key team members who will be there for you on a daily basis? Does it serve you to know that help is just a phone call away? Consider the size and time frame of your project, ask for what you need, and find the people who can give it to you.

7. Keep your eyes open for new team members. As the dream moves forward, keep sharing your passion and be open to new resources showing up. Continually ask your current team members to do the same.

   This phase can be exciting. As you accomplish the projects leading to your dream, new doors will open and new frontiers will become available. Take advantage of this. Encourage and allow your dream to be adopted by others and enjoy the enhancement of your original vision. This is no time to be stingy or to let your ego get in the way. Allow the dream to grow and flourish while you ensure that its integrity remains intact.

8. Start the process again. As the dream takes off and changes, so will the way you speak about it. New projects will emerge, different requests and needs will become apparent, as more and different resources become available. Keep breathing and growing with your vision and goals.

   If you feel that a project is becoming bigger than you, I recommend you find a coach or a mentor who can assist you. Once the ball is rolling, do everything in your power to keep it going. And be sure to honor yourself by continually getting the support you need to keep this process fun and exciting.

## HOW TO MAKE SPECIFIC REQUESTS

This point warrants a little more discussion, because we want to make it easy and appealing for people to help. Most of us enjoy making a contribution or being supportive, but often we are busy and overwhelmed. If you can make it uncomplicated for people to respond affirmatively to you, you will have mastered a powerful skill for having great ease.

When someone says to me, "Hey, I'm writing this great book. Can you help me?" my first response is "Egad, I wonder what he wants me to do?" If I'm very busy or caught up in something else in that moment, I'll probably just say, "Sorry, but I don't think so." Wait, don't think of me as a bad guy just yet. If someone says, "I'm writing a book. Would you mind introducing me to your agent or publisher?" my response to this question usually is "Sure, here's the number. Feel free to use my name."

Can you hear the difference? These two requests are worlds apart. Rather than just making a broad, sweeping request for help, be specific. Laurel was about to close on her dream home when she realized that the closing costs were thousands of dollars higher than she'd anticipated. She called me in a panic with a very specific request.

"I have an Erté print. Who do you know who might want to buy it right now?" I gave her the home number of an art-dealer friend. He bought it and she easily got her house. By using her resources and by being specific, Laurel produced a fast and big result.

Here are some other examples of specific requests:

"I want to get married. Who can you fix me up with?" Pretty bold, huh?

"I'm looking for a new job as a computer assistant. Who do you know who may be hiring?"

"I've been wanting to meet that CEO for a while. Would you please call him and make the introduction?"

"I want to attend your workshop but can afford only half the fee. How else can I pay for this? Are you willing to accept a payment plan? Can we trade services?"

"I'm looking for startup capital. Who do you know that makes this type of investment?"

Remember the basic steps of team-building: Identify what you need, decide who you think can help, and make it as easy as possible for people to say yes. This may require a little legwork or research on your part. If you're asking someone to make a call for you, try to have the number handy. If you're setting up a lunch appointment, pick a restaurant near the other person, make the reservation, and call beforehand with all the pertinent details. Faxing, sending self-addressed and stamped envelopes, and leaving your phone number even though you know the person has it are little things that make a difference.

What is essential for doing less and having more is to build an extraordinary team of people around you. Find people you trust, people you can count on. Look for people with the values you need.

Then honor these relationships as gold. Take great care of these resources. They are what make the difference between a life of ease and joy and one of frustration and exhaustion. Make your life easier by surrounding yourself with a winning team.

Roadmap Stop #5 — Teams

Who is an essential person for you to have on your Ease Team?

_____

By_____(date) I will share my dream or project with this person.


Who are three more people who would be helpful?

_____

_____

_____

## FUNDAMENTALS OF EASE

1. The number-one way to experience ease in your life is to share your dreams with others and ask for help. The best way I know to do this is to build teams.
2. I know what you're thinking: "I will not share my dream because people might laugh at me, think I'm lazy or crazy, steal my idea, or (*here's the biggie*) they might expect me to do something about it."
3. The problem is that unless you're sharing your dreams, they remain a secret. And an unspoken dream is frequently forgotten.
4. As you feel in your heart what matters to you most, it then gets formulated into ideas, in the form of thoughts, goals, and projects. When we give voice to our dreams, they begin to live.
5. Passionate living can be defined as aligning our head and heart through action. The voice is often the launching pad, since our thoughts turn into words, and our words then become actions.
6. Our voice and our words are two of the most awesome tools we have. What often sets us apart is how and when we use them.

7. Imagine if you took a stand on how you wanted your life to be and built a team that would help you, support you, and even hold you accountable to this vision. This could be your Ease Team.

8. What's essential in the beginning of this process is that you find at least one other person who believes in the dream and is willing to support you. The strength of the team grows exponentially if the interest is mutual.

9. It's your prime Ease Team that will truly make the difference in your daily life. These are the people whom you know you can count on. These people are the resources you need to make your life easier.

10. Create a robust Rolodex. Make sure your own fabulous resources are only a phone call away.

11. Communication is an essential strategy for any project. Talk to the people in your life, even the negative people. Find out what they're thinking and feeling. Give them some space to have their concerns and reactions.

12. Break down your dream into projects with due dates. This will help you identify exactly what you need and where you can use some assistance.

13. Identify people who share your dream of having greater ease and who can help you. Whether it be people in your family, at work, in your community, or even strangers, when you team up with other like-minded people, you can find ways to share resources, as well as inspire each other.

14. Most of us enjoy making a contribution or being supportive, but often we are busy and overwhelmed. If you can make it uncomplicated for people to respond affirmatively to you, you will have mastered a powerful skill for having great ease.

15. What is essential for doing less and having more is to build an extraordinary team of people around you. Find people you trust, people you can count on. Then honor these relationships as gold.

# PART III

# TOOLS
# FOR
# MAINTAINING
# EASE

# 12

# The Completion Corner

A s YOU realize what matters to you, it will also become evident what doesn't matter. Learn to recognize what's true for you and what's not. As you recognize false securities, illusions, and what no longer serves you, you can learn to release people, ideas, and things that just plain don't work anymore.

You can use The Completion Corner, anytime and anyplace, to free your mind and experience great ease by following three simple steps. The Completion Corner is a place inside you where you can practice emptying yourself out and clearing the clutter of your mind and life. If you want to have a dream-come-true life, you need to create space for your desires, not just in your closets or in your office, but in yourself. Make room in your life for your dreams!

Kim Johnson Gross, coauthor of *Chic Simple*, writes, "Quality of life comes not in accumulating things." We tend to gather a tremendous amount of stuff because we don't discriminate between what's valuable and what's not. Throw away and give away and feel the freedom of being unburdened. Weed the garden of your possessions, get rid of extras, and shed old skin.

The challenging part about creating space is completing what's been left undone. Learn to surround yourself with the things that really please you and work for you, and edit out the things that don't. As you do this, you'll see where your life is not working at maximum potential and you'll see places where you feel stuck, sluggish, perhaps confused. Lack of clarity or focus usually is a sign that something is incomplete.

As you complete what is incomplete, amazing things happen. Life begins to move easily, and then it's easier to keep it moving. When we get buried alive under burdensome annoyances, either we become incapacitated or we become motivated from a sense of fear and survival. This is a painful and sometimes dangerous way of living, and it's about as far away from ease as you can get.

At different times in our lives, many of us have been the victim of a pileup of incompletions. One man I know didn't pay his taxes for two years. The IRS put a lien on his assets, so he looked like a bad credit risk. He couldn't buy a house or rent an apartment. Eventually he lost his credit cards. He was caught in a downward spiral that also undermined his confidence and self-esteem.

Another woman I know let her parking tickets pile high. She never got around to paying them. She became afraid of driving her car because she might get towed. Concerned about driving to work, she eventually lost her job. A small detail led to a bigger concern, which led to an even bigger problem.

The secret to a life of ease is to clean up our messes and then design a personal practice or system that doesn't allow them to recur. This is not difficult, and we can take it a step at a time. Let's look at the process of finding where you have some cleaning up to do. We'll identify exactly what needs to happen for you to get complete. You'll create your completion list and, as quickly as you can, get it handled. I promise you this: Once you do your completions, you'll feel so good and so free that this process will change the way you deal with life.

## INCOMPLETIONS

Let's take a look at incompletions: things in your life that are unresolved and left hanging. Are there big incompletions in your life? They can be notorious and contagious: One incompletion leads to another and so on, as we saw earlier. It's difficult to focus on creating and dreaming when you have bills that are overdue or clutter all over your home.

We don't need to be obsessive about order. We just want to recognize signs of disorder. When you have clothes or shoes strewn all around the house, dishes piled in the sink, or a desk buried under paper, you may feel out of sorts. When life is overly cluttered, often so are we. Learn to see objectively what's in your mental and physical space. Recognize where you're sloppy and clean it up.

Then, in the morning, when you're enjoying your quiet, dreaming time, you won't be distracted. Or in the evening, you'll be delighted and free to focus on *you* when you come home, rather than tending to a mess. Complete what you start, when you start it, even if part of the completion process is to decide not to do it anymore. Keep your mind relaxed and available for the things that matter to you. You'll find this a life-changing practice.

As we become well rounded, we have access to more. The quality of people we choose as friends and colleagues, and the level of integrity by which we live our lives, will increase. And wherever we are incomplete, especially in our relationships, it will show up more clearly.

## TAKING INVENTORY

Let's look at all the important areas of your life. Explore what's up, what's in progress, what might be stuck, or what is just plain "not happening." The more honest you can be with yourself, the more powerful this process will be. And the more detached you can stay from the procedure, the less painful it will be. What I mean is, you don't have to judge or belittle yourself because some part of your life is in disarray.

The better you are at defining your current reality, the easier it is to accomplish the task at hand. Clarity about where you are helps shine a bright spotlight on what needs to be done, created, or accomplished. Remember, our goal here is to clear out the clutter, emotionally and physically, and make plenty of room for ease and flow.

Here is the three-step formula for using the Completion Corner. Use this formula as a guide in scrutinizing your whole life.

Step One: Write down what you feel incomplete about with anyone or anything. You can recognize something as being incomplete by how you feel about it. Is the matter settled? Do you think about it or worry about it? Is this affecting other areas of your life? When we are complete with something, often we don't even think about it. There is no agitation or energy wasted. If you think of something and you feel little or no internal reaction, then you're not incomplete with that thing. Only you can define if something is incomplete or not. You set the standard here.

Step Two: Write down what it is that is incomplete or describe what happened. Do this for each item on your list.

Step Three: Next to each item, write down what you need to do to complete it. On some items you may need to write a letter or make a phone call. For some items you may need to forgive someone or just declare "it's over." For some, you might not yet know what you need to do to realize completion.

My friend Carol had a room in her home that she called the "black hole." It was filled with incomplete items. She and her husband were trying to sell their house and move overseas, and she knew it was time to empty that room.

She decided it would be a great symbolic gesture to handle the black hole of her life. She followed the Completion Corner procedure and came up with a list of over three hundred "items to do." They included returning things she had borrowed, writing letters, returning phone calls, and even mailing back an inexpensive bracelet that she had stolen from her neighborhood drugstore when she was a teenager.

It took some time and effort initially, but with each item she handled, Carol felt lighter and freer. Within a few weeks of completing her list, they easily sold their house and made the big move. *Completion creates freedom.*

Decide which items on your list you intend to accomplish. I recommend doing them all, if that's what will honor your process. Practice doing completion from a place of grace rather than turning into a control addict. Having a sense of humor and keeping a sense of lightness about this process is useful. Your goal is completion and ease, not an obsessive compulsion. Life is easier and flows better when it's intact, when you are whole. It's just that simple.

## AREAS TO CHECK

Body—How's your health? When was the last time you had a physical or had your blood pressure checked? Are you at your desired weight? Do you like your hairstyle and color? How's your skin? How about your posture? Are you flexible and strong? What would you like to change? What would you want to be different?

Mind—Are you relaxed or stressed? How do you sleep at night? Do you meditate or otherwise quiet your mind? Do you have a psychological or spiritual path for growth? Is it working for you? Have you considered therapy or retreats? Are you learning?

Home—Are you living in the home or apartment you want? In the location and city you want? How's the view? Do you have enough space? Do you feel safe? How's your storage space? Do the walls need painting? How's the carpet or the drapes? What would you like to change? Are you thinking about moving? Are you financially or logistically free to go where you want? Are you living in your dream home? What changes would get you closer, if not there?

Car—Do you have one, need one, or want one? Do you want to get rid of it? Do you own or lease? What kind of shape is it in? Do you get regular maintenance and oil changes? Is your insurance current? Does your car have dents and dings? Does that bother you? How do you feel driving it? How about parking tickets or moving violations? Are you legal and safe?

Work—How do you feel about what you do? How is the environment? How do you feel about whom you work with and for? How long does it take to get there? Do you work reasonable hours? How's your energy while you are there? Are you happy about what you do?

Finance—How's your debt? Are you current on your finance payments? Do you have an IRA or retirement fund? Do you save money regularly? Do you spend more than you earn? How do you feel about your financial position? What are you wanting to change? How are you at managing your money? Do you have someone to help you?

People—Survey all your relationships. Look at work, home, friends, family, people from your present and people from your past. Do you have borrowed items to return, calls to make, letters to write, apologies to offer? Are you overdue with a wedding gift or a belated birthday card? Is there anyone you are hiding from? Is there an unfinished conversation, or a request you need to make? Are you willing to initiate it at this time? What do you need to do to heal or complete this relationship?

## THE BIG PAYOFF

The sense of accomplishment you'll feel as you clear off your list is amazing. This is not the same process as simply checking things off a laundry list. You're in the process of cleaning up your entire life.

The big payoff here has to do with integrity. Integrity is defined as the quality of being complete, whole, and unbroken; being sound, honest, and sincere. When we are whole, people can count on us and we can count on ourselves. Practicing integrity is one of the greatest ways to build self-confidence.

When you're not looking over your shoulder at all the incompletions in your life, you can be focused on moving ahead. When you're not hiding skeletons in your closets, you can be open and take risks. And when you're not cleaning up messes from the past, you're free to create and design big, new wonderful dreams for the future. When your energy isn't diffused or wasted in a fixing or fretting mode, you're available to play.

People start to see they can count on you, and you come through. Your word becomes extremely valuable and reliable, allowing you to tap into another level of ease and magic.

Keeping your word is how you show others that you're serious about your intention. Keeping your word is how you show yourself that you're accountable. You demonstrate to yourself that your word is powerful because you honor what you say. You use it to create, and it works.

The more your life is in order, the faster and easier your ability to manifest will become. You'll find that almost as soon as you say what you want or ask for what you need, it shows up. When your home, your business, and your relationships are solid and working, your integrity is fully intact.

Remember: Integrity means being whole and complete. Keep this picture in mind. If the integrity of a building or bridge is missing, it will fall down. It cannot stand. If there is some area of your life that is a mess, then ease and flow get stuck in the "gook." Keeping yourself at ease is a great incentive to keeping things honest, clean, and complete.

But let's not disregard the power of chaos as a force for change. Although I am an advocate of being clear and complete, let's honor and respect the energy behind a creative whirlwind. Let's be open to order *and* chaos, welcoming and practicing both!

## SPECIAL TIMES

There are times in our lives that require special attention with regard to completing. I'm sure you can look back on your own life and recall some of these. I'll mention a few, but it would be really valuable to think back on some of your own. Recall any memories of relationships or tasks that needed completing or finishing. How did you handle them? Was the completion process painful, joyful, or both? Did you celebrate or mourn? Did you ritualize the completion in any way, perhaps with a party or ceremony?

When our lives become chaotic, we sometimes don't take the necessary time to complete. We move from one event to another, from one job to the next, from one city to a new one, from relationship to relationship, and so on. It's an act of kindness, recognition, and an honoring of ourselves and others to acknowledge these times. In his wonderful book and television series called *The Power of Myth*, Joseph Campbell discussed how rites of passage and other rituals clearly marked initiation in days and cultures gone by.

Since we have few clear initiations into modern manhood or womanhood, we often don't realize that we have entered—or need to enter—a new phase of life. Here are some phases or experiences to consider, perhaps even to revisit. It's rarely too late to complete something, even if the event itself is long past.

**Completing a Relationship.** We might be defensive or judgmental about something someone has said or done, and our reaction may have little to do with them and everything to do with us. If there is someone with whom we are incomplete or to whom we have not said something that we need to say, it seems to get in our way again and again, often with different people. Practice "being complete" in all your relationships. This includes with your mom, dad, brothers, sisters, spouses, friends, lovers, and bosses.

With whom are you incomplete? When I ask this question, who pops into your mind? It is possible to clear the air with anyone. Harboring ill will is an energy drainer, and it often leads to greater incompletions. Notice if there is anyone with whom you are not being honest, whom you are hiding out from or avoiding. Are you withholding a communication or a hidden agenda? Whom is it time to deal with?

This process can be painful, depending on what happened, who was involved, and how the situation was handled. Ask yourself what specifically is incomplete. Are there unspoken feelings that need to be articulated? Do you need to write a letter (perhaps one that may never be mailed)? Be specific and decide what you are going to do about completing this relationship.

One woman I know was so angry when her boyfriend jilted her that she wrote a scathing letter, letting her rage roar. Then she burned it and flushed the ashes down the toilet. She felt complete. That's the measurement of success. You decide when you are complete. Learn to recognize your signs of feeling complete. They may include peace of mind, a sense of relief, or feeling physically lighter. You may feel more confident and happier. Use these internal cues to declare when you have completed something.

Just be aware of the pitfall here of never feeling complete, which I will discuss in greater detail in a moment. At a certain point, there's just no energy or "charge" on something, unless we artificially impose it. You don't need to get worked up over old business. Your goal here is to complete. Focus on that. It is healthy, essential, and thoughtful to be clean and complete with one relationship before attempting to cultivate another.

Perhaps you are incomplete with someone who has died. Death is never easy, especially on those of us who are left behind. Is there is a ritual to create, to pay homage or to release someone? Recognize the gifts those who have died gave you, the lessons they taught you, and the experiences you shared. Get out any feelings, including anger, sadness, and disappointment. Your goal is to complete these relationships. Mind you, this in no way suggests you need to forget them. You'll probably wind up feeling differently about them, but you never have to stop loving them.

I know a woman who had a dear friend die of AIDS at a young age. She missed him terribly and decided to go to his grave site and have a conversation with him. She brought bubbles and flowers. When she got there, she was so surprised to hear what came out of her mouth.

She was filled with rage. She had planned on having a lifelong friendship with this person, and now he was gone. After two hours of yelling, crying, laughing, and blowing bubbles, she was finally able to put it to rest. Her friend lives on in her heart, and she doesn't have such an intense reaction when she hears the sad news of someone having AIDS or any other illness.

**Completing a Job or Career.** We seem to be leaving or changing jobs more often and faster. You've heard people groan after fifty years on the job, "All they gave me was this watch." Whether you left after a few months or many years, how did you leave? Whether leaving was your choice or theirs, try to leave complete.

Do a brief inventory. Was anything left undone or unsaid? Was there anyone you needed to thank or acknowledge? Recognize what you learned, what you contributed, and what new skills or ideas you took with you. Ask yourself why you were there and how it contributed to your growth.

How do you feel about leaving? Are you happy or sad? Should you throw yourself a "moving on" party or do you need quiet alone time to reflect? What will honor you and help you complete this transition?

Where will you go from here? Is it time to think about what's next? Try not to go there too quickly. Of course, if what's essential is that you produce an income, do what's necessary. But sometimes taking a simpler, interim job may give you the required time to recharge and consider what's next.

If you're starting a new job or moving to a new city and are feeling nervous, you could invite close friends over to create a Power Circle. While seated or standing in an intimate circle, they could all toast you and speak one by one about your talents and abilities. With each toast they make, take a sip from your cup and ingest their good wishes. Allow this ceremony to fill you up with self-confidence and power.

**Completing Phases of Life.** A birthday with a zero on the end, such as thirty, forty, fifty, sixty, and so on, can bring up many feelings. Passages of life can be exciting or depressing or bring up a whole array of other feelings. What phase of life are you in? Are you moving into eldership? How do you deal with the aging process? Do you celebrate this rite of passage?

I wrote earlier about the luncheon that honored Women of Achievement, Vision and Excellence. Besides living an exemplary life, the criterion for eligibility for this award is that you must be at least seventy years old. I was inspired to hear the words of Dorothea Walker, whose three careers have spanned sixty years. At ninety, she started a new career as a media spokesperson. She's passionate about beauty and design and serves on the Council of the War Memorial Opera Board and chairs the Rosalind Russell Arthritis Research Center. Dorothea said, "Unless my mind and voice give out, I'll just go right on talking."

You can choose how to meet and greet life. You can also choose to celebrate aging with grace and dignity. And at any age, we can commemorate life. One way to do this is with ritual. Ritual is as old as time and allows us to feel and more fully experience whatever we are doing.

We observe most major initiations with some form of ritual. A baptism or naming ceremony celebrates the initiation of new life, a wedding is the ritual for celebrating marriage, and a funeral is one of the rituals for mourning a death.

Ritual allows you to experience deeper meaning in everything you do. A ritualized life takes on another dimension, with full texture and richness. Rituals are great for completing and for initiating. They can be done alone or with others. They require some time in which to feel what you want to create in the ritual, and they often require some planning. What rituals will you use to celebrate your next birthday or passage?

There are many good books on how to create a ritual. The basics are these: Get still and quiet, set an intention for what you want, open to or decide the process you will use, do what you think will serve, and then formally close the ritual.

At my engagement shower, I was preparing to complete life as a single woman. As a ritual, my women friends all gathered around me in two circles. The inner circle was comprised of the married women, and circled around them were my single friends. Each one spoke words of wisdom to me. The married women told me to have fun with my new husband and to remember to "date" him. The single women reminded me to flirt with my new husband and still have nights out with the girls. This went on for about twenty minutes. I said some closing words and we were done. Through this ritual, I felt more prepared for marriage.


NEVER COMPLETING

There are two common experiences associated with completing. One is fulfillment and satisfaction. The other is depression and loss. Both come up often when we undertake a creative endeavor. I know poets and writers who love the creative process so much that they never complete anything. They fear that completion means the end of their creativity. Since we have the tendency to avoid emotional discomfort, successful completion may never occur.

When you are in the flow of life, you must see that at one level there is no beginning and no end. But on the other hand, in order for something new to come into being, what came before it must be complete. No play or movie would ever be seen, or any painting viewed, if someone didn't complete them. In a creative process, completion is not the end of the road. Once you get used to the ebb and flow of life, you can ride this expressive wave and create again and again. As Robert Fritz wrote in *The Path of Least Resistance,* "Your life can be a series of creative acts that beget other creative acts."

I have seen this process occur with dreams. Fear of completing can be energy-draining and can kill the dreamer inside you. "If I realize my dream, *then* what will I do?" How about creating another dream? If you have fear about completing, reread the chapter on beliefs. Format a powerful belief that will help move you out of your fear. Consider, "As I complete the old, I am free to create the new."

Please trust me on this: Completing is just as important as beginning. Begin, do or express, complete, and begin again. This is an organic process. To omit any portion will leave you unfulfilled or frustrated.

This process does not have to be linear. You don't have to complete one thing before moving ahead on another. Completion can happen at many levels, and in many dimensions of life. You can overlap your projects and dreams, allowing the force and momentum of completing each to support the completion and creation of others.

Just keep in mind that when you complete something, it is whole. It has integrity and it holds together. Learn to appreciate your creations. See the beauty before you, and allow it to reflect to you your beauty as a creator.

## FUNDAMENTALS OF EASE

1. As you realize what matters to you, it will also become evident what doesn't matter. Learn to recognize what's true for you and what's not.
2. If you want to have a dream-come-true life, you need to create space for your desires, not just in your closets or in your office, but in yourself. Make room in your life for your dreams.
3. As you complete what is incomplete, amazing things happen. Life begins to move easily, and then it's easier to keep it moving.
4. Complete what you start, when you start it, even if part of the completion process is to decide not to do it anymore. Keep your mind relaxed and available for the things that matter to you. You will find this a life-changing practice.
5. The more honest you can be with yourself, the more powerful this process will be. And the more detached you can stay

from the procedure, the less painful it will be. Don't judge or belittle yourself because some part of your life is in disarray.

6. Clarity about where you are helps shine a bright spotlight on what needs to be done, created, or accomplished. Remember, our goal here is to clear out the clutter, emotionally and physically, and make plenty of room for ease and flow.

7. Completion creates freedom. Having a sense of humor and keeping a sense of lightness about this process is useful. Your goal is completion and ease, not an obsessive compulsion.

8. Life is easier and flows better when it's intact, when you are whole. It's just that simple.

9. When you're not looking over your shoulder, at all the incompletions in your life, you can be focused on moving ahead. When your energy isn't diffused or wasted in a fixing or fretting mode, you're available to play.

10. Keeping your word is how you show yourself that you are accountable. You demonstrate to yourself that your word is powerful because you honor what you say. You use it to create, and it works.

11. The more your life is in order, the faster and easier your ability to manifest will become. You'll find that almost as soon as you say what you want or ask for what you need, it shows up.

12. Let's not disregard the power of chaos as a force for change. Let's honor and respect the energy behind a creative whirlwind. Let's be open to order *and* chaos, welcoming and practicing both!

13. There are two common experiences associated with completing. One is fulfillment and satisfaction. The other is depression and loss. Both come up often when we undertake a creative endeavor.

14. If you have fear about completing, reread the chapter on beliefs. Format a powerful belief that will help move you out of your fear. Fear of completing can be energy-draining and can kill the dreamer inside you.

15. Completing is just as important as beginning. Begin, do or express, complete, and begin again.

# 13

# Moment by Moment

WITHOUT a doubt, the single biggest contributor to stress, or lack of ease in our life, is time. How we spend it, use it, and perhaps waste it has become a problem of epidemic proportions. A frequent complaint is "When I'm not buried in work, I have time, but then I don't have the money I need. If I'm working all the time, I have money, but no time to enjoy it." Does this sound like you? Do you feel caught in the loop of never enough time, or money, or both? Do you feel that there's always a price to pay for having more time?

Do you play a sophisticated version of *Beat the Clock?* An over-scheduled life creates stress. If we think we don't have enough time, we keep ourselves mentally and physically very busy, trying to accomplish the impossible feat of catching up.

On the other hand, too much idle or leisure time also causes undue stress. Time has such a grip on us that we can get agitated when we have nothing to do. Time is a manmade concept, initiated by the Maya, the creators of calendars. Brilliant in mathematics, they were able to calculate the length of the earth's orbit around the sun with an accuracy of a thousandth of a decimal point, according to modern calculations. The Maya gave each month of their calendar a special meaning and paid tribute to important days and moments. We, on the other hand, went on to sanitize time, divorcing it from the flow of life. Our society measures time in hours, minutes, seconds, nano-seconds (one billionth of a second), and even picoseconds (if you could imagine trillionths of a second). We are way out of control when it comes to controlling time.

We live as though we don't have anything to say about time. In-deed, when the sun goes down, that's pretty much the end of that day. But although the clock will tick at the same old pace, we must learn to shift our relationship to time. This is something we absolutely can do. We can make the most of time by actually experiencing life as opposed to doing as much as we possibly can.

Ben Franklin said, "Do not squander time, for that is the stuff life is made of." An extremely productive man distinguished as an inven-tor, scientist, writer, publisher, and statesman, Franklin retired at age eighty-two. He also said, "Be not disturbed at trifles or at accidents common or unavoidable. Lose no time; be always employed in some-thing useful; cut off all unnecessary action." Franklin followed his heart, doing what he loved, staying centered, and knowing how to say no.

## UNTIMELY MANAGEMENT

When we shift our relationship to time, we shift our relationship to life and the way we live. Stress and anxiety about time occur when we relate more to the future than to our present. We are usually here, thinking about there. To get from here to there, we turn to time management. The trouble with most time-management programs is that they focus on how to get things done more efficiently. Time management doesn't give us more time. Although it speeds up the treadmill and we may become more productive, we're only doing more, not living more. Time management may even worsen our stress because we're not actually shifting our relationship to time. We're not creating more flow or more freedom by doing more. We actually need to do less, in order to have more quality of life. The question more important than "How can I do more?" is "Why am I doing this?" In order to do less and have more, you must focus on the things that most matter to you.

USA Today polled adults, asking if they had one more hour a day, how they would spend it. Eighteen percent said they would spend time with family, 17 percent said they would sleep, 13 percent would read a book or magazine, 7 percent would exercise, 6 percent would participate in a non-sports leisure activity, and 5 percent said they would pray or go to church. If you had a twenty-five-hour day, what would you do with that precious extra hour?

Have you been to New York City lately? The pace there just seems to get faster and more chaotic. Everyone is rushing like crazy and trying to schedule you in. "I'll 'calendar' you in for lunch," one agent told me. At Elizabeth Arden's Red Door Salon, women bring laptops or clients so they can do business while having their toes done. Yet although the Big Apple appears to be moving at lightning speed, nothing seems to happen quickly. There's this illusion that life is sped up, yet the lines are longer than ever, and things in general take longer. Just how long is a New York minute?

A movie-producer friend told me that Jeffrey Katzenberg, co-founder of the media production company DreamWorks, used to have four breakfasts in a row at the Regency in Manhattan when he was in New York on business, starting before 8:00 A.M. and finishing at 10:30. He's also been known to have two back-to-back lunches. The other coast is equally notorious. I've heard that Sam Cohn, the superstar agent and vice-chairman of International Creative Management, has multiple phone lines that keep callers in a holding pattern, because he's too busy to return calls.

In Hollywood, the assistants to the stars have "limo logs," which are detailed reports of the comings and goings of their celebrities, to-the-second appointment calendars, and portable everything. On any given day they'll screen hundreds of calls, make last-minute reservations, and reshuffle a dozen or so appointments. Many even belong to the Association of Celebrity Personal Assistants, which helps the more than three hundred members cope.

And while traipsing between these two power cities, busy airborne executives can now receive calls during their flights. Downtime has been abolished through the wonders of technology. You can do business anywhere and anytime, and this is the problem. With cell phones, beepers, e-mail, fax machines—even car fax machines—the only way we can have quiet, quality time is if we turn the world off. Do you dare?

You can loosen technology's grip on your life by not living for your fax machine, e-mail, voice mail, and pager. Use them only when necessary or when you choose to. Decide what your hours of operation are and tell people when you're available. It doesn't have to be twenty-four hours a day. Don't become addicted to technology. If you already are, get help and break the habit. Take control of your time again by learning not to answer immediately. Put some space in your life.

## NATURAL TIMING

The reality is, time is a rhythmic dimension of life. In some countries these measurements that we swear by don't even exist.

Do you ever take off your watch? At least on weekends, do you practice tuning in to your innate body clock? Do you live as much of life as possible without checking the time? Or do you live in neatly scheduled one-hour increments?

Wait a second. What *is* a second? Your heartbeat takes a second. Most of us run at about sixty beats per minute. So what are you tuned in to? Are you run by a manmade calculation or by an internal clock, a natural rhythm? Who is setting the pace of your life?

What's your sense of time? When does time fly and when does it drag? When do you feel timeless and when do you feel timebound? By becoming aware of your natural rhythm, of your innate clock, you can begin to create and shift your relationship to time. You can begin to use time as a gift for creating ease.

We need to find our own rhythm, our own flow, and we need to learn to shift into the right rhythm for each of us. Your rhythm feels right for you. It puts you at ease. "If a man does not keep pace with his companions, perhaps it is because he hears a different drummer. Let him step to the music he hears," Henry David Thoreau wrote.

We can shift to internal time by recognizing and acting on what is true for us. It's this simple: Eat when you're hungry, sleep when you're tired, play or do something fun when you're bored. When we each learn to live on the beat, results happen effortlessly. All the pieces of our life symphony come into accord, there's a beautiful pulsation, and life works. You can find your rhythm through nature. Notice what works for you. Are you listening to birds, ocean, and wind or pagers, phones, and jet planes?

## WHAT ABOUT NOW?

For many of us, living "now" isn't okay. The sin of the century seems to be free time. Many people overschedule as a way of proving their worth. An open hour or, God forbid, a free day leaves some feeling nervous or useless. I know it sounds odd, but it's a matter of programming. There is something about *now* that we have an aversion to. It has to do with acceptance. Once we learn to accept where we are, what we're doing, and who we're being, we'll begin to reclaim great power and ease.

Funny thing, that "now" concept. In the present moment there actually is no stress. Stress comes in our resistance to this present moment. If you could just relax into it, allowing this precious moment to be whatever it is, it would be a priceless gift. But we are so resistant. We hold on for dear life to some obscure memory of the past or desire for the future that keeps us eternally scrambling and, unfortunately, dissatisfied. I'm forever questioning where I am and wishing I were elsewhere, when *all I really need to do for ease is to get still, get present, and realize that where I am is the perfect place to be.*

The moment you get this—really get it in the fiber of your being—your life will be altered and you will always have access to ease. We can take back our lives in small ways. Small steps build confidence to take larger leaps. Less stress means more success. When you're healthy and stress-free you can dream, play, and have time and energy for the people and things you love.

Create a life that allows for more ease and grace. Be where you are when you're there. Be here now. As noted author Louise Hay often says, "The point of power is in the present." Be where you are now.

Use your breath as a barometer. Are you huffing and puffing, or perhaps forgetting to breathe fully and deeply? This may be a sign of rushing and forgetting about your needs. Learn to slow up, rather than slow down, which means that relaxing can lift you up and give you more energy. Taking extra time for yourself will actually give you more time.

Create something in your life that you allow to unfold naturally. Write a poem or a story, plant a garden, or learn to paint. Let it take as long as it takes. Do it as often as feels right. It will teach you deep lessons about unstructured structure and timeless time.

You have the ability to practice "being in the now" all day long and every day. When you make tea or coffee, or when you're cooking, smell the aromas and notice the colors, textures, and shapes. Recognize when your thoughts drift from the present moment and gently bring your attention back. When the phone rings, use even it as a chance to breathe. Take a full, deep inhalation and exhalation each time before you answer the phone.

When you are waiting for the elevator, begin a breathing meditation, as discussed in Chapter 3. Find ways throughout your day to bring your attention and awareness gently back to here and now. The phone ringing, waiting for the elevator, even sitting on the toilet can become trigger points to remind you to breathe and see where your mind is. Gentle reminder notes around the house and office can also be useful: "Remember to Breathe" and "Are You Here?" are a few of my personal favorites.

Awareness is that state of mind that observes without condemnation. It's called being mindful, and every great master and teacher has spoken about it as the path to peace of mind and greater ease. Learn to infuse the spirit of ease into everything you do in everyday life by cultivating awareness.

How about taking "time out"? Often used as a disciplinary action for young children, I have found time out to be one of the greatest gifts we can give to ourselves. When do you take time out, and how do you take it? Consider naps, romantic novels, short meditations, a foreign movie, or afternoon tea with a pal.

And bring back spontaneity. Sometimes it's time to drop everything and indulge a whim. Are you really that busy that you never have time to change plans on short notice? When a friend urges or a child pleads, can you respond?

How often I hear, "I can't take the afternoon off or stop working on this project. I have to stay in control." Sometimes taking a break is the best possible thing you can do for a project, even though you may not think so. A little burst of spontaneity and breaking routine will help you feel refreshed, invigorated, and more "in control." Spontaneity, in moderation, can give you a breather, reignite your passion, and give you a new perspective. Give spontaneity a shot.

## LIVING FROM YOUR PASSION

Practice using passion as your barometer. If you are asked to do something and you don't have to do it and you are not passionate about it, say no. I'll explore this in more detail in Chapter 16, when I discuss the Ease Meter. It is possible to live more from your passion and a little less from your calendar.

Passion can be the ultimate timesaving tool for two good reasons. First, when you're doing what you love, who cares about the time? When you're with someone you love, or listening to a great piece of music, or painting, or volunteering, doesn't time just fly by? Don't you feel as if you have slipped into timelessness?

Second, when you are doing what you love, it often gets done faster than when you are doing only the things you need to do. Your challenge is to free up your life from some of the deeds you are doing. When you have a choice of accepting or declining a task, do you ever use your passion as the reason for saying yes or no?

Here's a quick word on calendars: Do you live in mortal fear that you might lose your Filofax or whatever is your chosen organizational tool? I started out with a small calendar. Friends ridiculed me, saying I needed a bigger book to hold bigger dreams and ideas. I switched to an elaborate personal-planning system. Soon I outgrew that and it was time to get "high tech." I transferred everything—all my dates, contacts, records, and phone numbers—to a notebook-size computer. It was wonderful, until one day when the computer crashed and I lost everything.

I am now back to a small and simple calendar. I juggle very large projects with this mini-marvel. If I notice it's becoming too full or busy, I stop, sort, toss out and rearrange my priorities, based on my passion and my dreams. I have learned to keep life pretty simple. I do not compromise on my vision, just on how I schedule my time.

My computer did have a cool capability that gave me great insight. It had a T button for transfer. Whatever tasks I didn't complete could simply be transferred to the next day with the touch of a key. After several days of transferring, I could simply move the task to the following week. If after two weeks I was still moving it around, I would switch to the D key, which stood for delete.

This program made me realize how much time I was wasting juggling incidental tasks that I never intended to accomplish. Now I am more aware and don't schedule things I don't plan on doing. Awareness is one of the greatest timesaving tools I know.


## TIME-SAVER "BASIX"

Here are six ways I practice being in control of my time and my life. I call them my Basix—because they are basic and there are six of them. As you make fundamental changes in the way you live, when you say yes or no, and how you take care of yourself, you will develop your own Basix. Here are my biggest and most basic time-savers.

1. Clarifying—Whenever and as much as possible, I have a clear picture of what I want or need, or what I am trying to create or accomplish. Clarity helps me accomplish the other things on my "to do" list faster and with much greater ease.

2. Setting priorities—If I lived strictly from my calendar and "to do" list, I could feel overwhelmed daily. Each morning, I decide what the three most important things are for me to accomplish that day. Then I list them in order of priority and I begin working on item number one. If it's a big task, it may be my only priority for the day. Completing it allows me to feel good, even if I've completed only one task. Practice not overscheduling.

3. Performing multiple tasks—I have developed the fine art of accomplishing multiple tasks at once, by being extremely organized. With little effort and intentional focus, I can get so much done, so efficiently. Living in the city helps. In less than two hours I can go to the post office, the dry cleaner, and the bank, eat a little lunch, and even get a manicure. If I attempt to do this at high noon, when everyone else is doing their errands, it takes longer. Part of my effective use of time and creating ease in my life includes deciding when would be the best time to accomplish these tasks. This is an important point.

4. Bundling—This is a continuation of multiple tasks, but it has more to do with the layout of your tasks. Set your life up for ease by using services that are near you, near each other, or easily accessible. Access, if you live in the city, may mean that it's within walking distance or that there is parking nearby. My favorite butcher is on the other side of town, but is located near my facialist. On days when my skin is glowing, I'm usually having a delicious dinner. Twice a month, this has turned into a "Take Care of Me" day.

See where bundling can save you time. Do you have certain days you go to the dry cleaner? Do you work out on particular days of the week? Can you eat out that night or is there a good carry-out restaurant nearby? What activities are

scheduled into your life that could be bundled with other activities, resulting in greater ease for you?

5. Just say no — If you don't *have* to do something and you don't
*want* to, why are you doing it? Practice saying no. And practice doing it with grace and ease. Pain and discomfort come
from resistance to something, not from the release of it. Do
you resist saying no? Take the pressure off yourself. This simple little word, no, will allow you more time to stop, look, reflect, and practice a new way of living.

Pressure is contrary to ease. If you feel suppressed, re-
pressed, depressed, or compressed, strongly consider saying no
(thank you).

6. Using resources — This is by far my favorite and most powerful
time-saver. If I need something, I don't always know where to
find it, but I usually do know whom to call. Don't reinvent
the wheel. Call your friends, family, colleagues, and others
who can share their best and favorite resources with you.

When I was under deadline to complete my last book, I
needed several powerful quotations on specific topics. I could
have gone to the library and spent hours researching. Instead,
I called my friend Caterina Rando, who has produced a soft-
ware program called *Words of Women Quotations for Success.*
Within minutes, she faxed me dozens of quotes, saved me
tons of time, and received an acknowledgment in the book.
When I needed a liability release for my business, I called a
business-owner friend who sent over one that she uses, with
her permission to modify it to my needs.

Nothing makes life easier and saves more time than using
your resources. And remember, the more you give, the more
you receive. You are also a resource to many.

## OTHER TIME-SAVERS

One of my colleagues, Odette Pollar, is president of Time Management Systems. She is the author of 365 *Ways to Simplify Your Work
Life* and writes the nationally syndicated column called "Smart Ways
to Work." Odette asked me to share her timesaving wisdom with you:

"You can do something easily or efficiently, which may not meet your goal of simplification. Simplification has to do with reducing the volume of tasks and complexity in your life." Three ways to simplify your life are:

1. Get rid of clutter and excess. Piles of things tend to distract you and make you feel guilty. The more you own, the more you have to transport, insure, store, dust, and maintain. Things can take over your life.

2. Say no to things, people, tasks, and opportunities that clutter up your life and distract you from your objectives.

3. Simplify decision-making. Don't agonize over minor decisions. They are still minor, with or without the agony. If you're making the same decision over and over again, you really need a rule, rather than a new decision.

## TIME TO LIVE

When I speak about changing our relationship to time or making room for our dreams, people get a little nervous. It makes sense to be concerned. What are you going to do with these new ideas and desires? How are you going to have time to do what you really want? Your calendar is already jammed with all the other stuff you need to do. Unless you have made a conscious effort to clear some space, there is probably little or no room to add passion and dreams to your life.

We live from our reactions, rather than from our dreams. When something happens or needs to happen, we go to our calendar in search of an open slot to squeeze one more task into our already very full life. By the time you do all the things you have to do and need to do, is there any time left to do what really matters to you? Do you get the leftover precious moments, assuming there are any? And what do you do with them?

How do you spend most Sunday evenings? Frequent responses include: planning the week ahead, doing laundry, or watching TV. Do you have any time scheduled for what you love? Do you have time for you?

I'm going to ask you to consider turning your life upside down. This is what the Passion Pyramid was designed to help you do. Don't panic, this doesn't have to happen all at once. It doesn't have to be drastic, unless you say so. I want to show you how to live a little more from your passion and a little less from your Day-Timer. Then you will feel in control of your life and really know the true meaning of ease.

Moment by moment is the only way we can live life. The better we are at this, the richer our lives will be. Savor life and you'll understand the true joy of doing less and having more, every precious instant of every priceless day.

## FUNDAMENTALS OF EASE

1. Without a doubt, the single biggest contributor to stress, or lack of ease in our life, is time. How we spend it, use it, and perhaps waste it has become a problem of epidemic proportions.

2. Too much idle or leisure time also causes undue stress. Time has such a grip on us that we can get agitated when we have nothing to do.

3. We must learn to shift our relationship to time. This is something we absolutely can do. We can make the most out of time by actually experiencing life as opposed to doing as much as we possibly can.

4. When we shift our relationship to time, we shift our relationship to life and the way we live. Stress and anxiety about time occur when we relate more to the future than to our present.

5. Time management doesn't give us more time. Although it speeds up the treadmill and we may become more productive, we're only doing more. Time management may worsen our stress because we're not actually shifting our relationship to time.

6. You can loosen technology's grip on your life by using your fax machine, e-mail, voice mail, and pager only when necessary or when you choose to. Take control of your time by learning not to answer immediately.

7. By becoming aware of your natural rhythm, of your innate clock, you can begin to create and shift your relationship to time. You can begin to use time as a gift for creating ease.

8. We need to find our own rhythm, our own flow, and we need to learn to shift into the right rhythm for each of us. Your rhythm feels right for you.

9. In the present moment there actually is no stress. Stress comes in our resistance to this present moment. If you could just relax into it, allowing this precious moment to be whatever it is, it would be a priceless gift.

10. Is this you? "I'm forever questioning where I am and wishing I were elsewhere, when all I really need to do for ease is to get still, get present, and realize that where I am is the perfect place to be."

11. We can take back our lives in small ways. Small steps build confidence to take larger leaps. Less stress means more success and more time and energy for the people and things you love.

12. Learn to infuse the spirit of ease into everything you do in everyday life by cultivating awareness.

13. Spontaneity, in moderation, can give you a breather, reignite your passion, and give you a new perspective. Give spontaneity a shot.

14. Passion can be the ultimate timesaving tool for two good reasons. First, when you're doing what you love, who cares about the time? Second, when you're doing what you love, it often gets done faster than when you're doing only the things you need to do.

15. Moment by moment is the only way we can live life. Savor life and you'll understand the true joy of doing less and having more, every precious instant, of every priceless day.

# 14

# Ease in Real Life

AS YOU begin to develop your skills for having greater ease, life will offer you many opportunities for practice and perfection. A little later in this chapter, we'll look at a larger-than-life yet still very simple philosophy about ease. But first, let's explore some of the day-to-day aggravations that can drive us to dis-ease and make us crazy. It's hard to look at the big picture of life when we're operating out of aggravation.

Daily occurrences in life provide us with unlimited opportunities to try out what we are learning and to sharpen our skills. I'm sure you're aware of some of your own personal "hot buttons," the circumstances when you seem to lose your cool or go off center. Some of the most common places for these include airports, in line at the post office, or in traffic. Here's a little extra ammunition for dealing with these potential detours:

## AIRPORTS

I arrived at the small Teeside airport in Northern England just before my flight departed. I was flying to Heathrow, where I'd board a connecting flight for my long trip back to San Francisco. As I was being dropped off by my client, I commented that it was such a delight not to have to check in hours prior to my flight. And how impressed I was that I was going to able to fly in this bad weather.

I spoke too soon. Stepping up to the counter, I learned that the flight was delayed two hours due to London fog, which would cause me to miss my flight home. I breathed and asked about options. The attendant informed me that there were no seats available on any later flights to the States, and she hoped I would enjoy one more evening in their country.

I considered my choices. I could visit friends in London or see a bit of the countryside. I could lose my temper and insist that someone in charge find me a seat. I told her I was often lucky and asked if she could please check one more time. Sure enough, she found me a seat on a later flight.

Upon landing very late in London, I was told if I ran to the gate, I might make my connecting flight. Dashing through the airport is not my idea of ease. Although I fully intended to make the plane, I have learned not to pin myself in to "do or die" circumstances. I walked quickly and directly to the gate and easily made the plane.

What I didn't do was panic, have an unnecessarily big reaction, lose my cool, blame or attack, or make matters worse. I stayed centered and went with the flow and everything turned out fine. I remained calm in the midst of chaos. This is what ease is about. I realized what was happening, what was possible, and I made simple choices along the way.

I am definitely someone who used to hate waiting. I thought it was a waste of time. The real time-waster, I discovered, was my frustration and stress from often scheduling myself too tightly. Showing up early for appointments, even for airplane flights, allows for experiencing the joy of winding down.

By the way, the best way I know to minimize or eliminate jet lag is through meditation. Fellow speaker and trainer Dr. Jerry Teplitz told me he meditates several times on a long flight and has been able to eliminate virtually any signs of jet lag. He claims he has flown from Virginia to Australia and has arrived rested and in synch with the appropriate time zone.

## TRAVEL EASE TEAM

We spoke earlier about Ease Teams. Who are the members of your travel Ease Team? Their job should be to make your life easier and, ideally, to make your travel experience a pleasant one. If you travel a lot and don't have this team in place, I strongly recommend that you create one as soon as possible. For example, does your travel agency take great care of you? Do they have a profile on you that includes your frequent-flyer numbers and meal and seat preferences? Do you get great service, quick turnaround, and your tickets delivered to your door? Or do you have to chase them down? Do you spend a long time on hold?

Do you purchase tickets electronically? You can earn free miles if you use the airport's on-site computer check-in system. You can even use a travel Web site, such as Travelocity (www.travelocity.com), Flifo (www.flifo.com), and Preview Travel (www.previewtravel.com). These services offer bargain airfares and no-hassle booking. Each lets users enter their itineraries and book the cheapest tickets available. They can typically match or beat travel agents' prices. These days, the travel savvy use the Web to scout destinations and prices, then pick up the phone. Personally, I'd rather speed-dial my trusty travel agent or even the airlines, but as Preview spokesman Ron Pernick says, "If a fare war is on, the Web is more fun than sitting on hold."

Who else makes a difference in your travel ease and should be on your travel team? How about your car-rental company? Does the clerk at the rental desk know you as a preferred traveler? Do you belong to an airport club, so if you get stuck at the airport, you can relax or do some business? Does the skycap recognize you as a frequent flyer? Ask yourself who can help make your life easier. Get them on board and consider remembering some of them at Christmas. Get into relationships with the people who can bring ease and, with it, great happiness into your life.

## TRAFFIC

Being in traffic gives you a great opportunity to practice being fully present. In his book *TimeShifting*, Stephen Rechtschaffen, M.D., suggests a new approach for ease on the road. "Slow down your driving by 10 mph and just enjoy the ride. Let someone cut in line in front of you." Relax and breathe. Traffic time could be your daily practice for just being.

Whether you are commuting by bus or train, sitting in traffic, or driving, this can be a great time to listen to music or language tapes, even books on tape. You can dictate an idea into a recorder or think through a problem. You can enjoy the scenery or flirt with a nearby driver. You can fantasize about your future, think about a pleasant memory, or make up a new dream. And you thought you had no time to relax!

The biggest stress reliever in my life, by far, is my cellular phone. I can alert people to where I am and give them a status report if I'm running late. I rarely experience anyone being upset if I call ahead to let someone know that I am stuck in traffic or lost. For me, a cellular phone is a great investment in ease.

I even use my phone to have people "talk me in." I ask them to stay on the line with me, giving me directions. And if you've ever been lost or received confusing directions, or hate to wrestle with a map, you can once again go high-tech. Some cars now come with a Satellite-Linked Navigation System, an in-dash guidance program that directs you to virtually any business or residential address. You can customize the program, storing up to a hundred personal addresses. You can even select your destination and, using your touch screen, access a database that locates nearby restaurants, hotels, airports, hospitals, banks, and points of interest.

Here's another high-tech device for making the roads and your drive a little safer. It's a computer that detects driver fatigue. Placed inside the car, the sensors pick up weaving motions and launch into a series of warnings, ranging from a gentle voice saying "Wake up" to loud beeps accompanied by a peppermint-scented spray, shown to increase alertness.

Speaking of scents, aromatherapy may be hitting the highways now that the National Highway Traffic Safety Administration is spending $1.6 million to keep drivers awake at the wheel. A squirt of lemon-menthol scent spritzed on your dashboard could save you a ticket or worse. Research shows that people tend to be more helpful and happier when surrounded by pleasant odors. Just the smell of fresh-brewed coffee can put some of us in a better mood.

If long drives fatigue you, shorten them whenever possible. Try not to drive more than three hours at a stretch. Make more frequent stops. Enjoy the scenery and the towns you're driving through. Don't always travel via the superslab highways. Adjust your work or vacation schedule just a bit. Plugging in breathing space can completely alter your on-the-road experience.

## POSTAL SERVICES

Do you know your letter carrier? When you are away or awaiting a special-delivery package, is he or she looking out for you? Or do you play tag, passing that little yellow slip back and forth via your mailbox? If you have a neighborhood post office that you frequent often, do you know anyone there by name? Do they know you?

My secret to success at the post office comes from talking to the agents. I ask them when business is slowest, and that's when I show up. Usually at 10:30 A.M. or 2:30 P.M. they have extra windows open and agents available. The after-work rush hasn't started yet, and I can walk right in and get right out. If I miss that window of opportunity, either I don't go or I use the local Mail Boxes Etc. (MBE). I pay a little extra, but I save so much time. They'll even pick up outgoing mail at my home for a modest fee. I don't always use them, but in a pinch, it's a great resource.

Did you know that the post office too will pick up mail at your house or office for a nominal fee? You can even buy stamps by phone by calling 1-800-782-6724. If you have a big in-house mail department this may not matter to you. But perhaps this information may help another member of your Ease Team, as you share shortcuts, tips, and resources.

Ease is easiest through relationships. United Parcel Service (UPS) went on strike the day that I needed to ship ten boxes across the country. Since my publisher often sends me large shipments of books, I've become friendly with Jan Olson at Roadway Express, a freight company.

"Hi, Jan, it's been a while since we spoke. How are you doing on your dream?"

"Marcia, it's great to hear from you. I have your book next to my bed. I'm working on it."

"I need your help. I have to get these books out to Florida, and with UPS on strike, I'm really in a bind."

"I'm sorry, we're inundated and not taking any more clients."

I paused, took a breath, and asked, "Do you have any ideas?"

"Hold on," she said, then, "Marcia, we'll have someone there today to pick up your boxes. You focus on writing your books and we'll take care of the shipping."

Thank God for Jan and all the other wonderful people in our lives who contribute to our sanity and well-being. I hope you cherish and honor the everyday people who make your life easier.

## DOWN-ON-THE-FARM LOGIC

Often I have the pleasure of speaking at different Young Presidents' Organization chapter meetings. I really enjoy being with these people because many of them are visionary leaders. They are creative (that is, they have dreams), they take risks, and they are passionate.

The most successful members use their passion to engage others, or use it to influence and make changes. But as mighty as they may be, there is something else that I have been struck by. They are down-to-earth, real people.

One such man is Roger Valine. He is the president and chief executive officer of Vision Service Plan, the nation's largest vision-care company, with more than fifteen hundred employees providing services to at least twenty million employees and dependents under group plans. Sales this year exceeded nine hundred million dollars. Roger has been married to Marie for more than twenty years, has three children, and lives in Sacramento, California. His family has been farming there for four generations.

Roger attributes much of his success and happiness to what he calls "down-on-the-farm logic." I interviewed him, and he shared some wonderful wisdom with me. What I love about his wisdom is that it's so simple. Here are wonderful ways you can do less and have more, no matter where you are, whom you are with, or what you are doing.

1. **Take care and pay attention.** If you have or use something, take good care of it. For example, treat the land with respect. You can't keep pulling crops without replanting. You have to put something back. On the farm, or in life, take care of your equipment all the time, so it's ready when you need it. Whether it is your body or a machine, maintenance is easier and often cheaper than repairs. "An ounce of prevention is worth a pound of cure." Trite but true.

2. **Do your best.** Work at least as well as others. Give it your best shot. On the farm, it didn't matter how old or how big you were. Size and age didn't hold you back. Roger was driving a tractor at the age of twelve. He learned to pull his own weight. He strove for things that were beyond his reach and strove to learn new things all the time. Doing this built great confidence and self-esteem.

    Roger's grandfather was a farmer his whole life. He had only a sixth-grade education, but he was a wise man. He taught this: "There's only one thing you can take to your grave. It's not your wealth or your debt. It's your reputation."

3. **Get out**. Roger recalls that good farmers didn't ride around all high and mighty. They were engaging in activities, not just supervising. They got out and hung around with other workers. They got dirty with the rest and had a firsthand understanding of what was happening, what worked and what didn't. They were part of the team. It didn't matter what they had, what they owned, how rich or poor they were. "When we were on the farm," Roger noted, "we were all farmers."

4. **Hard work won't kill you, but smart work is easier**. Working smart requires you to deal with challenging situations. Smart work is also primarily about planning. If you are a farmer, you have to consider in detail what you'll plant, when you'll plant it, where, and even why. You might take a risk and plant a unique plant. It might thrive, really stand out, and get you a better price. But it might fail and wipe you out. If that was all you planted, you'd be in trouble. Working smart yields better results.

5. **Respect your people**. Respect everyone you meet, not just customers or people who have something you need. Go out of your way to have great relationships with your suppliers. You don't have to do business with everyone, but generation to generation, maintain your precious resources. The farmers Roger knew were not out to make the biggest profit and didn't always look for the lowest bid. They honored their relationships and were really there for each other. They could count on one another completely.

If a piece of machinery broke down, he recalls, suppliers would scurry to find the part. Once they even took it off one of their own rigs. They bent over backward for each other. Whether you are among family or friends or employees, treat others with respect.

6. **Take the first step.** Getting out of a warm truck on a cold, blustery morning is hard. On the farm, you learned to adapt a "just do it" attitude. There was always plenty to do, and often tasks seemed overwhelming. You roll up your sleeves and dive in. You learn to take the first step, then you take another and still another. Eventually you look back and the job is done.

7. **Mistakes are not the end.** Roger told me mistakes were expected on the farm. They were a chance to learn, to risk, and

to grow. We often have such a fear of failure that it keeps us from taking action. On the farm, you couldn't run from things. If a machine broke, you had to get creative. You had to try something. If you were already stopped, you couldn't get more stopped, so you often adopted a "what the heck" approach. If you made a mistake, you lived with it.

From surviving mistakes, you develop the ability to think creatively and take risks. You try all kinds of wild things. Sometimes they work and sometimes they don't. That's just life. You learn to roll with the punches. You don't beat yourself up when you screw up. You acknowledge what you've learned and you move on.

8. **Nature does her thing.** We can work hard and work smart, but still we have no control over Mother Nature. There is no such thing as "fair." Life is not fair and doesn't care. If there is a storm and you stay out in it, you will get wet. Learn to have the sense to literally come in from the rain, when you can.

Roger told me he once spent an entire season planting and tending prize-winning tomatoes. They were almost ready, but not quite perfect. Unforeseen rains came, torrential rains the likes of which you don't often see. It was disastrous. The entire crop, a whole season of work, was destroyed in a few hours. There is nothing you can do about something like this. You learn to bow your head. You feel humbled by the power of the forces of nature and you feel grateful that at least you're alive. You begin anew. You pick up whatever remaining pieces you can and take that first step once again.

In life, you can do everything "right," but as a result of events beyond your control, everything can still go wrong. You have to learn to deal with it and just let it go. When we stop trying to control, or getting upset about, situations that are out of our hands, we are practicing surrender and ease.

9. **Appreciate where you are.** Sometimes the most mundane jobs make us crazy. Riding a tractor for hours at a time can be monotonous. If you think you have it bad mowing your lawn, think about Roger. The farm covered forty acres, and it all had to be cut by Roger. He found a wonderful peacefulness in this task. He had time to dream, to think, and to plan.

Recently, Marie bought Roger a great birthday present. She

gave him a beautiful Harley-Davidson motorcycle. When Roger rides it he has that same feeling as when he rode the tractor. He sees beauty everywhere. He smells fragrances and feels free. Roger's imagination (and his Harley) can take him anywhere.

10. **Strive for balance.** On the farm, in business, and at home, when we do not balance our activities for any extended period of time, everything seems to fall apart. Learn to make time for all the things that matter to you. A successful life includes work time, family time, self time, and spiritual time.

At work, be the best you can be and empower others to be even better than you. Use your family to learn to appreciate all the different types of people and personalities that make the world whole. Put their priorities high on your list. Once-in-a-lifetime events, like your kid's sixth-grade class play, won't ever happen again. Be there.

If Roger wanted to throw a ball with his dad, no matter how tired his dad was after a full day of farming, he somehow found the time and the energy for his son. Often the activity would recharge his battery, and he would even outlast Roger.

Your personal needs are important, too. Play as hard as you work, and let playtime be whatever you need for you. And schedule or make time for your soul, whether that be in church or in a meadow. Give yourself the time you need, so you can be there for everything and everyone else.

11. **Follow your dream.** Roger was the first generation in his family not to become a farmer. He tasted it growing up, but that dream time he had on the tractor allowed him to imagine other things. Although farm life taught him amazing lessons and heartfelt values, it was hard work and a hard life. Joe and Lorraine Valine (Roger's parents) did it. Roger chose not to. He wanted to find his own way. With all that rich guidance learned down on the farm, he has emerged as a successful entrepreneur, a loving husband, and a supportive dad.

One last note on ease. Roger told me he avoids waiting in lines at all costs. If he's leaving a ball game and there's a backup of cars, he'll look for another way out. He'd rather be moving than sitting in one spot. See what years of mowing the farmland taught him.

## CITY GIRLS ON THE FARM

Roger's wisdom and insight came from years of experience on the farm. Mine came in an instant and were never forgotten.

I was driving with a friend in New Mexico. We were on our way to the Taos Pueblo. It was getting late, and we wanted to arrive before nightfall. I rounded a sharp bend, to find the butt of a large black bull. He was trotting down the middle of the road.

"Should I honk?" I asked my friend. She didn't think so. I tried to sneak around to its left. It halted dead in its tracks ten feet in front of us, turned, and stared right at us. I stopped the car. It turned and continued on its way. It seems this massive animal was herding cattle, and he was bringing up the rear.

"This is crazy," I said. "We're not going to let this bull stop us from our mission, are we? I'll just speed by and we'll be done with this silliness."

As I put my foot on the gas pedal, the bull stopped suddenly, looked me squarely in the eye, and let out a very loud and booming bellow. His presence was so solid and his energy so powerful that I was instantly convinced of his message and intent. He was clearly saying, "Don't even think about it."

I coyly smiled at my friend and said, "Let's let him set the pace. We'll just hang back here taking it nice and easy."

He continued ahead, guiding the cattle into a corral. Only then did he allow us to pass.

The lesson of this bull story? No matter where we are or what we're doing, life provides wonderful opportunities and lessons. To push and resist is to learn the hard way. On the farm, at the post office, stuck in traffic, or behind a bull, if we remain open, centered, and available to the lessons life is handing us, we experience ease.

### FUNDAMENTALS OF EASE

1. As you begin to develop your skills for having greater ease, life will offer you many opportunities for practice and perfection.
2. Don't panic, have an unnecessarily big reaction, lose your cool, blame or attack, or make matters worse. Remain calm in the midst of chaos. This is what ease is about.
3. The best way I know to minimize or eliminate jet lag is through meditation.

4. The job of your travel Ease Team should be to make your life easier and, ideally, to make your travel experience a pleasant one. If you travel a lot and don't have this team in place, I strongly recommend that you create one now.

5. Get into relationships with the people who can bring ease and, with it, great happiness into your life.

6. The biggest stress reliever in my life, by far, is my cellular phone. I can alert people to where I am and give them a status report if I'm running late. For me, a cellular phone is a great investment in ease.

7. This information may help another member of your Ease Team, as you share shortcuts, tips and resources.

8. The most successful people use their passion to engage others, or use it to influence and make changes.

9. There are wonderful ways you can do less and have more, no matter where you are, whom you are with, or what you're doing.

10. "There's only one thing you can take to your grave. It's not your wealth or your debt. It's your reputation."

11. Hard work won't kill you, but smart work is easier. Working smart requires you to deal with challenging situations and includes planning.

12. In life, you can do everything "right," but as a result of events beyond your control, everything can still go wrong. You have to learn to deal with it and just let it go. When we stop trying to control, or getting upset about, situations that are out of our hands, we are practicing surrender and ease.

13. Strive for balance. When we don't balance our activities for any extended period of time, everything seems to fall apart. Learn to make time for all the things that matter to you.

14. A successful life includes work time, family time, self time, and spiritual time.

15. No matter where we are or what we are doing, life provides wonderful opportunities and lessons. To push and resist is to learn the hard way. If we remain open, centered, and available to the lessons life is handing us, we experience ease.

# 15

# Six Steps for

# Ongoing Ease

B Y THIS time, you get the point about ease. It's clearly something you understand and desire. Now you have to take it out
into your daily life. If this gives you concern, it's no wonder. We can
count on life for certain things. Life will test us. Life will keep us
busy and too often distracted. Will your life keep you too busy to
have ease?

When life shows up with all its distractions and annoyances, as
well as its opportunities and rewards, you can be ready with your ease
tools. What follows is a clever system of tips you can use on a moment's notice and under any circumstance, to assist you in maintaining and practicing ease.

When something happens that throws you "off-center," follow this
six-step formula: *Recognize* what's happening when it happens; *realize*
and *reflect* on what you are doing and where or how you have done
this before; get into *relationship* with the people and situations involved; *respond* and *re-create* the scenario.

This formula will offer you ease. Just noticing or realizing what's
happening, when it's happening, is a life-changing skill that you already possess. But have you forgotten to use it? Making these unconscious skills conscious is simple to do. Soon you will find yourself
automatically using these points to remember your inherent capacity

and to reclaim your power. You will notice that you are more in control, are much more relaxed, and have a much greater capacity to deal with challenging situations.

As you begin to live with greater ease, this six-step process will support your daily maintenance of ease. When you hear the word *maintenance*, do you think, "Uh-oh, this is going to be work," and run and hide? For many of us, maintenance is a term that has been used to describe our diet or fitness regime. It connotes arduous workouts and food deprivation. Maintaining good grades meant many hours of studying and no fun. Car maintenance, to me, still means big expense and inconvenience.

But when we talk about maintaining ease, it's a different story altogether. I would never suggest a complicated or energy-draining approach for maintaining ease. It would obviously be counterproductive. The idea behind this maintenance program is to incorporate these habits *easily* into your existing repertoire, so you can *easily* practice ease on a daily basis, and especially during stressful times. Let me share a personal example.

## MY WEDDING

I *recognized* that I was going to Bali to get married and had none of the details planned. We had no rings, no written vows, no outfits, no location, no minister. We literally had nothing planned. Typically a control freak, I normally would have all the specifics planned, down to the color of the napkin rings. Yet here it was, one of the most important days of my life, and I promised myself and my fiancé that I would let the wedding unfold in Balinese fashion. I would trust the unknown and practice ease.

I *realized* that my behaviors included feelings of fear and disappointment. I saw my desire to control and how uncomfortable I was with being out of control. I *reflected* on how this made me feel and saw I was starting to get uptight, moody, even downright mean. I didn't like who I was becoming and made a commitment to try something new. If I had stuck to my typical control mode, I would never have had the opportunity to develop unfamiliar parts of myself. Learning to trust and relinquish control without going into mental chaos or confusion is essential for ease.

I took a few very long and very deep breaths to help me relax. I saw how I was behaving. Rather than react with fear, defensiveness, and aggression, I could actually "lighten up" and make a conscious choice to respond from a different place. My fiancé and I decided to do what many locals do to relax. We went to carve masks. It was here that we met Oka, a famous Balinese artist and respected mask carver. Because we were relaxed and centered, we created a wonderful *relationship* with him. While talking to him about all kinds of things, we casually spoke about our wedding. That's when the ease began. Oka offered to take care of everything and told me to relax. There was something about the way he said it with a gentle smile that allowed me to truly surrender. Now I was *responding*.

From my newfound sense of ease, the most remarkable events unfolded and we *re-created* our vision of the perfect wedding day. Oka hand-carved us wooden ceremonial rings. His mother made beautiful flower arrangements. He found the perfect priest. One week later he drove all of us two hours away, so we could be married on the most beautiful beach in Bali.

With all the details flowing with such ease, I knew the other pieces of the ceremony would come together. Open, at ease, and trusting, we even met an American designer named Nadya who owns Puri Naga Studios. (In case you ever need a great little outfit from Bali, I want you to be able to find her easily.) As a gift, she gave us stunning ceremonial costumes, and on the day of our wedding someone just showed up to fix my hair and makeup in traditional fashion.

What usually is one of the most stressful events imaginable became one of the most magical days of my life. It taught me unbelievable lessons about ease. Once again, I used the six R's: *Recognize, Realize, Reflect, Relate, Respond,* and *Re-create.*

When something upsets, confuses, or scares you, or just plain throws you into a tailspin, turn to any one or all of these steps. Sometimes all you need is one step. Sometimes walking through the entire process, as I did for my wedding, will offer the greatest ease:

*Recognize* what's happening when it happens. *Realize* and *reflect* on what you are doing and where or how you have done this before. Get into *relationship* with the people (including yourself) and the situation involved. *Respond* appropriately and *re-create* the scenario or outcome.

Let's look at each of these steps individually.

## STEP 1: RECOGNIZE

To recognize something is simply to see it. How do you recognize your behaviors, feelings, and patterns? Recognition is the first step and the key for restoring balance. Recognition gives you access to more of who you are, what you need, and what's happening. Without it, we often "spit into the wind" or make situations harder for ourselves. When you are in tune with what you're feeling and what's going on, you are more present and available to face reality.

Here are five simple suggestions for recognizing what's happening or what you are feeling. First, learn the proper use of your breath (as discussed in detail in Chapter 3). Second, close your eyes and focus your attention inward. Third, put your attention fully on the situation. Fourth, simply sit down and get still. Or fifth, write in elaborate detail about what you are experiencing. Any of these methods will help you become more present. And in the present moment is where you need to be, as often as possible, to experience ease.

## STEPS 2 AND 3: REALIZE AND REFLECT

Realizing what's happening when it's happening may sound difficult, but it's actually easier than many expect. We are so influenced by our past and so colored by our experiences that just seeing "what's so" is an important skill to practice. This skill already exists inside you, but by consciously naming it and using it, you are shining a bright light on it. We perfect our skills and techniques through our awareness of and use of them. As you develop this part of yourself, you will have instant access to greater ease.

Realization begins with stopping. Stop and notice what you're feeling. As you realize what's happening, as it is happening, you can begin to use life's encounters as a resource for growth and to have ease in your life. To realize something is not just to see it, or have a thought about it, but to feel the emotions associated with these thoughts, and, when necessary, to take appropriate action.

Carey wanted a new boyfriend, but saw she was sabotaging the chances of this happening. When Carey finally accessed her feelings, she realized that she was angry because her husband had died, leaving her feeling lonely and abandoned. She carried that unresolved anger around for nine years. Once Carey realized what she was feeling, she immediately felt free and alive, and met a new man within a few months.

Kristen is a successful woman who had wanted to make a career change for quite some time. She couldn't understand why she was struggling to live the life she wanted. After listening to her for a half hour, the problem was evident to me. Every time she said what she wanted, she immediately came up with a list of reasons she couldn't have it. She was sabotaging herself with doubt. But here's the kicker. She had no idea she was doing this. I fed back to her what she was saying, when she said it. She was shocked. She had not been listening to herself. Realizing that she had this bad habit was the first step in breaking it. Kristen listens to herself carefully now, which helps her realize what she's thinking and feeling.

Realizing the situation you're in is one way to free up blocked energy or to remove obstacles. Once something is realized, it can be released. "The truth will set you free." All the great yogis, masters, and teachers who speak about enlightenment are also speaking about self-realization. The ultimate realization for a life of ease is to know yourself. A spiritual path will help you begin to ask and answer important questions like Who am I? Who am I not? Why am I this way? and What will make me happy?

To realize something is to give yourself the potential to shift it, or at least to shift your relationship to it. For what you once could not see, hear, recognize, or understand now exists in your conscious awareness, to be examined and understood.

Often as we begin the journey to know ourselves, we see things that we don't like or don't want to believe about ourselves. My friend Tom realized that his relationship with money was not good. Actually, it was awful. He would do things like lose it, get angry about it, and always be late paying his bills, even his taxes. He just hated money and everything about it.

With a commitment to understand himself, Tom began to face his financial issues. He remembered a painful childhood memory about money. When he was six years old, one of his young buddies stole a jar of quarters from his own father. The two boys spent the afternoon bingeing on candy and soda pop. When their fathers found them, they beat the daylights out of them.

The moment Tom remembered the incident and realized his pain, the block on money released. He no longer loses cash and is able to balance his checkbook. Sound farfetched? Within twenty-four hours of the realization, Tom was offered a new job making thousands of dollars more than in his current position. His remembering released his negative money attachment and freed him to create a new relationship with cash.

Once you realize what's happening, you can reflect upon what this situation means and how you are reacting to it. Ask yourself, When have you been here before? What did you learn? What is this revealing about yourself? Do you trust yourself and feel confident, or do you need to take some time for yourself to reflect more deeply? See how your ability to trust yourself either empowers or impedes your new relationship with ease. Learn how to confide in and fully trust yourself. This can be done only through practice. It is through the ongoing practice of asking and answering questions and acting on what you think, believe, and know that you will deepen your intuition, instincts, and risk-taking abilities. Practice minimizing stress around important decisions by exploring options and deepening your self-trust. Think new thoughts, try new ways, and recognize what works. These are essential tools for building the kind of life you want.

A few months ago I spoke at the Governor's Conference for Women in California. More than two thousand women gathered in a room to hear my speech, entitled "Insight, Inspiration, and Impact." It was a lively and interactive discussion. About halfway into it, one woman raised her hand.

"Marcia, how can you have ease when you're torn between two mutually exclusive options? It's finally time to take my home-based business and move it out of the house. But I have a problem. I love spending time with my children, and I want to be a good mother. To me, this means being there for them when they need me. What should I do?"

Another woman in the audience asked for the microphone and gave her opinion. She felt we should not give our lives up for our children. She emphatically said, "We have to pursue our own dreams as we encourage our children to pursue theirs." Half the room cheered in agreement.

I presented another point of view. (There are always at least two, usually more. Whenever we want more ease, we need to explore options and opportunities, while still honoring what is true at any given moment.) I invited the first woman to reflect on her needs. I asked her to make up her ideal career scenario, playing it out fully with either outcome, or with a combined picture including the best of both worlds. I asked her to feel which scene honored where she was in her life and what she needed now. I reminded her that it didn't have to be an either/or situation.

I asked what would give her ease. We saw that she could get creative, perhaps creating child care right in her new office. By asking for help, she began to see new possibilities, and by taking a breath, she could honestly recognize, from a centered and calm place, what action to take. The rest of the room applauded. They witnessed how recognizing old behaviors and reflecting on new ideas created ease and opportunity. It didn't have to be all or nothing.

This either/or theme is not part of the American culture alone. I recently spoke in England to the British Association of Entrepreneurs. A woman in the audience said she loved what I was saying about passion and dreams, but asked, "How could I ever put my needs before the needs of my family?"

I felt much compassion for her. Her heart was in the right place. Unfortunately, many of us take care of everyone else first. Our families, clients, employees, friends, and pets get all we have. If there's anything left over, perhaps some of our needs get met. It's darn near impossible to live a life of ease if your needs are always the last to be identified, heard, or fulfilled.

Listening to her question, an image came to my mind. If you're on an airplane and the cabin experiences a pressure change and, God forbid, the oxygen mask falls down in front of you, what does the flight attendant tell you to do? "Please secure your mask first, so you are available to help others around you."

The oxygen mask offers an interesting metaphor. If you look up the word *inspire* in the dictionary, you'll see it means "to breathe." Without inspiration, we would expire, or die. Taking care of some of your needs and recognizing and realizing some of your own dreams is essential. Talking about your dreams and passions is not a frivolous conversation. It inspires you and has everything to do with ease.

How are dreams related to ease? Remember, a dream is defined as a fervent hope or desire. Living a dream-come-true life requires ease. The whole rationale behind ease is to be able to do less, use less effort, and waste less energy, while having more. Don't you want more time, energy, creativity, love, and happiness? Wouldn't this be a dream come true?

Without passion and inspiration we become depleted and run out of "juice." But when we take care of ourselves, which includes reflecting on our own needs and living more inspired lives, we have more joy and vitality to give to the people we care about. "I'm taking good care of me, so I can take good care of you" is a motto many of us need to adopt in order to have ease. If this is true for you, please open your calendar right now and schedule a day (or at least an hour) that is time just for you. Use this time to recognize, realize, and reflect on who you are, how you feel, and what you need.

## STEP 4: RELATIONSHIP

How you relate to life, to the people you meet, and the circumstances you encounter will determine how much ease you have. Before you can be fully available to relate to others, you need to be in what is called "right relationship" with yourself.

How do you get there? Quality, quiet time is invaluable. During quiet time, you can begin to explore personal healing and awakening, which includes being open-hearted, available, and trusting. Concurrently, others will be on their journey to become more of who they are. Although we may follow similar or different paths, the more we know ourselves, the more available we are to be with each other. From this place, we can see and hear each other. We can help and support each other. We can even help make each other's lives easier and richer.

In relationship, as we share with each other our differences and preferences, the people we interact with are mirrors to help us see, understand, and learn about ourselves, especially our disowned selves. Your disowned self is the part of you that you don't know, can't see, don't recognize, and don't understand. Regardless, this is the part of you that tends to have the biggest reactions to other people and often wastes huge amounts of energy by blaming others for something that lives inside you. We must get into relationship with our disowned selves in order to experience ease and to have more peace of mind. We all possess these parts, and perhaps one of the sacred functions of being human is to come to know these parts of ourselves.

Here's a story I recently heard a rabbi tell: Thousands of years ago, when God was creating the earth and life, he asked the angels, "Where on earth should I put love? It's so precious I want to put it someplace safe." The angels thought for a while, and then one said, "Put it in the food. Surely the humans will find it there and cherish it." Another angel said, "Put it in the ground. Every time they walk they will feel it." A third angel said, "Put it in the sky. That way it will be everywhere." Finally God said, "I know—I'll put it in their hearts. Right there inside them. It will be safe there. But it will be the last place they look."

As we reveal ourselves and see others, we can heal and grow and become more whole. True love is not a destination, not a place to get to or a goal to obtain. Love is about bringing wholeness forward. It is about opening our hearts and letting our magnificence and beauty be expressed and witnessed. At the center of you and at the center of me exists perfect love.

One of my favorite tarot cards is called the Lovers. The deck I have shows a man and woman being blessed by a hermit. It represents the union of opposites, an acceptance of one another, and the image that we are one soul. It reminds us that our goal is to become whole, total individuals. The bliss we seek outside ourselves is to be found and developed only in ourselves. When we find our inner harmony, we will know ease.

Until we get into right relationship with our wounds and deal with all of ourselves, we are not complete; we are distorted and dismembered. Until we begin to recognize and realize that we are more than we can see or touch; until we begin to feel our feelings and relate to ourselves, we will not know true inner peace. And without inner peace, ease is impossible.

How we relate to what's happening in our lives, to the people with whom we are involved, and to what we are trying to create can provide much ease or much stress. Every day we meet people who can have great impact on us, who can help us know ease. How we use and honor our relationships affects who we are and who we become.

Here's a simple example of how relationships provide ease: When my friend John started his new job as a salesman, he called the man whom he replaced. John asked for help, and his predecessor introduced him to all his old accounts. He began closing deals and making money immediately. John has healed the parts of him that feel unworthy of asking for help and the parts of him that believe life has to be hard. He is in right relationship with himself, which makes it possible to be in right relationship with others. This is a key for having ease.

I'll say it again: How you relate to life, especially to the situations and people you encounter, is directly related to the amount of ease and joy you will have on a daily basis.

## STEPS 5 AND 6: RESPOND AND RE-CREATE

When you respond to life from a centered and mature place, you have options such as reacting or relaxing. Sometimes the appropriate response may be to retreat. In retreat, we can find peace and quiet. Being alone may enhance your concentration and creativity. Solitude has inspired innovation from many famous figures like Buddha and Sir Isaac Newton, as well as many poets, philosophers, and computer gurus.

But assuming you don't retreat, or when you return, there are other ways you can respond. You can re-create your desired outcome and have what you really want.

Remember to play. (Sometimes skipping directly to this step will give you the greatest ease.) Reenergize and keep going by recuperating through rest and relaxation. Although many people think that play time is unproductive, it really is necessary. Momentum gained during "downtime" of no work or worries can be used as a wave you ride to even greater ease. Learn to enjoy and appreciate both playtime and downtime. Perhaps we should rename it "uptime."

Even in the most desperate of times, these skills will help. I received a heartfelt and moving letter from a man named Jim. In his thirties, with a beautiful wife and two young children, he had achieved a high degree of success in his life, including ranking as high as fourth place as a body builder in the Mr. USA Competition. But last year he lost his focus and his confidence after his mother committed suicide.

Jim couldn't eat, became very depressed, and began thinking about driving his car off the road to end his own life. He realized he was out of control and needed help. He didn't know where to turn, so he turned inward. And somehow he found the inner strength to recognize what he was feeling. He reflected on his entire life, what he had accomplished, and who he was. He reconnected to his love for his family and the relationships in his life. He felt how deeply he loved and cared for them.

From this place he responded. He wrote to me saying how he had been drawn to my book *Life Is But a Dream*, and how, although he wasn't an avid reader, he read the entire book in two days. It gave him a whole new meaning for life and a new perspective. He remembered and reconnected to his dreams and he decided to re-create his future. He is currently back in training, as he puts it, "to win the U.S. Championships in body building."

At any moment, we can reconnect to what we love, to what matters to us, and we can use our talents, resources, and passion to move forward easily in life. Whether you feel overwhelmed by life or by death, by little details or huge obstacles, you can experience ease by remembering to recognize, realize, reflect, relate, respond, and re-create. Using this formula or any aspect of it provides ease.

## FUNDAMENTALS OF EASE

1. Life will test us. Life will keep us busy and, too often, distracted. When life shows up with all its distractions and annoyances, as well as its opportunities and rewards, you can be ready with your ease tools.

2. When something happens that throws you "off-center," follow this six-step formula: *Recognize* what's happening when it happens; *realize* and *reflect* on what you are doing and where or how you have done this before; get into *relationship* with the people and situations involved; *respond* and *re-create* the scenario.

3. Just noticing or realizing what's happening, when it's happening, is a life-changing skill that you already possess. Soon you will find yourself automatically much more relaxed and have a much greater capacity to deal with challenging situations.

4. The idea behind this maintenance program is to incorporate these steps *easily* into your existing repertoire, so you can *easily* practice ease on a daily basis, and especially during stressful times.

5. When something upsets, confuses, or scares you, or just plain throws you into a tailspin, turn to any one or all of these steps. Sometimes all you need is one step.

6. Recognition is the first step and the key for restoring balance. Recognition gives you access to more of who you are, what you need, and what's happening.

7. Realization begins with stopping. Stop and notice what you're feeling. As you realize what's happening, as it is

happening, you can begin to use life's encounters as a re-source for growth and to have ease in your life.

8. To realize something is not just to see it, or have a thought about it, but to feel the emotions associated with these thoughts, and, when necessary, to take appropriate action.

9. To realize something is to give yourself the potential to shift it, or at least to shift your relationship to it. For what you once could not see, hear, recognize, or understand now exists in your conscious awareness, to be examined and understood.

10. It is through the ongoing practice of asking and answering questions and acting on what you think, believe, and know that you will deepen your intuition, instincts, and risk-taking abilities.

11. Practice minimizing stress around important decisions by exploring options and deepening your self-trust. Think new thoughts, try new ways, and recognize what works. These are essential tools for building the kind of life you want.

12. Recognizing old behaviors and reflecting on new ideas creates ease and opportunity.

13. Without inspiration, we would expire, or die. Taking care of some of your needs and recognizing and realizing some of your own dreams is essential. Talking about your dreams and passions is not a frivolous conversation. It in-spires you and has everything to do with ease.

14. As we reveal ourselves and see others, we can heal and grow and become more whole. True love is not a destina-tion, not a place to get to or a goal to obtain. Love is about bringing wholeness forward.

15. Until we begin to recognize and realize that we are more than we can see or touch until we begin to feel our feel-ings and relate to ourselves, we will not know true inner peace. And without inner peace, ease is impossible.

# 16

# Your Personal Profile

I N *Super Joy*, Paul Pearsall writes about the joy crisis in our society, which he says is caused by the belief that more is better. "We think doing everything is the same as enjoying everything. We mistake external stimulation for spiritual intensity. When we pressure ourselves to do all that we should be able to do, we fail to fully experience and enjoy what we are doing."

What will give you the greatest ease of all is to know yourself— your personal needs and timing, your hopes and desires, your doubts and concerns—and to honor these. It is imperative that you learn and understand what works for you. This chapter is designed to assist you in developing your own personal and simple practices that you can access anyplace and anytime.

## YOUR TYPICAL DAY

Begin by assessing how a typical day in your life looks and feels. I'll describe a scenario I often hear.

The alarm clock jolts you out of bed. You race around getting breakfast prepared for your family or housemates. You yourself skip eating because you just don't have the time. As you get the kids off to school, you have a very tight time frame to shower, dress, and pull your look together.

You get to work only a little late and spend much of the morning reacting and responding to others' needs, putting out fires and handling problems. You are very good at this, so everyone comes to you for help.

Today you don't have a business lunch, but you take time to wolf down a sandwich at your desk. You are thirsty, but opt not to bother getting any water. You just keep working.

The afternoon may be more of the same. Every so often a really big zinger of a problem arises, just to keep you on your toes. Although you handle each situation well, little on your "important things to do" list seems to get done.

You creep home in rush-hour traffic, arriving home just in time to prepare dinner. You miraculously get a good meal on the table, do the dishes, and pass out exhausted. In the morning, you do it all again. Sound like anyone you know?

Or how about this twist: A friend said to me, "Hey, tomorrow's Tuesday, which means I'll have sex instead of going to my health club. I can sleep half an hour later because sex takes less time."

I've seen many variations on this theme. Some of us do set priorities: We eat well, we drink enough water, we go to the gym or for a walk, we've learned to schedule fun or play time, and we're less reactive and more proactive about how we spend our time and live our lives. Where do you fit in?

Comedienne Lily Tomlin says, "The problem with the rat race is, even if you win, you're still a rat." Do you schedule time for your own needs? Granted, many things feel out of your hands. Your boss needs a bid or proposal, your clients need your help, your employees need guidance. We do many things that are expected and required. But what about the things that aren't? Besides looking at what can wait, what can be handed off to someone else? And how do you handle the things that you must?

Let's begin with the dream-versus-reality approach discussed in Chapter 8. The scenario you just read is an example of one person's reality. What's yours? Write down or at least picture what your typical day is like. (Include as much detail as you can stand!)

## YOUR IDEAL DAY

Now imagine the day of your dreams. What does it look like? Since most of us work, it's useful to include both the office and home in our dream day. Have some fun as you imagine and create your ideal day. Start with work. Imagine doing what you love, with creative and fun people. Picture a simple commute, listening to your favorite music, inspirational or educational tapes, or your favorite radio show. Have you created flexible hours, so you rarely travel during rush hour? Keep dreaming and imagining.

Do you telecommute? Andersen Consulting eliminated fifteen hundred cubicles by setting up a telecommuting system, and staff at all levels work from laptop computers. Is working from home part of your ideal day? Does a twenty-yard commute appeal to you? Perhaps sometimes you want the personal contact of coworkers. In your dream, include what you want and leave out what you don't.

Picture your office and desk or work space. Imagine the interactions you are having, on the phone and in person. See yourself easily accomplishing important things. Notice how throughout the day, you take time out for water, air, small talk, or to do nothing.

See yourself sitting comfortably, moving easily, and standing tall. Do you want to design a midday break, in which you exercise or even go home to be with your kids or dog?

How do you feel at the end of the day? How do you wind down? Is someone else cooking the meals and cleaning the house? What are the things you look forward to in the evening? How do you feel when you lie down to sleep and upon awakening in the morning? In your ideal day, I hope you wake up refreshed and rested, eager to start a new day.

## PRIME TIME

Discovering your personal prime time is a simple awareness tool that can be really helpful in reclaiming your life and having more ease. Are you a morning person or evening person? First answer this question; then delve deeper.

What do you love to do in the morning? If I haven't worked out by 11:00 A.M., I won't work out that day. However, I have learned that I love yoga stretches in the late afternoon. And on days when I feel really energized, going dancing at night is fabulous. I now know that different forms of exercise are available to me at different times of the day.

When is the best time for you to eat? I tried that "nothing but fruit before noon" approach. It made me ravenous. And if I'm not putting something in my mouth every four hours or so, my energy level crashes. What do you know about your creature comforts, and how do you take care of you?

What are the best things for you to do at night? Soon you'll be able to use the Ease Meter (that you are about to design), so you know when to get up and go. Doing less and having more is all about designing your life. You can directly affect the way you live.

Finally, don't forget sleep. Are you getting enough? Do you wake up feeling well rested, before your alarm clock goes off? If not, pay extra attention to what you're doing before you go to sleep. Bad news, heavy food, intense work—all these things stress your adrenal glands and can get you so wound up that sleep is disturbed or impossible.

Spend the next week noticing who you are: when you're hot and when you're not. I'm not suggesting that every day and the rest of your life turn into one big, boring routine. When I have creative ideas, I write. When I can't sleep, I may turn on my computer and e-mail friends. This week I found myself painting in the middle of the day. Yesterday I took a nap after lunch.

Ultimate ease is finding what works for you and, wherever you can, designing it into your daily life. Do more of what you love, when you love to do it. Do less of what you don't like, or do it when you can get it done quickly.

## YOUR EASE METER

Now study the differences between your dream day and your reality. Doing this may result in some startling news. You may wonder whose life you are living and how it got this way. Most important, you'll want to know how you can regain some balance and control. We must learn how to say no. The simplest solution I can offer is the Ease Meter.

Create a short list—I recommend three elements—of things that are most important to you. You may have one set of criteria for work-related projects and another for your personal life.

What follows is a list of the most common criteria that people mention to me. Select the three most important criteria for you to say yes to a request. Sometimes you have no choice, but often you do have a vote. The Ease Meter is designed to help you make quick decisions, freeing up time and energy.

My personal rule is this: The issue, opportunity, or request must meet at least two of my three criteria. If it does, I say yes. If it doesn't, I say no. At different times in my life, my criteria have changed. For example, years ago when I was building a big business and success mattered most, my criterion was that a project had to be profitable, highly visible, or fun. If it was fun and profitable or highly visible and fun, I'd participate. If it was just fun, or just profitable, I would decline.

Now my needs and priorities have changed. My business criteria are these: The situation has to be easy, fun, and profitable. For a personal decision, I have a different set of criteria: It has to be inspiring, nurturing, and easy. Two out of three will get me going. This handy tool can help you set priorities instantly. Decide what your criteria are for saying yes. This is now your Ease Meter.

Here are some criteria to consider. Of course, feel free to add your personal preferences to the list.

| | |
|---|---|
| easy | inclusive of others |
| fun | intimate |
| creative | spiritual |
| profitable | heartfelt |
| expressive | new |
| inspiring | challenging |
| worthwhile | fast |
| risky | healthy |
| adventurous | funny |
| nurturing | beautiful |
| simple | luxurious |
| visible | educational |
| rewarding | unique |
| playful | |

## PASSION PULSE

Sometimes using my Ease Meter comes down to one very clear question: "Will this make my life easier?" My response is often linked to my Passion Pulse. If there is something that I love or am excited about, I may be willing to give up some amount of ease. Passion and ease are two important criteria to consider in most circumstances. When I want one final, comprehensive check on how I feel about something or my level of interest, I take my Passion Pulse. First, I picture, feel, or sense the situation at hand. I imagine myself doing what I'm being asked to do, or what I'm considering embarking on.

I then take my Passion Pulse. I rate my level of excitement, joy, or enthusiasm. I know that passion and commitment go hand in hand, so I don't treat this response lightly. By testing my level of passion, I'm really checking out my level of intent and willingness for serious participation.

Life is just too short to keep saying yes when what's in your heart is no. But do you ask your heart what it wants? And, more important, do you follow its advice and guidance?

Design your own passion scale for use in taking your Passion Pulse. Rate your passion level from 1 to 5. Or use expressive adjectives. Let 1 be "turned off," 2 is "no interest," 3 can be "interested," 4 is "turned on," and 5 is "red hot." At different points along the way on any project, use your passion scale to take your Passion Pulse.

If your passion begins to wane, don't despair. It doesn't have to be the end of your involvement or participation. Simply refer to Chapter 7, where we discussed how to revisit, remember, and reignite your passion. This can often be done very easily and quickly.

## YOUR INTERNAL TRACKING SYSTEM

This is not new, it's been said a thousand times, yet it's still true. In order to have ease in your life, you need to take care of yourself. Pay attention to the basics. Here are the five basic requirements for survival. When you feel exhausted or depleted, or life seems hard, check these areas first. See what's incomplete or missing and make it a priority to do whatever it takes to recharge your battery.

Incorporating these five basics into your day will help you be strong and resilient, confident and curious. When we are healthy, wealthy and wise often follow.

I recommend you use the following fundamentals to develop your own Internal Tracking System (ITS). Learn to recognize what you need, at the moment you need it, for more immediate ease in your life. When your ITS says it's hungry, eat; when it's thirsty, drink; when it's tired, sleep or rest; and so on. Look for clues in your body, mind, and soul that will instantly connect you to what will make you feel good. Make taking care of yourself a priority and it soon will become second nature.

1. **Sleep**. Deep, restful sleep and as much of it as you need is the first essential component for having ease and energy. How many hours of sleep do you average a night, and how soundly do you sleep? How do you feel in the morning? Are you up before your alarm clock rings?

   Our bodies need sleep to replenish and to heal. The more nonstop your life, the more important your rest is. Don't rob yourself of sleep. Fatigue is dangerous to your well-being and to the people around you. Sleep deprivation is a tactic of war. You are not a prisoner or victim of circumstances unless you choose to deprive yourself. My wish for you is "pleasant dreams, regularly."

2. **Food and Water.** For the first time, there are more Americans who are overweight than of average size, according to the National Center for Health Statistics. Proper nutrition based on your body size, needs, and temperament will give you maximum efficiency. You can eat quickly without eating fast food. Try menus from The Simple Living Network (www.slnet.com). They even run on-line monthly contests for the fastest, cheapest, and most nutritious recipes.

   Water is the sustenance of life. When you feel thirsty, you are already in the dehydration danger zone. I could never drink eight glasses of water a day, but by keeping a filled Big Gulp cup nearby, or a glass with a straw in it, I sip water all day. Everything works better when it's well watered. Without enough water you will perish, slowly.

3. **Exercise.** Your body is your temple. Exercising is a chance to honor your temple and take care of your machine. The bottom line is, if you take care of it, it's available and ready to take care of you. Being fit will help decrease your stress levels. Exercise will add years to your life and life to your years.

   Once again, find what works best for you. If you hate the routine of going to the gym, take up a sport. Whether you like slow, gentle movement or something rigorous and challenging, there's probably some sport that's right for you. Explore your options, as well as the range of motion of your body. Exercise expands your capability and capacity. Your lungs can breathe more air, you increase your strength and your flexibility. Flex your muscles and keep your body supple. Exercise is a stress buster, mentally and physically.

This is the one area where more is better. The more you exercise, the better you'll feel. You can accomplish more, with less effort. The better you feel, the easier it is to move through life.

4. **Rest.** The pause that refreshes, from my point of view, is a nap, but you also can rest without going to sleep. Closing your eyes for a few minutes can give you a burst of energy, or can help shift you out of a negative mind-set. Resting can put a little emotional space between you and an upsetting or confusing situation. Meditation can have the same effect, in a short period of time. Especially when you can't lie down, closing your eyes and "watching" your breath go in and out can be transformational. You'll feel clearer of mind, relaxed, and available for whatever is next.

For many of us, rest is a skill that needs a bit of improving. Start where you can. Reading a good book, even watching television can be restful. Just notice what you're putting into your system and how you respond to it. Do what works.

5. **Fun.** Too often omitted from our daily existence, and yet essential to our well-being, fun is priceless. What do you do for fun, and how do you design it into your day, both at work and at home?

Do you laugh and make others laugh? Have you developed the fine art of laughing at yourself? Being with others, just having a good time, is rich and rewarding. Share good times with friends and family.

Explore being of service and contributing to others, which builds self-esteem and a very full life. If risk-taking is fun for you, schedule an adventure or two.

## DAILY PRACTICE

How you begin each day, and the practices you follow throughout the day, can help or hinder you. There's tremendous power in developing daily rituals and practices. Learn what works for you and incorporate this into your day.

Each morning I take some quality time to be with myself. I begin with a twenty-minute meditation, either in silence or with music. Often I put my hands on my heart and use my breath to get still. If my day starts without this simple practice, my energy and thinking are much more scattered.

I know this works for me, so I do it. On days when I meditate first, I am on top of things and much more at ease. On days when I get on the computer or phone first, I realize I have forgotten to pay attention to my own needs.

After meditating, I take a few minutes to pray. I ask for what I want and need. Sometimes I visualize my goals, or use this focused time to write them down. I also use my prayer period to give thanks for all the wonderful people and gifts in my life.

Then I open my journal. I write down what I'm feeling or thinking. This morning ritual is often the most exquisite time of my day. It restores my equilibrium. It also sends an important message to my psyche. The message is: My needs matter, and I make time for myself.

Other things I do every day include taking time outside in nature, eating healthy meals, drinking water every time I think of it, and making time to be with my husband, face to face or at least by phone.

Whenever possible I take a bubble bath and linger in the tub. We light candles on the dinner table, put on soft music, and turn off the ringers on the phones after 9:00 P.M. I exercise at least every other day and take a walk, even a short one, every day.

Look for ways to combine your favorite things, like having a candlelight dinner with someone you love, taking an easy walk to meet a friend for lunch, or playing golf with your kids or clients. You get extra points for doubling up, as you experience doing less and having more.

## CREATING YOUR DAILY PRACTICE

What is the one thing, or perhaps a few things, that you could do for yourself each day? Having a simple daily practice, usually in the morning, before your day becomes too chaotic, can offer you so much. Consider it a significant gift, and imagine what would make your life easier and more joyful. The key here is to keep it simple.

Just adding one thing to your life, that you will commit to doing daily for one week, will begin to build an awareness.

The best place to find guidance on this is inside you. Ask, "What do I need most now? What simple thing can I begin to do today that will give me ease?" Close your eyes, take a few breaths, and see what comes up. You have great wisdom inside you. Use this to guide you. Then act on what you feel, think, or know.

If nothing comes up as the obvious "thing," I recommend taking five minutes each day, for one week, to do an inventory. The inventory is as simple as asking these questions.

"How do I feel?"

"What do I need today?"

"What can I do today to have ease?"

"Is there anything that feels incomplete?"

"What shall I do about this?"

## EMERGENCY EASE CHECKLIST

When life becomes overwhelming, or if a crisis is throwing you for a loop, take a Personal Pause. In a hot situation, give yourself a chance to cool down. Rather than doing or saying something you may regret, take a little time to check in, reflect, and consider your options.

The very act of pausing can be life-changing. Think about it as interjecting some space, a little breather, into your life. A pause can mean the difference between war and peace or ease and dis-ease. Here are some actions to access when you're in the heat of the fire. If you can use these in truly trying times, you'll be masterful at using them in daily life.

1. Assess your state of mind. What are you thinking and feeling? Go beyond the surface reactions. Consider using the six steps from Chapter 15 to delve a little deeper.

2. Use delaying tactics. Try taking a single deep breath rather than giving in to a knee-jerk reaction. Resist the need to respond instantly. Patience is much more than a virtue. It is a skill and a sign of mastery to wait until you are ready to move forward.

3. Arm yourself with an arsenal of appropriate responses: "I'll get back to you on that." "I can't talk now." "Let me think about

this." These are useful, socially acceptable lines that can buy you some time to consider your options.

4. Vent safely. Sometimes the safest time to really let go is when we are by ourselves. It's usually not necessary to spew all over others, or in public. When you're ready, use friends and people you can confide in to yell, rant, and cry with. Don't forget to turn also to professionals, mentors, and coaches.

   Write down your feelings or yell into a tape recorder. Hitting a punching bag or pounding a pillow is a great way to hammer out your frustration. Dancing and exercising are useful ways to get this gook out of your system and body.

5. Physically change locations. Change your environment and you'll change your mood. Go to one of your energizing places (beach, mountains, park, lake) as soon as possible. Use this power spot as a well to drink from.

6. Utilize the Completion Corner (see Chapter 12) to identify exactly what is needed to resolve this situation. What words can be spoken or what actions taken so this problem no longer continues and you feel empowered again?

7. Check in with your Ease Meter and use your criteria to decide if you want to deal with this issue. Walk away when you can. Whether you move ahead or away, complete your Personal Pause by taking three deep breaths and slowly drinking a glass of water.

8. Recognize what you have learned here. What did you do to cause this situation, and how will you do things differently in the future? Ideally, write down what you learned. Enlightenment comes one lesson at a time. It's self-affirming to identify what you've learned. Have compassion for others and for yourself while you're learning, a process that will continue for your entire life.

9. Acknowledge that you didn't get sucked into the drama, that you honored yourself and that you completed the situation.

10. Be grateful it's over.

## FIVE THINGS IN FIVE MINUTES

Even when you're extremely pressed for time, you can access ease. Whether you're stressed out over a decision, running late to an event, or in "overwhelm mode," help is instantly available.

Here are five things you can do in five minutes to regain your center and your composure.

1. Use your Ease Meter to see if this situation is something you choose to participate in. If not, see who might love to take the project or effort on, or be willing to help you. Guiltless delegating often comes from finding the perfect person for the job.
2. Take your Passion Pulse. Use what you know about passion to reignite your excitement or interest.
3. Breathe deeply to change your heart rate. Or use any of the tools from Chapter 3 to access and shift energy. Some include: feeling, expressing, deciding, and dreaming.
4. Drink water. I'll say it again. Drink lots and lots of water. It will rejuvenate you on the spot. Sorry, tea and coffee don't count.
5. Take action. Do something. Take a walk or a nap, write a letter, make a call, schedule a date. Acting gets blocked energy moving and makes things happen.

The purpose of your Personal Profile is to know what works for you. With this knowledge, in any situation, and with any person, you can tap into ease. By understanding your needs, you can develop good and simple habits for taking care of yourself. You need to know what your ideal day looks like, and strive to live it. Small changes can have great impact, especially when they are based on what truly matters to you.

I encourage you to develop your own daily practice, to create an Ease Meter based on your individual criteria, and to take your PassionPulen. These simple practices will help you do less and have much, much more. Make them a part of your life.

## FUNDAMENTALS OF EASE

1. What will give you the greatest ease of all is to know yourself—your personal needs and timing, your hopes and desires, your doubts and concerns—and to honor these.
2. Discovering your personal prime time is a simple awareness tool that can be really helpful in reclaiming your life and having more ease.
3. Doing less and having more is all in designing your life. You can directly affect the way you live.

4. Bad news, heavy food, intense work—all these things stress your adrenal glands and can get you so wound up that sleep is disturbed or impossible.

5. Ultimate ease is finding what works for you and, wherever you can, bringing it into your daily life. Do more of what you love, when you love to do it. Do less of what you don't like, or do it when you can get it done quickly.

6. Sometimes using my Ease Meter comes down to one very clear question: "Will this make my life easier?"

7. When I want one final, comprehensive check on how I feel about something or my level of interest, I take my Passion Pulse. I rate my level of excitement, joy, or enthusiasm. I know that passion and commitment go hand in hand, so I don't treat this response lightly.

8. By testing my level of passion, I'm really checking out my level of intent and willingness for serious participation. Life is just too short to keep saying yes when what's in your heart is no.

9. In order to have ease in your life, you need to take care of yourself. Pay attention to the basics. When we are healthy, wealthy and wise often follow.

10. Develop your own Internal Tracking System (ITS). Learn to recognize what you need, at the moment you need it, for more immediate ease in your life. When your ITS says it's hungry, eat; when it's thirsty, drink; when it's tired, sleep or rest.

11. Explore being of service and contributing to others, which builds self-esteem and a very full life. If risk-taking is fun for you, schedule an adventure or two.

12. How you begin each day, and the practices you follow throughout the day, can help or hinder you. There's tremendous power in developing daily rituals and practices. Learn what works for you and incorporate this into your day.

13. Imagine what would make your life easier and more joyful. The key here is to keep it simple. Just adding one thing to your life, that you will commit to doing daily for one week, will begin to build an awareness.

14. When life becomes overwhelming, or if a crisis is throwing you for a loop, take a Personal Pause. Rather than doing or saying something you may regret, take a little time to check in, reflect, and consider your options. The very act of pausing can be life-changing.

15. Even when you're extremely pressed for time, you can access ease. Whether you are stressed out over a decision, running late to an event, or in "overwhelm mode," help is instantly available.

## 17

# Wisdom from Ease Masters

AN EASE Master is someone who has learned how to do less and have more. Ease Masters have learned the art of simplifying their lives. They come in all sizes and all ages, have diverse backgrounds and beliefs. They have time to share their wisdom and are willing to impart their knowledge.

They may be living or dead. The living ones can be interviewed. Some Ease Masters may be living very close to you. You can ask them questions and reap great rewards from their experiences. They may be willing to teach or mentor you. Some may even serve on your Ease Team.

The ones who are not living also have great wisdom. Through books and tapes we can read or hear what they knew. Through stories and legends we may learn what they knew. Your own family members, past friends, and teachers are good resources to consider.

So are the people you have read about or look up to. History has delivered us many wise men and women. In your heart, feel who has inspired you, and seek out their teachings. We can learn from their examples. A wise lesson in ease is this: We don't need to reinvent the wheel.

## BECOMING AN EASE MASTER

Each of us has the ability to become an Ease Master. That is what we are seeking. Cull your pearls of wisdom. Use what works and try new things. Develop the habits and behaviors that will make your life easier.

Model others. Try what worked for them. Be open to the simple, small changes or suggestions that can have a big impact on you. Mine for the gold, don't just gloss over things with a know-it-all attitude. What follows in this chapter are firsthand interviews with many different kinds of Ease Masters. There are also stories, quotations, and excerpts from people who have inspired me. Whether they're dead or alive, I consider them masters and resources. They help me and can assist you, too.

Share what you learn. Teach others through your example. Model being an Ease Master and you will come to know yourself as one. As you are identified with ease, more ease will find you. When you are clear about what you want, you attract it to you. This is a level of mastery. There are no blocks and obstacles in the way. You are in the flow of life and are experiencing the ultimate high in ease.

## MEET THE MASTERS

### *Ease in Success*

Mark Victor Hansen is the coauthor of the *Chicken Soup for the Soul* series, which has sold more than twelve million copies. He has spent a lifetime dedicated to making a profound difference in people's lives, teaching how to triple your income and double your time off. He shared this wisdom with me:

> The goal for each of us is to simplify. We need to learn to do more with less, so we can live rich and fulfilling lives. We know how to do more with more. That's not the game.
>
> We have a choice in this world. Choose higher complexity or more simplicity. Our real goal is to accomplish so much, to get so much done, with so little effort. Then we will have the time and money to do what we love.
>
> This is the most spiritual and prosperous time in history. People who know how to do more and have less will have great freedom.

This includes money freedom, time freedom, relationship and spiritual freedom.

The secret here is to find your genius. Find where you excel and delegate as much of everything else as you possibly can. I'm a genius in writing, speaking, promoting, husbanding, and fathering. I spend as much time as possible doing these things. Everything else goes to someone else.

If you don't have the money to hire a big team, your passion will go a long way. Help others find their genius and see how you can partner to support your goals.

By choosing simplicity, you are freed up to focus on a mega home run. *Chicken Soup for the Soul* is the bestselling book series in history and still going strong. Every day Jack Canfield and I keep our dream alive and growing. And we keep it real simple and fun.

We innovate at all levels. Every book we write is totally physiological. It gives you goosebumps, happy tears, and sighs. Our unique gift in our work is that we use stories to change your inner image and outer reality.

Here are a few tips: Journal your uniqueness. Ask ten friends what they see in you that you don't. Elaborate on what's special about you. Then build a great team based on everyone's unique talents. Find people with the core competencies you are missing. Support each other in simplifying your lives.

*Ease in Relationships*

John Gray is the bestselling author of *Men Are from Mars, Women Are from Venus; Mars and Venus in the Bedroom;* and *Mars and Venus on a Date.* As one of the leading relationship experts of our time, he told me how we can have ease with our loved ones:

The greatest element for ease today is to understand that people are different. We can't expect others to think and feel like we do. But when we learn to validate their experience, cooperation is achieved. Rather than give your partner what you want, take time to discover what they want. And practice patience.

Here's a simple technique for doing less and having more: A man needs to understand that with a woman, lots of little things go further than a few inconsistent big things. Without this knowledge, men put a lot of effort into grand things, assuming this will make his woman happy. Focus on the little things like flowers, cards, and compliments, as well as affection, eye contact, and asking her questions about her day. Sympathetic listening is all that is needed, not fixing her problems. Don't make it harder than you need to.

For women the greatest gift you can give your man is how you respond to what he does for you. Don't focus on doing more, but pay attention to the quality of your response. It is a gift of love when he makes a small mistake and you simply overlook it. Be sensitive to his needs to feel successful in your relationship. Take time to acknowledge him with a smile. He'll feel greatly loved.

## Ease in Creativity

Julia Cameron is the bestselling author of many books, including *The Artist's Way, Vein of Gold, Heart Steps,* and *The Right to Write.* She has been a working artist for more than twenty years, serving in Hollywood as a film and television writer, director, and producer. Julia passionately shared this with me:

> Ease is a question of priority. We feel stressed and frustrated because we are doing a great deal, but little of it is what we choose. Have a life where you focus on your inner wealth and draw on it freely. Rushing around and not asking what will give you joy makes it hard to feel the sweetness. As a single mom, many of my tools came from what appeared to be "much too much to do." I needed a way to move from the inside territory, mining my inner wealth, bringing it out, over time. Build a life that resembles your wishes and dreams.
>
> I recommend doing what I call the Morning Pages, writing longhand, three full pages. This helps prioritize your day so you are doing more of what you love and less of what you feel roped into. You can run a stream of consciousness about anything. When we siphon off worry, guilt, and preoccupation, the result is clarity, activation, and a finer tuning to our own inner promptings.
>
> This is not about being irresponsible to others, but about being more responsible to ourselves. Ease is peacefulness, the byproduct of living according to your own value system. You really can't live out of alignment with your own needs and values and expect to have peace or ease.
>
> Morning Pages are my active meditation, while walking is my receptive participation. I do a walking meditation, which is my clearest way to listen. Sitting and being quiet isn't for everyone,

since most of us are too skittish. Even just fifteen to twenty minutes a day will make a difference. Life is holistic: Whatever is on our mind goes with us on the walk.

I listen to my inner teachings. Ease comes from practice. I have a structured life even though I'm a freelancer. Every day I do my pages, walk my dog, and check in with friends. This all helps structure my life. Some call this discipline, which I think is such a loveless word. I like the word structure. If we build with strong materials, we will have a solid, usable, happy day and life.

Using these tools and listening, most people find instant access to new resources in two or three weeks. When you feel supported, ease happens. As we check in internally and receive guidance, we realize we are not alone, although we feel alone. As we access and listen more and more closely, we find a supportive universe that manifests its support in many ways. Go inside yourself, find your dream, and listen. You will be given a hand-holding approach for what is needed to manifest this. The answers are in you.

## Ease in Spirituality

Wally Amos was the founder of Famous Amos Cookies. He is a national spokesman for Literacy Volunteers of America and recently started the Uncle Noname Cookie Company. He is the winner of the President's Award for Entrepreneurial Excellence. Wally shared these thoughts with me:

I found ease in my life when I enhanced my spirituality. I developed a relationship with God that I can relate to. Together with my wife of eighteen years, Christine, we practice this daily.

I have a simple routine that I use to maintain ease. Every morning I meditate. I get my body and mind still and find a deep inner connection. Then I take some time to pray, where I give thanks and appreciation for all I am and all I have. This whole process takes about half an hour; then I can really hit the ground running. I am energized and at peace.

Often I ask the following question: Do I want to experience peace or conflict? If I want peace I will be concerned only with giving. If I want to experience conflict, I will be concerned with trying to get something or evaluating why I'm not getting it.

In every communication I have I ask myself if this is a loving exchange between the other person and me. This was taught to me by Gerald Jampolsky, the founder of the Center for Attitudinal Healing. Now it has become a way of life. I do this automatically.

I don't work at my spiritual practice, or to be a spiritual person. By having a daily practice, it has become a way of life, a way of being. This is who I am, not what I do. What could be easier?

One hundred fifty million people knew me as Famous Amos. My style is just to be me, to be available and generous with myself and my time. Even with my cookies."

## Ease in Daily Life

Jeff Davidson, M.B.A., is the executive director of the Breathing Space Institute and the author of twenty-five books, including *Breathing Space: Living and Working at a Comfortable Pace in a Sped-up Society.*

Here are what Jeff calls Moments of Truth: Signs of Having Breathing Space in your life:

You wake up naturally, without an alarm clock.
You have time for reflection each morning.
You leave the workday on time, ready for what's next.
You play with your child for hours on the weekend, with no concern about time.
You eat dinner early in the evening, at a leisurely pace.
You resubscribe to the local community theater's fall series.
You re-engage in a hobby with renewed enthusiasm.
You make a new friend about once month.
You book a cruise or a vacation.
You volunteer for a charitable activity of your choice.
You notice your retirement account is in good shape.
You fit into clothes you once put away.
You take naps throughout the week and feel good about it.
You view a sunrise nearly once a month and see many sunsets.

## Ease in Attitude

Dr. Tony Alessandra has delivered more than two thousand speeches and presentations, has authored twelve books, has been featured in more than fifty films and videos, and still has time to enjoy his family.

He says attitude is a huge contributor to his ease and offers these three suggestions:

1. Personally, focus on simplicity, get rid of your junk. I don't worry about things I have no control over. As a result, I don't get stressed and distressed over things like the economy.
2. I pay attention to the things I can impact. No matter what happens, my mantra is "This too shall pass." I believe life is a roller-coaster ride of ups and downs. They don't last long, but the downs help me appreciate the ups.

   I regularly ask myself, "What should I do, or delegate, or not do?" Ask yourself, "What's the highest and greatest use of my time? There are many things I do and do well. Is this pulling me away from my goals? Is it allowing me to do something else? Do I want to do it, or not?"
3. I believe that what goes around comes around, so I try to always be there to help people. Then somebody else will be there to help me, too.

   One more important attitude adjuster is the proper use of ritual. Every night after 9:00 P.M., when I'm home, my wife and I bathe together. We talk about the day and we get connected. It's an anchor for us and provides peace of mind.

   As a result of a good attitude, I don't work as hard as many, but make more money than most. I focus on quality rather than quantity so I have more time with my wife and four kids.

*Ease in Business*

Grace McGartland is the author of *Thunderbolt Thinking*. Her company coaches Fortune 500 leaders with fresh, idea-sparking techniques, to rejuvenate thinking and improve performance. She shared a little of her philosophy with me:

   What gives me ease in business is to have faith in the people around me. Hire good people, perhaps who even have better credentials than you. Don't be intimidated by them; rather, seek talented and skilled people who challenge the way you think. As I teach, when we break down barriers we are building bridges.

   Be excited enough about something that you are willing to let go of it. In growing my company, I funnel my excitement so others can buy in, share it, and grow it. They run with my vision and often expand it.

Recognize your key learnings. At the end of the day, reflect on what you learned. After I give a speech, I seek someone who can debrief with me. I ask what worked well, what should I add, and what should I never do again. When there's no one around, I'll do this with myself. It gives me clarity and makes the next round easier.

On my daily planner, I have a Post-it note that says, pray, exercise, eat, and work, in that order. My day starts with some kind of prayer. I think faith gives us ease in all areas of life. We need to trust what we're doing at the time we're doing it, that it's the right thing. People waste so much energy worrying about things that never come to pass and second-guessing themselves.

I journal every morning by writing letters to myself. My "Dear Grace" letters can be wake-up calls, thankful or seeking help. I ask what's needed and have my own "Dear Abby" column. When I don't have the time to do it, that's okay, too. I let myself off the hook. I do it when I can, and when I can't I don't.

### Ease in Parenting

Jon Kabat-Zinn, Ph.D., is the author of *Wherever You Go, There You Are* and the founder of the Stress Reduction Clinic at the University of Massachusetts. This excerpt is from *Everyday Blessings: The Inner Work of Mindful Parenting*, a new book coauthored by his wife, Myla.

Here are simple suggestions for having greater ease with your children:

1. Imagine the world from your child's point of view, purposefully letting go of your own.
2. Imagine how you sound and appear to your child. How do you want to relate to them in this moment?
3. Practice seeing your child as perfect just the way they are.
4. Be mindful of your expectations and consider whether they are truly in your child's best interest.
5. Put the needs of your children above your own whenever possible. Then see if there isn't some common ground, where your true needs can also be met.
6. Learn to live with tension without losing your own balance. Bring

your full awareness to this moment. Practice seeing that whatever comes up is "workable."

7. Apologize when you have betrayed a trust with your child, even in a little way. Apologies are healing and demonstrate that you thought about what happened.

8. There are very important times when we need to practice being clear and strong with our children. Let this come as much as possible out of awareness, generosity and discernment.

9. When you feel lost, or at a loss, stand still.

10. Try embodying silent presence. Listen carefully.

11. Every child is special and has special needs.

12. The greatest gift you can give your child is yourself.

### Ease in Love

Gregory J. P. Godek has authored ten books on love. His best known is 1001 *Ways to Be Romantic*, and his latest is *Love — The Course They Forgot to Teach You in School*. He has sold more than two million books and is proud of his one-and-only marriage. He shared with me these six keys for Ease in Love:

1. Honor your own uniqueness — your love blossoms as you express your own soul.

2. Treat your partner as an individual — not as a stereotype; our essential differences come from much deeper than our upbringing.

3. Act on your feelings of love — every day, in little ways, in different ways.

4. Tap into your creative side — it is a boundless source of energy, joy, and innovation.

5. Nurture your relationship — the "us" that is created by the two of you — and you will always be serving the best long-term interest of each of you as individuals.

6. Remember that time is your most valuable resource; your partner wants more of *you* than he or she wants more gifts.

### More Ease Masters

Grandma Fritzi with her red hair and flawless skin used to say, "Nothing ages you faster than stinkin' thinkin'."

Mother Teresa said, "Kind words can be short and easy to speak, but their echoes are truly endless."

Alice Roosevelt Longworth, daughter of Theodore Roosevelt, wrote, "I have a simple philosophy. Fill what's empty. Empty what's full. Scratch where it itches."

American poet and historian Agnes Repplier wrote, "It is not easy to find happiness in ourselves, and it is not possible to find it elsewhere."

The suffragist and psychologist Florida Scott-Maxwell wrote, "It is not easy to be sure that being yourself is worth the trouble, but we do know it is our sacred duty."

Actress Ruth Gordon said, "So easy to fall into a rut? Why should ruts be so comfortable and so unpopular?"

The *Tao Te Ching*, a five-thousand-year-old book of philosophy, tells a wonderful story that offers a whole new perspective on the process of judging something as good or bad.

One day, an old Chinese farmer and his young son were given the gift of a horse. "Oh, Father, isn't this wonderful! This horse will make it so much easier to plow the land." "It could be good, it could be bad," replied the old farmer.

The son was on the horse plowing the farm, when a field mouse ran by, causing the horse to throw the son to the ground, breaking the son's leg.

"Oh, Father, this is such a terrible thing that our horse has done to me." "Could be good, could be bad," replied the old farmer.

Soon after that, the country went to war and the army came knocking on their door to take the son away to battle. But alas, the son's leg was broken and he was unable to go. Still the old farmer said, "Could be good, could be bad."

One day the horse ran away. "Could be good, could be bad." It returned with three other mares. "Could be good, could be bad." You get the idea.

Consider the next time something happens to you that you might label good or bad and recognize that perhaps it just "is." Notice what's actually happening without labeling and judging and you will have access to a whole new perspective and new ideas.

The ability to see a bigger picture can be a huge stress reducer. You will be less "in reaction" to things and more at ease and available to resolve any situation. You can tap in to your creativity and actually start to develop prowess for problem-solving from a more powerful place.

Marcia Wieder says:
   Expand yourself.
   Sit, breathe, center, open.
   Compassion is a most useful practice while you are learning.
   You can always do better, but at what cost, and for whom?
   At what point is enough enough, and good enough?

The American writer Laura Ingalls Wilder wrote, "I am beginning to learn that it is the sweet, simple things of life which are the real ones after all."

Louisa May Alcott wrote, "Love is the only thing we can carry with us when we go, and it makes the end so easy."

# 18

# Parting Words

WHEN I finished my last book, *Life Is But a Dream*, my publicist asked whose name I would like on the back cover in the form of an endorsement. What a fun thing to think about.

One of the people I wanted to approach was an author named Paulo Coelho. He wrote one of my favorite books, entitled *The Alchemist*. I love his work and thought this would be a thrill. Besides being acknowledged by someone I admire, I could also help promote his work. So I went for it.

I was apprehensive and nervous while preparing the package for him. Finding out that he lived in Brazil almost became my excuse for dropping the idea. But what the heck? I mailed him a copy of my manuscript along with a cover letter. Then I forgot about it. Do your best, go for it, then let it go.

Weeks later, I was typing at my desk when the phone rang. "Hallo, Marcia?" an accented voice asked. "This is Paulo calling from Brazil."

I was grateful those picture phones from the World's Fair never really took off, because I was caught so off guard. My face surely would have shown my shock and delight. He went on, "I would be honored to endorse your book, after all, we are . . . simpatico."

By now I was swooning. "You and I," he continued, "know how important it is to inspire people to dream." I took a breath and told him I agreed and was thrilled.

"Just one more thing, my new friend. How else can I help you?" he asked.

At this point, I'm sure I wasn't breathing. I initially had had trepidations about just approaching him. He turned out not only to be very accessible, but so generous. We wound up including a passage from his book in mine.

Is there someone you need to reach out to? Are you holding back? Take it from me, you have nothing to lose by asking and much to gain. One small step soon can turn into a stride. This book is filled with the wisdom of many wonderful and famous people because I now have the courage to ask for help. Sometimes I get a resounding response and sometimes my call doesn't get returned. But what goes around comes around. As they help me, I'll help you and you'll help someone else. Pass it on.

## UP, DOWN, AND ALL AROUND

I just returned from the annual convention for the National Speakers Association. Imagine stepping into a room of two thousand professionals, in this case speakers. Many are extremely successful, have books and radios shows, and make a lot of money. Harvey Mackay, Stephen Covey, and Wally "Famous" Amos were a few of the keynote presenters.

I consider myself successful and yet I noticed how I shrank and deflated in the company of all these pros. I took myself aside and sat quietly. I connected to my passion, my dreams, and my philosophy. When I was ready, I began to approach people like Mark Victor Hansen, who allowed me to interview him on the spot for this book.

I spent the next three days talking to everyone I could and sharing everything I had. I asked for ideas and help and offered the same to others. I gave first-timers encouragement, while many seasoned experts gave me specific guidance. Everywhere I turned there were people helping each other. We generously shared our resources.

This was such a powerful experience. It made me realize that there are always people ahead of us, behind us, and all around us who have something to offer. Will you ask? Will you be willing to reach out to people at all levels and in all walks of life and say, "This is my dream" or "This is what I need" and "Can you help me?" Or, in the face of someone who seems more successful or experienced, do you lose your confidence?

And when you are on the other side—perhaps the one with the answers or resources—will you encourage the people in your life, the people you love, the people you play with and work with, to share their dreams and goals with you? Will you be the one who reaches out and says, "How may I help you?"

What are you giving back? If you truly want a life of ease, a life that is filled with magic and grace, what are you willing to give? What specific gifts will you provide? Whom will you reach out to? Whose team will you serve on and whom will you ask to be on yours?

In the face of our biggest dreams, doubts often arise. They're just opportunities to check in and step up to the plate once again. I dedicate my life to inspiring people (including you and me) to dream our most heartfelt dreams and to have the courage to make them come true.

Remember, when Martin Luther King, Jr., gave his awesome speech, he didn't say, "I have a strategic plan." He didn't say, "I have a goal or a hope or a need or a desire." He said, "I have a dream." And so do you.

MARCIA WIEDER travels around the world reminding people to dream. She speaks to clients such as AT&T, American Express, the Young Presidents' Organization, and many direct-selling companies. She also speaks to teenagers and prisoners.

Marcia is the author of two other books, *Making Your Dreams Come True* and *Life Is But a Dream*. She appears frequently on national television shows like *Today* and *The Oprah Winfrey Show* and writes a column called "Dream Achievers." Her infomercial is televised nationwide.

She is an active member of the National Speakers Association, the National Association of Women Business Owners, and the Direct Selling Association.

Marcia lives in her dream city of San Francisco, where she is pursuing her favorite dream: balancing work and play, with much more emphasis on play.

## MARCIA WIEDER—INSPIRATIONAL SPEAKER

MARCIA WIEDER gives speeches and presents fun and inspiring workshops worldwide. She speaks on dream fulfillment, team building, and visionary planning. She is known for her live-on-the-spot coaching of audiences from fifty to five thousand.

**Speeches and workshops:**

Big Dreamers: The Secrets of Leaders and Top Performers

Igniting Passion in Your Work and Life

On Your Way in Just One Day: The Business of Making Dreams Come True

Doing Less and Having More: The Roadmap to Ease

Teamwork Makes the Dream Work!

Mapping Your Leadership Vision

**If you would like to know more about these or other workshops, please call 1-800-869-9881.**

or

**visit Marcia's website: www.marciaw.com**

MEMBER

NATIONAL SPEAKERS ASSOCIATION

## MARCIA WIEDER'S DREAM UNIVERSITY

**Dream University** is a rare opportunity to work with Marcia in an intimate, small-group setting. You will dive in deep to reclaim your heart and soul, and emerge a very different person. This curriculum provides the structure to design a dream-come-true life.

In a beautiful and exotic environment, learn the ancient art of manifestation from an expert. Use this retreat to recharge and regenerate, to nurture yourself, and to grow.

**Dream University** is for you if:
* You want to create or realize an important personal or professional dream.
* You desire new clarity, insight, and resources for the twenty-first century.
* You want to express your voice as a visionary or leader.
* You dare to dream big.

This curriculum will:
* Offer an in-depth process for connecting to your life's purpose, providing renewed passion, vitality, and enthusiasm.
* Crystallize your most heartfelt dreams.
* Reveal where and how you sabotage your dreams and teach how to remove obstacles.
* Show you how to build and inspire the ultimate DreamTeam.
* Blend movement, meditation, soul work, and Marcia's own powerful technologies to fulfill your dreams.

**For more information call: 1-800-869-9881 or visit www.marciaw.com**

# INDEX